Consumer Defense: A Tactical Guide To Foreclosure, Bankruptcy and Creditor Harassment

The Luxury of the Informed

Matthew Hector, Esq.

Ahmad T. Sulaiman, Esq.

Sulaiman Law Group, LTD

DEDICATION | INNOVATION | COMPASSION | EXCELLENCE

Visit our website at www.sulaimanlaw.com

Published by
Sulaiman Law Group, Ltd.
900 Jorie Boulevard, Suite 150
Oak Brook, Illinois 60523
(630) 575-8181
(630) 575-8188 fax

ISBN 978-1475267341

Notice

This book is designed to provide information about the subjects covered. The information herein should be used only as a general guide and not as the ultimate source or authority on the subject matters covered. While every effort has been made to make this guide as complete and correct as possible, the law does change over time.

The authors and publisher shall have neither liability nor responsibility to any person or entity with respect to any loss or damage caused or alleged to be caused directly or indirectly by the information covered in this guide.

The information you obtain in this guide is not, nor is it intended to be, legal advice. Any information provided in this document is not intended to create a lawyer-client relationship.

All the documents, forms, and information on these pages are generic in nature and must not be regarded as legal advice, accordingly you use this guide at your own risk.

The authors are licensed to practice law only in Illinois and the United States District Court for the Northern District of Illinois. You are strongly advised to consult an attorney for individual advice regarding your own situation. The author makes no guarantees or warranties as to the quality of the forms listed.

The authors and Sulaiman Law Group, Ltd. are a federally defined Debt Relief Agency, and help people file for bankruptcy protection under the U.S. Bankruptcy Code.

The names of individuals used in this document are entirely fictitious, and are not designed to bear any resemblance to any persons living or dead. Any resemblance to persons living or dead is entirely unintentional. All hypothetical examples in this document are merely for illustrative purposes and do not reflect the specific facts related to any person living or dead.

Table of Contents

11

How to Use This Book

The book that you currently hold in your hands contains a vast amount of information about foreclosure defense, bankruptcy, and consumer defense law. While it is possible to read it cover-to-cover, you may also benefit from reading the sections that are most relevant to you first.

The Table of Contents contains the majority of the headings and sub-headings used in this book to make navigating its contents easier. Once you have found a section that is relevant to you, pay special attention to the examples that illustrate each point.

These hypotheticals have been specifically crafted to provide "real-world" applications for the concepts discussed in the book.

As with any other legal guide, do not assume that by reading this book, you are an expert on the law. Consumer defense law is a broad field with many nuances. It is always advisable to consult with an attorney licensed in your state before implementing the strategies described in this book. Proceeding on your own can save you money; it can also be the worst decision that you have ever made.

Introduction

"In America's capitalist economy, borrowing can be a path to prosperity . . . borrowing can also be a path to poverty."[1] America's middle class is under attack. Stagnant wages and alarmingly high levels of consumer debt have created an unsustainable economic reality: many people fund their middle-class status with increasing consumer debt. People are no longer working to build wealth; they are working to pay interest. Quite simply, consumer debt is the new serfdom. Many Americans of all income levels are discovering that their debt burdens are impossible to pay off. Instead of spending money that would stimulate the economy, we are increasingly spending our money to repay what we have already spent. John Maynard Keynes described increased consumer savings during an economic recession as "the paradox of thrift." When individuals save money, they do not spend it, decreasing demand in the economy and slowing recovery. What we are currently witnessing in middle-class America is the paradox of debt.

Like the stereotypical loan shark from a gangster movie, debt collectors are increasingly aggressive in their pursuit of repayment. Nowhere is this more evident than in our current housing crisis. Home owners are underwater, underemployed, and over leveraged. Home ownership is increasingly becoming a bad investment for many Americans. If there is no equity in your home, you are not building wealth; you are maintaining the property for the bank. People seeking assistance from their mortgage lenders are turned away each and every day. Even home owners who find help discover that the help they receive is simply kicking the can down the road. Servicers offer loan modifications with their left hands while initiating foreclosure proceedings with their right hands. With no end to the housing crisis in sight, and with the economy still struggling under its burden, it seems like financial freedom is nothing but a fever dream.

Nothing could be further from the truth. Powerful consumer defense remedies exist for those who take the time to find them. However, finding useful information about subjects like bankruptcy, foreclosure and other consumer defense issues can be difficult. The goal of this guide is to put a large amount of potent and useful information in one place. Although everyone has the same rights under the law, consumer rights are truly the luxury of the informed. Those who know their rights have very powerful tools at their disposal to prevent creditor harassment, get rid of bad debt, repair their credit, and save their homes and other property. Great effort has been taken to make this guide useful and relevant by providing the reader with a practical foundation. From this foundation, you can begin to exercise your rights.

If you are contemplating filing a bankruptcy, or are facing foreclosure, you need to make an informed decision about your options. If your home is deeply underwater and you are contemplating exiting your property gracefully, this guide can help you. If you want to stop an abusive creditor from harassing you, you have rights. The worst thing that you can do is make a decision based on fear. The economic downturn has affected most Americans; you don't have to be a victim. You have rights under the law than can improve your bargaining position with your creditors. Don't let the behavior of creditors and debt collectors intimidate you. Everyone deserves a fresh start, including you.

We hope that you find this guide a useful and reader-friendly resource. Regardless of whom you hire to assist you with your financial affairs, let this guide be your starting point for achieving financial freedom. If you are interviewing an attorney who cannot explain the concepts contained in this guide, you are interviewing an attorney who is probably not the right fit for you. Make sure that you hire the best attorney you can; settling for less likely will lead to headaches in the future.

Debt – A National Problem

During the second quarter of 2011, the total value of outstanding student loan debt surpassed the total amount of credit card debt carried by Americans.[2] The topic made it into President Barack Obama's 2012 State of the Union Address. Over 1 in 4 homes is underwater nationwide[3]; 47% of homes in the City of Chicago are underwater.[4] As of November 2011, the U.S. Department of Labor's Bureau of Labor Statistics pegged the unemployment rate at 8.6%.[5] With so many people unemployed and underemployed, it is no wonder that many of us are facing an ever-growing mountain of debts. When corporations get into financial trouble, they ask Washington for a bail out or they enter into a Chapter 11 bankruptcy, a process which allows a corporation to reorganize its debts, repay its creditors over time, and emerge in a stronger, more viable condition. Companies that successfully reorganize walk away from bad investments to profit another day.

So why don't more consumers walk away from bad debts? For innumerable reasons, our national psyche is ingrained with a moral theory of contracts. Based upon this theory, those who do not honor their debts are "bad people." We generally use terms like deadbeat and loser to define these people. Yet when a corporation emerges from a Chapter 11 filing, the financial press praises the corporation's management for turning things around. The same managers are often rewarded with large bonuses and an increase in their stock price. General Motors is a great example. In 2009, this icon of American ingenuity was on the brink of disaster. With the help of the federal government as a debtor-in-possession lender, General Motors successfully reorganized, innovated, and emerged from bankruptcy as the world's number one automaker by 2012.

Aren't we missing the bigger picture? If we were all informed, and were aware of our rights, then we could all emerge from a bad financial situation and succeed. Politicians, performers, billionaires, and others have filed for bankruptcy or used the other protections outlined within these pages and thrived. Plenty of educated, well-informed people have sought protection under state and federal law and prevailed. This is why consumer defense is the luxury of the informed. The U.S. Bankruptcy Code's stated purpose is to give the honest yet unfortunate debtor a fresh start. Everyone is entitled to equal protection under the law; having the information to exercise your rights tactically and purposefully is invaluable. What prevents most people from making sound financial decisions is that they are unaware of the true impact that debt has on long-term financial security.

Evaluating Your Options

Any good consumer defense strategy involves a serious evaluation of your financial situation. If you are facing a mortgage foreclosure lawsuit, there are multiple strategies available to you. The best strategy depends on the specifics of your finances and your individual goals. For example, you may have legal claims against your creditors that can offset some of what you owe. If you are considering filing for bankruptcy, there are non-bankruptcy options that may work better for you. In some situations, there are hybrid strategies that might better serve your needs and assist you in achieving your long-term financial goals. Underneath all of this is the power of being informed. Informed decision making requires evaluating several strategies, dissecting the pros and cons of each, and arriving at a decision that reflects the most cost-effective and predictable solution.

When you make informed decisions, you act from a position of strength. The uninformed may panic when they receive robo-dialed collection calls and threatening letters from debt collectors. In fact, the reason for the barrage of calls and threats is to keep the consumer scared and making bad decisions. For example, Ocwen Financial, Inc. employs social psychologists to aid its employees in collection efforts.[6] Armed with the knowledge of your rights and the tools available to you, you can confront these situations without fear. This is why it is critical to have a dedicated, experienced, and compassionate professional assist you in determining a strategy that is best for you. When you are in the middle of a difficult situation, it is often hard to see a way out. Taking the time to get informed is the first, most important step. Finding and securing good advice from a professional is the second. Attorneys, accountants, debt management counselors, friends, and family will all give you conflicting opinions. The best way to filter these opinions and make the best choice for you is to get informed. Once informed, you can take the path with the most predictable outcome. There is no greater luxury than being informed. Before leading troops into battle, where each decision is measured by the lives lost or saved, a general first secures information about the battlefield. Being uniformed and allowing fear to dictate and influence your actions will inevitably lead to more stress and, ultimately, financial ruin. The goal of this publication is to replace fear and unpredictability with information and methodically researched strategies for achieving financial freedom.

Non-Bankruptcy Debt Relief Options

There is no shortage of debt relief gimmicks. While some of these methods may work for certain people, they tend to lack predictable outcomes. It is important to note that the debt relief industry is not immune to the presence of scammers. Always thoroughly investigate any professional you hire to assist you with your financial affairs. Searching an organization or person's name on Google or another search engine can often yield a wealth of knowledge, but that is only a start. If you are investigating a licensed professional, the state's licensing body will provide unbiased information about that professional.

Debt Settlement Companies

Debt settlement companies work with borrowers to settle debts with their creditors. In general, a debt settlement company will tell borrowers to stop paying their creditors and instead make monthly payments to the debt settlement company. Once enough money is built up in the borrower's account, the debt settlement company will attempt to work out a settlement amount for the borrower's debts.[7]

This method is typically utilized for unsecured debts like credit cards, but does not work for secured debts like mortgages and auto loans. This is because secured debts allow the creditor to essentially repossess the asset (the house or car) if the borrower fails to make the required loan payments. The debt settlement process does not protect borrowers from being sued by their lenders. If you stop making payments to your creditors, then they will likely pursue you in court for the balance due. Before the lawsuit is filed, you will also incur serious negative credit reporting as your lenders will begin to report your accounts as delinquent. Remember, most debt settlement companies will not make periodic payments to your creditors; their goal is to pay one lump sum to each creditor. This means that your creditors will not be paid until you have given the debt settlement company a large sum of money. In the meantime, you will be incurring interest and late charges on your unpaid accounts.

If you decide to hire a debt settlement company, watch out for companies that want to charge you large fees up front. Not only is it a red flag for a debt settlement scam, but you may end up paying money to the company while never settling any debts. The most reputable companies should only charge you after a settlement is made; the charge should be no more than 20% of the amount by which the debt's balance was reduced. Debt settlement is unpredictable because it depends on several variables such as the ability of the debt settlement company and the creditor's willingness to reduce the debt owed. These types of negotiations rely heavily on human to human interactions that are out of your personal control.

Dave Jones, Lombard, Illinois: A Typical Debt Settlement Strategy

Dave has $45,000 in credit card debt spread across five cards ($9,000/card). His monthly minimum payments are higher than he can afford. He signs up with DebtSettlers, Inc.[8] to help him settle his debts. Instead of paying his creditors, Dave begins to send his monthly disposable income to DebtSettlers. In six months, Dave has amassed $10,000 in his DebtSettlers account. Dave is receiving daily calls from his creditors, even though the creditor knows that DebtSettlers is representing Dave. DebtSettlers attempts to negotiate a small settlement amount for each of his credit cards, using the $10,000 to pay them all. At the end of the process, Dave still has a mortgage on his underwater home, and DebtSettlers has managed to settle three out of five of his credit card debts. The remaining two credit cards have filed lawsuits against Dave.

In this scenario, Dave may have been better served by filing a Chapter 13 bankruptcy or a Chapter 7 bankruptcy, depending on the equity in his home and car. For instance, if Dave only has $5,000 of equity in his home, he could likely file a Chapter 7 bankruptcy and use the Illinois homestead exemption to protect his home from liquidation. The Illinois homestead exemption allows every person with an ownership interest in a home to protect up to $15,000 in equity from liquidation. A married couple would have a $30,000 exemption. However, if Dave's home is deeply underwater, and it seems that he could complete a Chapter 13 plan, a Chapter 13 may provide more tools to restore some equity in his home and potentially eliminate his credit card debt by paying a fraction of the debt owed over time. If his disposable monthly income is low enough, he can settle his debts for less than 10% of the total amount owed.

Debt Consolidation Companies

Debt Consolidation is basically the practice of taking out one loan to cover all of your outstanding debts. Instead of settling with each creditor separately, debt consolidation companies will generally pay off the debts you wish to consolidate, leaving you with one payment to make as opposed to many payments to make.[9] The main risk with debt consolidation is finding a company that is reputable. Some debt consolidators will purchase outstanding debts from creditors at a discount. The better ones will pass some of the savings along to the borrower. It is also risky to convert unsecured debts (like credit cards) into secured debts (like a mortgage). While it may seem attractive to many borrowers, these loans end up costing more money over time – if a typical mortgage lasts 30 years, the debts consolidated into that mortgage are paid off over that time period while interest accrues. Consolidation loans replace one debt with another; they are inherently unsustainable. The authors have never advised a client to consolidate debt because it is simply the financial equivalent of kicking a can down the road.

Mike Thompson, Joliet, Illinois: A Typical Debt Consolidation Strategy

Mike owes MasterCharge $3,000 at 29% interest. He also owes Gracy's Department Store $5,000 at 30% interest and Big Box Electronics $10,000 at 18% interest. Mike shops around and finds a debt consolidation company that will put him into an $18,000 consolidation loan at 20% interest. Although he is increasing the interest rate on his largest debt by 2%, this is largely offset by the savings on his MasterCharge and Gracy's debts. However, Mike may be better served by a bankruptcy – it all depends on what he purchased from Big Box Electronics. If the items are no longer worth much money, a Chapter 7 trustee may not attempt to liquidate what Mike cannot exempt. Other factors come into play as well. When did Mike purchase the goods at Big Box Electronics? If the purchases were relatively recent, his behavior may appear to be an abuse of the bankruptcy code if he files. This is why it is highly important to evaluate your financial situation before rushing to file a bankruptcy – there may be actions you have taken that must be remedied before you can successfully file for bankruptcy. Those who make full disclosure of their financial affairs rarely need to worry about abuse.

What If I Do Nothing?

Doing nothing is the worst-possible option. Ignoring debt won't make it go away. Assuming that a debt is too small to be pursued is asking for trouble. Many credit card companies are taking advantage of Illinois's streamlined small claims court process to pursue debts that are small enough to qualify for small claims court. In some areas, small claims courts will hear cases up to $10,000 in value, so even an $8,000 credit card debt can be a risk. In small claims courts, it is possible to obtain a default judgment on the first court date if the defendant has been served with a summons and the time to respond has lapsed.

What Happens When a Creditor Sues You

Once a creditor determines that collection calls and letters are not working, it will generally proceed to litigation to collect the debt. To begin a lawsuit, creditors hire a collection attorney to file a lawsuit. The attorney will draft a document called a "complaint."

The complaint will set forth the facts necessary to assert, among other things, a claim against you. In some cases, the complaint will set forth multiple claims as separate counts. Once the complaint is drafted, it is filed with the Clerk of Court, likely in the county where you live. The Clerk generates a document called a "summons." This document is attached to the complaint and is delivered to the county sheriff or, in some cases, to a person known as a "special process server."

In order for the lawsuit to proceed, you must be served with the summons. If the sheriff is unable to locate you to serve you with the summons, a special process server will be hired. These people tend to be licensed personal investigators and will do more than the sheriff to locate you. If you still cannot be served, the creditor will obtain the judge's permission to publish a notice of the lawsuit in the local paper. After you have been served, you have 30 days to file your appearance and respond to the complaint, either by answering or by filing one of several motions. If you are sued in Federal court, you only have 21 days to file your appearance and respond. In small claims court, the summons will include a date at which you must appear. On that date, you will have an opportunity to file your appearance and either file an answer or set the case for trial.

If you fail to respond within the time allowed, or miss the first hearing date in a small claims case, the creditor will bring a motion for default judgment against you. This happens every day. Although the law gives you the right to defend yourself against a lawsuit, this right is not without a time limit. If you fail to respond to the lawsuit at all, the creditor will be entitled to a judgment by default. This means that all the facts alleged in the complaint will be taken as true and most of your defenses to the lawsuit will be waived. You will also be liable for the creditor's court costs and attorney's fees. This can turn a $2,000 debt into a $3,500 debt or more. In addition, many judgments accrue interest while they are pending. If a judgment is large enough, it may increase by hundreds of dollars a month.

Once a judgment is entered, the creditor is free to begin collecting that judgment. Judgment liens can be filed against your home. Creditors can garnish your wages. This means that your take-home pay can be docked until the debt is satisfied. Given that the debt continues to earn interest post-judgment, particularly large debts are mathematically impossible to pay off via wage garnishment. Creditors can also come after your bank accounts or other assets if they cannot garnish your wages. For example, if you are paid in cash or are self-employed. Many borrowers discover that their accounts are frozen when auto-draft payments return declined or when their debit card no longer works. When a creditor attempts a non-wage garnishment on your bank account, the account will be frozen up to twice the value of the judgment until the garnishment is approved. In the meantime, the borrower has limited or no access to his funds. Even if you manage to avoid all collection attempts, judgments can be renewed every 7 years. This means that determined creditors, and they are typically determined, can keep judgments alive and collecting interest for a very long time. In Illinois, judgments accrue interest at a rate of 9%.[10]

Quite simply, doing nothing is a great way to create more problems than you had before. The rest of this guide is designed to assist you in making informed choices regarding your financial affairs. Knowing the best way to exercise consumer defense to create more predictable outcomes is the luxury of the informed.

Strategic Default

Many people have read about the concept of strategic default. Sometimes, this idea is referred to as the "just walk away" movement. Home owners who owe more on their home than it is worth may want to get rid of their bad investment. One method is to perform a strategic default.

In some states, like California, lenders are generally not allowed to pursue home owners for extra money after foreclosing on their homes. California is what is referred to as a "non-recourse" state. Some Californians have chosen to stop paying their mortgages, find alternative living arrangements, and move out of their homes. Although their credit suffers the negative reporting of the defaulted payments and the foreclosure, they generally are not liable if their home is worth less than their loan balance.

Illinois, on the other hand, is considered a "recourse" state. This means that lenders can pursue home owners for the difference between the value of the foreclosed property and the loan balance. This is also known as a deficiency. When the lender chooses to hold the home owner liable for the deficiency, it requests that the foreclosure court enter a deficiency judgment against the home owner. This concept will be discussed further in the foreclosure defense sections of this book.

For Illinois residents, a truly strategic default is one where the home owner develops an informed, predictable strategy for gracefully exiting an underwater property. There are many ways to do this, but none of them involve simply walking away. In Illinois, a strategic default truly requires a strategy.

Consumer Defense Strategies

The rest of this book will discuss the various elements of a well-planned consumer defense strategy. Which elements a specific strategy may include will vary depending on your individual situation. For example, some people may determine that a foreclosure defense and loss mitigation strategy provides the most predictable outcome given their goals. Others may determine that a consumer bankruptcy best fits their goals. Some individuals may find that their rights are best protected by filing a lawsuit against an abusive creditor. In most cases, a well-planned consumer defense strategy will include elements of foreclosure defense, bankruptcy and general consumer defense litigation. The remainder of this book will discuss those elements in more detail.

Foreclosure Defense

A well-planned foreclosure defense strategy can help you stay in your home or gracefully exit from what has become a bad investment. One of the first things to consider is the current market value of your home. Many homeowners are underwater; their homes are worth less than what they owe. Regardless of whether you want to keep your home or gracefully exit your home, a well-planned foreclosure defense strategy can help you achieve your goals. This is because foreclosure defense is more than simply defending a lawsuit. Armed with the right information, it is possible to create a strategy that works best for your specific situation and goals.

While many attorneys will tell you that the only way to save your home is through a Chapter 13 bankruptcy, this may not always be the case. If you are behind on your mortgage payments, it is possible to get them caught up in a Chapter 13 plan. However, you must be able to afford the "catch-up" payments in addition to your regular monthly mortgage payment. For many homeowners, this is not a workable alternative, nor even advisable on an underwater or break-even property. If your goal is to return your property to the bank with no further liability, then surrendering your property in a Chapter 13 bankruptcy is one option. However, a Chapter 13 surrender does not place the property's title in the bank's name. You are still liable for ongoing expenses such as homeowner's association assessments as long as the property remains in your name.

Fortunately, there are other options. Defending against a foreclosure lawsuit can provide you with a very valuable commodity: time. As the foreclosure crisis deepens, the lifespan of a foreclosure case increases. As of December 2011, the average foreclosure takes 674 days to complete.[11] If you defend against the lawsuit, this timeframe can extend beyond that mark. That additional time is beneficial.

First, you have more time to work out a loss mitigation strategy with your mortgage lender. Obtaining a loan modification can be a lot of work, especially when the lender loses documents or requests information that you have already provided. Extra time eases some of the stress. Also, if your defense attorney is successfully fighting the foreclosure case, your lender may be more likely to work something out with you. A second advantage to additional time is that you may see your financial situation improve over time. This can improve your chances of obtaining a loan modification.

Mortgage Basics

Before digging into the subject of foreclosure defense any further, it is important to understand how a mortgage works. A home loan consists of two parts: the mortgage and the note. The note is also called a promissory note. It states the amount of money lent, what interest rate will apply to those funds, and represents a promise to repay a specific entity (the lender). The mortgage is recorded against the property becoming what is commonly known as a lien or secured lien. The mortgage creates no personal liability. It is the note that creates your personal liability to repay the debt.

In Illinois, the mortgage exists as a lien against your home. You are the legal owner of the title in Illinois. You remain the title owner of the home at all times, even during a foreclosure lawsuit. Your title interest in the home is only terminated by the judicial confirmation of a sheriff's sale, which happens at the end of a foreclosure lawsuit where the lender is the prevailing party. Even if the lender prevails in the foreclosure lawsuit and sells your home, your liability under the note is not necessarily extinguished by the sheriff's sale. If the home sells for less than the value of the loan, a deficiency judgment can be entered against you. This is because your obligation to repay the loan is tied to the note and not the mortgage. In many foreclosure defense situations, severing personal liability under the note is a primary goal. Under the Illinois Mortgage Foreclosure Law, lenders have a right to deficiency judgments based on in-hand personal service or abode service. Proper abode service occurs if someone who is a regular resident of the property, who is above 13 years of age, accepts service of the summons on behalf of the person to whom the summons is addressed. The sheriff or process server must also mail a copy of the summons and complaint to the property.

Karl Watson, Oswego, Illinois: The Difference Between a Mortgage and a Note

Karl purchased a home in Oswego, Illinois on August 1, 2006. In order to finance the purchase, he went to Local Prairie Bank to obtain a home loan. The selling price for the home was $300,000. Karl had $60,000 saved as a down payment. Local Prairie Bank lent Karl $240,000 at 7% interest to be paid off over

30 years. At the real estate closing, Karl signed a promissory note. This note represented Karl's personal promise to repay the $240,000, and also set forth the terms of the loan. Karl also signed a mortgage. The mortgage incorporated the terms of Karl's promissory note, and secured the value of the promissory note against the value of Karl's new home. This means that if Karl fails to make the scheduled loan payments, the bank can initiate foreclosure proceedings against Karl's house. The bank could also directly pursue Karl for the balance of the loan based on the terms of the promissory note. The seller, Sam, executed and delivered to Karl a general warranty deed, which vested title in the property in Karl.

After the closing, the title company recorded the Sam-to-Karl deed with the Kendall County Recorder of Deeds. Shortly thereafter, Local Prairie Bank recorded its mortgage with the Kendall County Recorder of Deeds. Local Prairie Bank's mortgage functions as a lien against Karl's property. If Karl attempts to re-sell his property to someone else, a title search will reveal that Karl has an outstanding mortgage on the property. This way, the public is on notice that Karl owns the property, and that the property is subject to Local Prairie Bank's lien interest. Once Karl pays off his loan, Local Prairie Bank, or the owner of the loan at that point in time, will record a release of mortgage with the Kendall County Recorder of Deeds. This document will release the mortgage lien on Karl's house. At all times after the closing, Karl is the title owner of his home.

A mortgage is a specific, voluntary lien. It is specific to the piece of property and is voluntary because it was agreed to by the homeowner. A judgment lien is an example of a general, involuntary lien. Judgment liens can be applied against any of an individual's assets. They are involuntary liens because they are not agreed to, but instead arise by law.

Suppose for a moment that instead of keeping Karl's loan on its books, Local Prairie Bank sold Karl's loan to a third party. This would free up the money that Local Prairie Bank lent to Karl, allowing Local Prairie to make another loan. In this scenario, Local Prairie Bank sells Karl's loan to Bank of New York Mellon, formerly known as Bank of New York. Bank of New York Mellon then deposits the loan into a trust, with Deutsche Bank as the trustee. Once Karl's loan is part of the Deutsche Bank trust, investors then purchase bonds issued by the trust. These bonds give their holders an interest in the profits generated by every loan in the trust. A more extensive discussion of mortgage securitization can be found later in this document.

Loss Mitigation

A good foreclosure defense strategy will generally involve loss mitigation efforts. Loss mitigation can involve loan modification, but there are other loss mitigation options available to you. In some situations, requesting a deed in lieu of foreclosure or a consent foreclosure may be the best option. Which strategy is right for you depends on your goals.

Loan Modification

Loan modifications are one of the most popular means of loss mitigation. The Making Home Affordable program includes loan modifications under the Home Affordable Modification Program (HAMP). HAMP is probably the best-known program, but lenders and servicers also have in-house programs that are available to those who do not qualify for a HAMP modification. It is important to note that the vast majority of loan modifications do not include principal reductions. If your home is significantly underwater, a loan modification will not necessarily restore equity in your home. However, a loan modification can provide for curing missed payments and lower your mortgage payment. If you are committed to keeping your home, a loan modification may be the right strategy for you, especially if you don't have any significant other debts.

The Two Types of Loan Modifications: Temporary and Permanent

Temporary ("Trial") Loan Modifications

It is important to understand the difference between temporary and permanent loan modifications. Generally, before a lender will offer a permanent loan modification, it requires borrowers to enter into a temporary, or trial, loan modification. These temporary modifications are designed to test a borrower's ability to make payments. Trial modifications are generally 3 months long. They do not change the terms of a loan. Successfully completing the trial period does not guarantee that the lender will offer a permanent loan modification. If a payment is missed, the lender can choose to reinstate the regular mortgage payment amount. It will also charge the borrower fees and penalties for making partial payments during the trial modification period. If a foreclosure lawsuit has been filed against you, a trial loan modification does not stop the lawsuit. A trial loan modification will not cause the lawsuit to be dismissed. If you are not actively defending the foreclosure lawsuit, obtaining a temporary loan modification provides you with little to no legal protection as the foreclosure lawsuit continues. Even when the lender tells you that the foreclosure is on hold, verify that information independently and continue to monitor the foreclosure case. Experience has shown that your adversary in court will not look out for your interests in any way. Their goal is to obtain a judgment for foreclosure of your home and to pursue a personal deficiency against you.

Although they are supposed to be short-term, some borrowers have experienced the "perpetual" trial modification. These "perpetual" trials are essentially multiple trial modification periods that run back-to-back. When a borrower is in a "perpetual" trial modification, it is often because the lender has misplaced paperwork or has taken too long to process the file and needs updated financial information. The longer a trial loan modification lasts, the bigger the penalty assessed against a borrower, especially if a permanent modification is ultimately not granted. If you are in a situation where your lender or servicer has placed you into several trial loan modifications in a row, consult with an attorney to help evaluate your options.

Permanent Loan Modifications

After successfully completing a temporary loan modification, a borrower may be offered a permanent loan modification. A permanent loan modification changes the terms of the loan and may include a reduced interest rate, reduced payments, and other terms. The specific terms of a modification will vary based on the lender and the borrower's financial situation. It is extremely rare to see lenders write down the loan's principal balance via a permanent loan modification.

In situations where the mortgage is in default, loan modifications will often cure the default. This is primarily done in one of two ways. The fees, penalties, and other costs resulting from the missed payments are added to the outstanding loan balance, or they are "tacked on" to the end of the loan. When the default is "tacked on" to the end of the loan, the fees, penalties, and other costs associated with the missed payments are set aside as their own loan balance. This balance is not charged interest, but must be paid off. The balance will be paid off at the end of the loan's lifetime, when the property is sold, or when the loan is refinanced. Even if a loan modification significantly reduces your monthly payment, it may extend the term of your loan. In other words, the time it will take to pay off your mortgage is extended. If your goal is to ultimately own your home free and clear, a loan modification may delay the realization of that goal.

A permanent loan modification will stop a foreclosure lawsuit. Once the permanent loan modification is granted, the missed payments are considered cured. Since the loan is no longer in default, the foreclosure lawsuit cannot proceed forward. This is because the default that triggered the lawsuit no longer exists. Do not assume that simply because a permanent modification has been offered, the case will automatically be dismissed. If you do not receive the loan modification documents, sign them, and return them, the lender will likely assume that no modification exists. Quite simply, if there's no paperwork, assume that there is no modification. If you are offered a permanent loan modification, but don't receive the papers, contact an attorney to discuss your options.

Making Home Affordable Programs

Making Home Affordable (MHA) is administered by the Departments of the Treasury and Housing and Urban Development (HUD). It includes several programs aimed at providing qualifying homeowners with different types of assistance. Although HAMP is the best-known program, there are other programs that can help homeowners refinance their loans, seek alternatives to foreclosure, modify second mortgages, refinance underwater mortgages, and provide relief for unemployed and underemployed homeowners. MHA also includes the Hardest Hit Fund, which provides targeted financial assistance to the housing markets most heavily affected by the foreclosure crisis.

HAMP is by far the best-known and most-maligned of the MHA programs. Although the government had projected that HAMP would assist millions, its early implementation was poorly-planned. After several revisions to the program's guidelines, HAMP remains as a viable option for homeowners seeking a loan modification from a lender that is participating in HAMP. The MHA website has a list of every lender that is participating in HAMP.[13] It can be found here: http://www.makinghomeaffordable.gov/get-started/contact-mortgage/Pages/default.aspx. If you have a government-sponsored loan like a Veterans' Administration, Fair Housing Administration, or USDA loan, you may also qualify for special HAMP programs.

Homeowners are eligible for HAMP if: 1) they are seeking a loan modification for their primary residence; 2) if the mortgage loan was obtained prior to January 1, 2009; 3) if their mortgage payment is greater than 31% of their pre-tax income; 4) if the balance of the loan is under $729,750; 5) if a financial hardship exists[14] and they are either delinquent on payments or in imminent danger of falling behind; 6) if they have sufficient, documented income to support mortgage payments; and 7) if they have not been convicted of various mortgage and tax-related crimes. Many people believe that they must be several payments behind to qualify for HAMP. **This is absolutely untrue.** If a representative from your mortgage servicer tells you that you must be in default to qualify for HAMP, then your servicer may be in violation of current HAMP guidelines.

HAMP modifications can cure missed payments by adding them onto the balance of your mortgage. It can also result in reduced monthly payments. These reduced payments can be the difference between an affordable mortgage and one that is destined to fail. Although HAMP guidelines also allow principal reductions, very few servicers offer principal reductions as part of a HAMP modification. As with most loan modification programs, there is a three-month trial period before a permanent loan modification is issued.

While it is possible to obtain a HAMP modification on your own, many homeowners seek assistance with the application process. This is because it can take many hours on the phone with a servicer's employees and repeated document submissions to get a file ready for review. A successful HAMP modification will also end any foreclosure lawsuit pending against you because a permanent loan modification cures any missed payments that triggered the lawsuit.

Second Lien Modification Program (2MP)[15]

If your primary mortgage was successfully modified via HAMP, your second mortgage may also be modifiable under the Second Lien Modification Program. The criteria for modifying your second mortgage are similar to those for HAMP. As an added requirement, you cannot have three consecutive missed payments on your HAMP modification. The program expires on December 31, 2012.

As of January 1, 2012, only seventeen servicers currently participate in this program. They are: Bank of America, N.A.; BayviewLoan Servicing, LLC; CitiMortgage, Inc.; Community Credit Union of Florida; GMAC Mortgage, LLC; Green Tree Servicing, LLC; iServeResidential Lending, LLC; iServeServicing, Inc.; JPMorgan Chase Bank, N.A.; NationstarMortgage, LLC; OneWest Bank; PennyMacLoan Services, LLC; PNC Bank, N.A.; PNC Mortgage; Residential Credit Solutions; ServisOne Inc., dba BSI Financial Services, Inc.; and Wells Fargo Bank, N.A.

The Home Affordable Foreclosure Alternatives Program is designed to provide homeowners who cannot afford to keep their homes with viable alternatives to a mortgage foreclosure. HAFA assists homeowners with securing a short sale or a deed in lieu of foreclosure. If your mortgage is backed by Freddie Mac or Fannie Mae, or if your servicer is a HAMP participant, HAFA is available to you as well. Although Illinois has its own deed in lieu of foreclosure, the HAFA version is useful for homeowners who do not live in a state that recognizes the remedy. Most attractive about HAFA is the HAFA short sale. Unlike a traditional short sale, a HAFA short sale completely satisfies a borrower's personal obligation to repay the loan. If your home is underwater, a HAFA short sale allows you to sell your property and not be faced with a balance due on your mortgage loan.

In order to qualify for HAFA, you must have been in your home for over 12 months and have not purchased a new house in the last 12 months. You must be able to demonstrate a financial hardship. HAFA is only available for loans that were originated prior to January 1, 2009. If you are unsure whether Fannie or Freddie backs your loan, you can find their loan lookup tools online.

To determine whether Fannie Mae owns your loan, go to: http://www.fanniemae.com/loanlookup/. To determine whether Freddie Mac owns your loan, go to: https://ww3.freddiemac.com/corporate/.

Home Affordable Refinance Program (HARP)[17]

The Home Affordable Refinance Program is available to borrowers who are current on their payments, but cannot find a refinance loan because their homes are underwater. Fannie Mae or Freddie Mac must own or guarantee your loan, and must have acquired the loan on or before May 31, 2009. The loan to value ratio for your home must be greater than 80%. This means that if your loan balance is at $75,000, and your home is worth $100,000, your loan to value ratio is at 75% and you are not eligible for a HARP refinance. If your loan balance is $125,000 and your home is worth $100,000, your loan to value ratio is 125% and you are eligible for a HARP refinance. The HARP refinance program also requires that borrowers have no missed payments in the last 6 months prior to applying and only 1 missed payment in the last 12 months. Refinancing while underwater is normally impossible, so this program offers a benefit in that regard. A HARP refinance will not lower your principal balance. If your home is severely underwater, a HARP refinance only makes sense if you are committed to keeping your home regardless of whether it has negative equity. In that case, HARP can help you secure a lower interest rate for the long-term.

FHA Short Refinance[18]

Refinancing while underwater is very difficult, if not impossible. If your loan is not backed by Fannie, Freddie, the FHA, the VA, or the USDA, you may be eligible for an FHA Short Refinance. If you are eligible for a new loan under the FHA's underwriting requirements, you may want to ask your mortgage servicer whether it participates in the FHA Short Refinance program. Participation in this program is entirely voluntary, so your servicer may not participate. In addition to qualifying for a FHA loan, you must be underwater, you must be current on your payments, and your total debt cannot exceed 55% of your monthly pre-tax income. If your servicer participates and you are eligible, the refinance loan must write down your first mortgage to no more than 97.75% of your home's current value.

Home Affordable Unemployment Program (UP)[19]

If you are unemployed and eligible for unemployment benefits, the Home Affordable Unemployment Program may be able to reduce your mortgage payments to 31 percent of your income or suspend your mortgage payments for 12 months or longer. Like the rest of the MHA programs, this program is only available for your primary residence. If you received a HAMP loan modification, you are not eligible for this program. If Fannie Mae or Freddie Mac owns or guarantees your loan, you are not eligible for this program, although both companies offer their own unemployment forbearance programs.

Other Loss Mitigation Methods

Deed In Lieu of Foreclosure

If you are not interested in keeping your home, or if you realize that your home is so far underwater that it will take years to see positive equity, you may be eligible for a deed in lieu of foreclosure. In Illinois, the deed in lieu of foreclosure is a remedy created by the Illinois Mortgage Foreclosure Law (IMFL).[20] It may be used before a foreclosure lawsuit is filed. It is also available once a lawsuit has been filed. If a lender accepts a deed in lieu of foreclosure, the homeowner literally deeds the property to the lender. In exchange, the lender waives the right to pursue the homeowner for any deficiency amount. A deficiency is the difference between the current market value of the home and the current balance of the mortgage loan.

While a deed in lieu is a powerful remedy, they are not frequently granted. Most lenders will not accept a deed in lieu if there is a second or third mortgage on the property. This is because the lender would be taking the property subject to the junior mortgages – it would not be obtaining free title to the property. In order to resell the property, it would have to pay off the other mortgages. Similarly, if there are other liens against your home such as judgment liens or mechanic's liens, the lender will require that you cure those liens before accepting a deed in lieu. In addition to that requirement, lenders will commonly require you to list your home for sale for a period of 90 days and provide financial documentation that establishes you have a valid hardship. Being underwater is not necessarily a financial hardship unless other circumstances help establish that a hardship exists. It is not possible to force a lender to accept a deed in lieu of foreclosure – it must be agreed to by both parties.

In some situations, a lender may send you an IRS Form 1099 reflecting the amount of the deficiency. In the past, this would have been considered taxable income as cancelled debt. However, if the home was your primary residence, and the value of the loan was under $2 million ($1 million for married couples filing separately), then this type of income is not taxable through December 31, 2012,[21] pursuant to the Mortgage Forgiveness Debt Relief Act of 2007[22].

Whitney and Bart Smith, Naperville, Illinois: A Sample Deed In Lieu of Foreclosure

Whitney and Bart Smith own a home in the DuPage County portion of Naperville, Illinois. They purchased their home in 2007 for $750,000. It is now worth $450,000 and they owe $600,000. When they purchased the home, both Whitney and Bart were both engineers for Tellabs and had a combined household income of $200,000 a year. In mid-2010, Bart was laid off. They managed to make their mortgage payments by tapping into their savings account when Whitney's income fell short. In early-2011, Whitney was also laid off. By then, Bart had found a replacement job, but only making half of his previous income. The couple continued to make their mortgage payments by tapping into their dwindling savings. In the summer of 2011, they decided that they were throwing good money after bad. They listed their home for sale, but had no luck finding a buyer. They finally asked their lender for a deed in lieu of foreclosure. After submitting their financial paperwork and demonstrating their economic hardship, their lender agreed to a deed in lieu of foreclosure. Whitney and Bart got a specific move-out date from the lender, and the lender avoided the costs of taking the property through the foreclosure process. The lender also waived its right to collect a deficiency, giving Whitney and Bart some clarity and peace of mind. This kind of certainty is the luxury of the informed.

If your lender has already filed a foreclosure action against you, the IMFL provides an additional remedy: the consent foreclosure.[23] A consent foreclosure is just what it sounds like. In exchange for the lender agreeing to waive any deficiency, you consent to a judgment of foreclosure being entered against your property. Title to the property vests in the mortgagee without conducting a sheriff's sale. Unlike a deed in lieu of foreclosure, this remedy is available even if you have multiple liens against the property. So long as those lien holders do not object to the consent foreclosure, the procedure has the effect of voiding those liens. However, the consent foreclosure does not terminate any personal liability on the debts that correspond with any junior liens.

At one point in time, a simple letter to the lender's attorneys was all that had to be done to secure a consent foreclosure. Some lenders are now requiring that borrowers list their home for 90 days and that they submit financial documentation before the lender will accept a consent foreclosure. As is the case with many loss mitigation strategies, defending against the foreclosure in state court is a key component to making a consent foreclosure work. Some lenders will realize that litigating the foreclosure will take a long time and agree to the consent foreclosure to cut their own expenses.

Kelsey Adams owns an investment property in the Lincoln Park neighborhood of Chicago, Illinois. When he purchased the property, a 4-unit brownstone, he had four tenants who paid their rent on time. As the economic crisis deepened, two of his tenants quit paying their rent, forcing him to default on his mortgage payments. Kelsey also owns his own home, and he was forced to prioritize his income on making the mortgage payments on his primary residence. Both properties are underwater. The investment property is now in foreclosure. Kelsey's attorney sends a letter to the lender's attorneys requesting a consent foreclosure. Within 45 days, the lender accepts Kelsey's offer and sends a set of stipulations to Kelsey's attorney for Kelsey's signature. The stipulations are agreed-upon facts that establish the statutory requirements for a consent foreclosure. Kelsey executes the stipulations and returns them to the lender's attorney. 45 days later, Kelsey's attorney appears in court when the consent foreclosure judgment is entered. The judgment vests title to the property in the lender, and Kelsey enjoys the certainty of knowing that he is not liable for any deficiency on the property. He has managed to rid himself of a failed investment and can comfortably make the mortgage payments on his primary residence. Since the property is not Kelsey's primary residence, Kelsey will want to consult with a CPA to determine what, if any, tax liability he may incur. Had the property included Kelsey's primary residence, his potential tax liability would have been waived so long as the consent foreclosure was to be completed before December 31, 2012.

Short Sale

Some defense attorneys will tell you that a short sale is a great idea. Some will tell you that it is a terrible idea. The truth is usually somewhere in the middle. A short sale does not necessarily provide you with protection from a deficiency. In a short sale, the deficiency is the difference between the selling price of the house and the balance of your mortgage loan (or loans). In some situations, borrowers must bring cash to the closing table just to get the money returned to the lender up to a level that the lender will accept.

Additionally, short sales offer very little predictability or certainty. A potential buyer may walk away if the bank drags its feet accepting the buyer's offer. Sales can fall through because the bank simply will not approve the sale price. It may be that the buyer cannot obtain financing due to a low appraisal value, among other reasons. At the end of the day, a short sale is probably the least efficient means of loss mitigation, but it can be rather lucrative for attorneys and realtors. Furthermore, the conflicts of interest that are inherent in most short sale transactions are unsettling. Typically, the seller pays the fees of all the parties involved. However, in your typical short sale, the realtor and attorney's fees are paid by the lender. The seller has less control over the transaction and, as a result, is exposed to less predictable, unsatisfactory outcomes.

Foreclosure Defense Strategies

Defending a residential foreclosure in Illinois involves more than simply replying to a complaint and going to trial. As with most situations that affect your personal finances, the best solution for you may not be the best solution for someone else. It is important that you make an informed decision after considering all of your options. Done properly, litigation is a powerful element of loss mitigation. This section offers a deeper discussion of the interplay between loss mitigation and litigation.

Litigation and Loss Mitigation

Many homeowners who want to keep their homes but aren't good bankruptcy candidates choose to fight their foreclosure case in court while pursuing a loan modification or another loss mitigation strategy. This approach can be effective in two different ways.

Stu fell behind on his mortgage payments after being laid off from his job of 10 years at the Chrysler Assembly Plant in Belvidere, Illinois. Stu has recently found a new job, and is making slightly less money than he was at his previous job. Stu's house is not significantly underwater, and he wants to keep his home. By defending his foreclosure case in court, which is his constitutional right, Stu will buy himself more time to obtain a loan modification. Since his income is only slightly less than it was before, he may have a good chance of getting a modification. If his lender refuses to offer a loan modification for any reason, Stu still has several possible safety valves: a Chapter 7 bankruptcy, a deed in lieu of foreclosure, or a consent foreclosure. While none of those options will save his home, they will both eliminate his potential liability for a deficiency in the future. Stu may also qualify for a Chapter 13 bankruptcy, which could save his home if he can afford to make monthly plan payments.

Amy Collins, Addison, Illinois: Chapter 7 Bankruptcy and
Foreclosure Defense

Amy's home in Addison, Illinois, is worth 25% less than
the value of her mortgage. She is currently employed as a nurse at
a local urgent care clinic. Amy has missed some mortgage
payments, but is not actively in foreclosure. She realizes that she
will likely lose her home and, given that the home is so deeply
underwater, she does not have any real financial benefit to keeping
the property. Amy's house has two mortgages, so she is not a good
candidate for a deed in lieu of foreclosure. She would have to settle
the second mortgage before being approved for a deed in lieu of
foreclosure. Amy has children in school and would like to remain
in her children's school district for as long as possible.

Amy has two main options for pursuing a foreclosure
defense strategy. Amy's income is within the limit for passing the
means test, so she is eligible for a Chapter 7 bankruptcy. She has
some unsecure debts that she could discharge and, like the vast
majority of Americans, does not have any significant assets other
than her cars and retirement fund. Filing a Chapter 7 bankruptcy
will help Amy get rid of her debts and will sever her personal
liability under the note, which would remain secured against her
home by her mortgage. If her lender then files a foreclosure lawsuit
against her, she is protected from any deficiency judgment that
may arise. Her credit has also started to improve because the

Chapter 7 bankruptcy discharge has forced her lender to stop reporting her mortgage as delinquent. More importantly, two years after her discharge, Amy may be eligible to purchase another home with a Federal Housing Administration loan.[24] With the FHA's lower interest rate and superior terms, she will have a better opportunity to pay off her mortgage. Paying off a mortgage as soon as possible is a critical goal of an informed borrower. Working to pay interest is never advisable, but that is what many Americans unwittingly do each day.

If the lender files a foreclosure action Amy now has options. She can ignore the lawsuit and begin looking for somewhere else to live. Even an uncontested foreclosure case can take a year to complete, so she has a great deal of time. If Amy wants to extend her time in the home, she can fight the foreclosure lawsuit. Defending a foreclosure significantly extends the time it takes a lender to complete the case, and may even result in the case being dismissed. If Amy's income increases or if she changes her mind, she may even be able to obtain a loan modification and remain in the home. Filing a Chapter 7 does not eliminate Amy's chances of obtaining a loan modification. No matter what she decides, she will have zero personal liability for the debt after her Chapter 7 discharge is granted. This kind of predictability is invaluable in a foreclosure situation and is one of the luxuries of being informed.

Many people think that a foreclosure case is a simple matter. The assumption is that if the homeowner failed to make payments, then the bank wins. In reality, foreclosure cases aren't that simple. The current foreclosure crisis has exposed many problems with the foreclosure process and homeowners typically have valid defenses against a foreclosure lawsuit. These defenses can cause a case to be dismissed. Here is a sampling of some of the most common defenses. Keep in mind that as the law develops, new defenses arise and some older defenses may not be as applicable. Moreover, every judge is different. In Illinois, there is no right to a jury trial in a foreclosure lawsuit, so the outcome of a specific defense is largely based upon a specific judge and whether he or she is convinced by the argument.

Lack of Standing

This specific defense is by far one of the most effective defenses to a foreclosure action. Long ago, most homeowners knew their loan officer. This is because loans used to be originated, held, and serviced by the same bank for the life of the loan. In the modern mortgage lending industry this is almost never the case. The lender whose name is on the note and mortgage may not be the entity that brings the foreclosure lawsuit. Illinois state law requires that the plaintiff in a lawsuit have a legitimate interest in the case. When a plaintiff does not have a legitimate interest in the case, the plaintiff lacks the standing to sue. A plaintiff that lacks standing cannot bring a lawsuit, and the case must be dismissed. Additionally, a plaintiff must have standing from the moment it files the lawsuit. If a plaintiff gains standing to sue during the pendency of the case, but after the date of filing, the case must be dismissed. In that instance, the plaintiff is free to re-file the lawsuit, but the case must be restarted from scratch. Some common standing issues are discussed below.

A Brief History of U.S. Mortgages

In the past, most homeowners borrowed the money to purchase their home from a local bank. The bank issued a short-term loan with a balloon payment at the end of the loan's lifetime. Some loans were for as short as 5 or 10 years. The longest-term mortgages were 15 year mortgages. After the Great Depression, the government created the Federal Housing Administration in 1934 to help repair the damaged housing economy. Another entity that helped transform mortgage lending was the Home Owners' Loan Corporation, which was established in 1933. Both agencies helped transition the mortgage market into 15 and 30 year fixed-rate mortgages, which were seen as a superior alternative to the balloon-payment mortgages that had been popular before the Great Depression.

In general, banks kept mortgage loans on their books as a liability, and balanced those liabilities by keeping enough assets on hand to cover all but the most catastrophic losses. This meant that once a lender had issued a certain amount of loans, it was unable to issue more loans without acquiring extra capital. Some banks would sell their loans to the secondary market, thus freeing up funds for issuing more loans. This secondary market allowed banks to sustainably lend money to homeowners for quite some time. Midway through the 20th century, some of the first mortgage-backed securities were issued. However, federal regulations kept the number low and limited the types of mortgages that could be securitized.

As time went on, regulations were lifted and more lenders got into the business of issuing mortgage-backed securities. The system worked well for a while, but further deregulation and the desire to keep increasing profits eventually led to the housing boom that preceded the 2008 collapse.

Mortgage Securitization Issues

One of the main causes of the financial crisis was the failure of mortgage-backed securities. Mortgage-backed securities are intended to be long-term, stable investments. Many mutual funds, pension funds and other investment vehicles buy mortgage-backed securities as part of their overall portfolio. These securities are supposed to be stable because the risk of loss is spread across a large pool of mortgage loans. If one homeowner defaults and the property goes into foreclosure, it does not destroy the entire pool. A mortgage pool that contains a large number of high-risk or subprime loans is a different matter. When many loans in a pool default, the value of the mortgage-backed securities plummets.

During the housing boom, mortgage lenders were securitizing the vast majority of the loans that were issued. However, many of these loans were poorly underwritten – the borrowers were given a loan that they could not afford, often without any documentation to support their financial status. Lenders pushed to create these loans to provide more mortgages for the securitization process. Since it is possible to increase profits by keeping overhead low, many mortgage lenders cut corners in order to maximize profits. In a perfect world, a mortgage-backed security trust would be properly established and funded. In the real world, many of these trusts were not.

A typical mortgage security trust involves several parties. The parties and their respective duties are defined by a document called the Pooling and Servicing Agreement (PSA). At the beginning of the chain is your original lender. This could be a small mortgage lender or a major bank. In securitization terms, this person is called the Seller. The Seller originates the loan and then sells it, for value, to another entity called the Sponsor. The Sponsor then sells the loan, for value, to a third entity called the Depositor. The Depositor then transfers the loan into the trust. This chain is necessary because mortgage-backed securities must be "bankruptcy remote." If the original lender goes bankrupt, the subsequent sales of the loan insulate it from being repossessed by a bankruptcy trustee. A typical PSA requires that each stage of this process is documented in writing and that the original documents all make it into the trust before its closing date.

In theory, loan securitization is a simple process that merely involves lots of paperwork. During the real estate boom, this process was generally mismanaged and did not work as intended. In fact, in 2010, an employee of BAC (Bank of America/Countrywide) testified in open court that Countrywide loans were never properly handled when they were securitized.[25] Instead of sending the original documents to the trustee, Countrywide held those documents in its warehouse. If her testimony is true for every Countrywide loan, then trusts holding those loans do not actually hold the loans. This is because, by law, a trust cannot take actions that are outside the powers granted to the trust by the trust documents. Since PSAs require that the trust or its document custodian[26] have actual possession of the original loan documents by the trust's closing date, a trust that is not in possession of the original loan documents by the closing date cannot own the loan.

This presents an interesting problem for trusts that are attempting to foreclose on a home. If the trust cannot demonstrate that it was in possession of the original documents pursuant to the terms of its PSA, then it does not own the loan. If the trust does not own the loan, it cannot enforce the mortgage or the note against the homeowner. In that situation, the trust does not have standing to sue and the foreclosure case should be dismissed. Depending on the documents that the trust attaches to its complaint, your foreclosure defense attorney should be able to make an initial determination as to whether this defense is available to you.

A Mortgage Loan in Orland Park, Illinois: An Example of Mortgage Securitization

Local Prairie Bank issues as many loans as it possibly can issue without over-extending itself. Local Prairie Bank regularly sells its loans to Midwest Mortgage Holding, LLC in order to free up available capital for issuing new loans. Midwest Mortgage Holding, LLC then sells large packages of loans to National Bank Depositor LLC, which is a subsidiary of National Bank Mortgage Trusts, N.A. National Bank Depositor LLC conveys each package of loans into separate securitization trusts. Each trust is governed by its own Pooling and Servicing Agreement. For example, a loan issued by Local Prairie Bank in June of 2007 became a part of NBMT Asset-Backed Securities Trust, Series 2007-3. This way, if Local Prairie Bank becomes insolvent, there are two "true" sales in between Local Prairie Bank and the securitization trust. This all but eliminates the risk of a bankruptcy trustee clawing back loans into Local Prairie Bank's bankruptcy estate. Bankruptcy trustees are impartial third parties tasked with overseeing bankruptcy cases. They have very broad powers designed to protect the assets of a bankruptcy filer (also known as the bankruptcy estate). Those powers include, among others, recovering assets that were sold shortly before a bankruptcy filing.

National Bank Mortgage Trusts, N.A. assigns its servicing rights in the mortgage loans to American Loan Servicing, Inc., which collects mortgage payments from homeowners and remits the payments to National Bank Mortgage Trusts, N.A. for distribution to the holders of the mortgage securities. So long as each entity in the chain followed the terms set forth in the Pooling and Servicing Agreement, the securitization trust properly owns the loans it holds and should be a stable, long-term investment.

Show Me the Note

At the beginning of the foreclosure crisis, the "show me the note" movement began. If the party attempting to foreclose on your home is not your original lender, demanding to see the original note is an essential tactic and a valid defense to foreclosure. If the party attempting to foreclose on your home is your original lender, you still want to demand that the original note be produced for inspection. What's the big deal about the original note? Only the original note can be enforced against a borrower. Notes are negotiable instruments. A negotiable instrument is a type of financial document that can be transferred from one party to another. This transfer generally involves signing it (indorsement) and then delivering the original to the new owner. Other examples of a negotiable instrument would be a personal check or a twenty dollar bill. No bank will cash a photocopy of a check, and nobody in their right mind would give someone two tens for a photocopied twenty. This is because only the original document has any value. The same goes for notes associated with home loans.

When you are being sued by a party that is not your original lender, the stakes are even higher. The plaintiff must demonstrate more than mere possession of the original note. The original note is payable only to one party – the original lender. In order to be enforceable by anyone else, the note must bear indorsements that either name a new party as the payee of the note or that make whomever holds the original note the payee. These are known as special and blank indorsements. If you indorse the back of your paycheck, you have just created a blank indorsement. By indorsing the check and not naming a specific payee, your indorsement converts the check to what is known as "bearer paper." If you drop your check on the ground, whoever finds it can cash it. If, instead, you indorse the back of your paycheck and write, "Pay to the order of Bob Smith," then only Bob Smith can cash the check because it is now specifically payable to him. This type of indorsement is sometimes referred to as "order paper" because it is payable to the order of the named individual. As with the original note, a photocopy of a note with indorsements is insufficient. The original document must bear the indorsements in order for the indorsements to be valid. Additionally, even if the note is indorsed, it must still be delivered to the new owner, otherwise, the indorsements have no true effect. This process is known as negotiation.

A Lockport, Illinois Property: An Example of Why "Show Me the Note" is Powerful

Let's say that in 1998 you purchased a home in Lockport, Illinois and took out a mortgage loan with Chase Bank. During the time you owned the home, you received a letter from MahnaMahna Mortgage Company, Inc. informing you that it was the new owner of your home loan. Being a responsible person, you began making your payments to MahnaMahna as requested. Years later, in 2010, you fell behind on your mortgage payments. After several missed payments, you received a knock at the door and were served with a summons by the Will County sheriff. The summons listed Washington Morgan Chase Bank as the plaintiff and indicated that it was a summons in a foreclosure action. Attached to the summons was a complaint with two exhibits. One of those exhibits was a copy of the note you executed in 1998. The note has no signatures on it besides your signature. In that situation, you would want to demand to view the original note. You'd also want to assert that, based on the face of its documents, Washington Morgan Chase Bank lacks the required standing to bring the foreclosure lawsuit. Unless Washington Morgan Chase Bank can demonstrate that it was in possession of the original note, which was either indorsed in blank or indorsed as payable to Washington Morgan Chase Bank, at the time it filed its lawsuit, it lacks the required legal standing to bring the lawsuit. Since a party must have standing on the date that it files its lawsuit, Washington Morgan Chase Bank can likely file a new lawsuit if it actually has standing. However, its current lawsuit must be dismissed as a matter of law. This is the heart of a solid standing defense.

If you are considering hiring an attorney to defend your home from foreclosure, make sure to ask whether that attorney is familiar with both mortgage securitization and standing issues in general. This area of law is constantly developing. For instance, some attorneys are now arguing that a home loan note cannot be transferred by indorsement and a change in physical possession. Although this argument has its merits, it is currently untested in Illinois and goes against the "common understanding" of most judges and attorneys.

Before a lender can initiate a foreclosure lawsuit against you, it must take certain steps to notify you of your default and that you are subject to foreclosure. This obligation may be imposed by state or federal law, but is also contained in almost every mortgage. In most mortgage documents, this obligation is stated in paragraph 22. The notice must be provided in the format described in the mortgage. If you received a notice that did not comply with the mortgage's terms, or if you did not receive any notice at all, your lender cannot bring a foreclosure action against you. Most mortgages and notes are the same. Many are Fannie Mae/Freddie Mac Uniform Instruments and are designed to keep terms consistent from loan-to-loan. In general, the lending industry uses form documents to keep loan terms consistent. This is also known as "boilerplate" language. The reason loan terms are kept consistent is to facilitate the sale and negotiation of the loans. Some mortgages and notes are exceptions to the rule, the terms contained in the standard paragraph 22 may be in paragraph 18 or paragraph 23. This is why attention to detail is an important quality for a foreclosure defense attorney.

This mortgage clause is one of the few clauses in the mortgage that protects you as a borrower. The vast majority of a mortgage's language is designed to protect the bank's interests, not yours. However, because this clause is contained in almost every mortgage, it is considered a "condition precedent" to filing a foreclosure lawsuit. In simpler terms, a bank must give you an opportunity to catch up on your missed payments before proceeding with a foreclosure lawsuit. Even if your lender insists that it properly notified you, it may not be able to properly document that it provided this notice. In that case, it is as if the notice was never provided. A mortgage foreclosure lawsuit is serious business, and you should make your lender dots every "i" and crosses every "t" if it is going to attempt to foreclose on your home.

Setoff

This defense alleges that you are owed money by the bank or that the bank has improperly applied your payments. While this defense does not necessarily defeat a lawsuit, it can offset the amount of money that the bank claims that you owe. This is particularly useful if you are trying to exercise your right of reinstatement or redemption. If you believe that you have a claim for setoff, inform your foreclosure defense attorney so that he or she can explore the issue for you.

Chet always paid his mortgage on time. When he had extra money, he would make a pre-payment against his loan's principal balance by sending a separate check with a letter indicating that he was making a pre-payment. Pursuant to the terms of his promissory note, this was sufficient to ensure that the bank was properly applying his prepayments towards his principal balance. In total, Chet pre-paid $45,000 towards his loan's principal balance over the course of 4 years. His goal from the time he took the mortgage was to pay it off as quickly as possible. In late-2010, Chet was laid off from his position with the U.S. Department of Education, where he monitored student loan providers for 15 years. Although he was able to make mortgage payments with a combination of his unemployment benefits and savings, Chet soon ran out of savings and was forced to default on his mortgage.

When he was served with a foreclosure summons and complaint, Chet hired a seasoned foreclosure defense attorney. After reviewing the complaint, Chet and his attorney noticed that the amount due alleged in the complaint was significantly higher than it should be. Chet provided his attorney with his mortgage statements from the past five years. After carefully examining the statements, it was evident that his lender had not been properly or accurately applying his pre-payments towards principal, but was instead applying those payments towards interest. In his answer to the foreclosure complaint, Chet asserted the $45,000 in pre-payments as a setoff against the total amount owed. Had his payments been properly applied, Chet would have a significantly lower amount of money to pay in order to redeem his loan. Given that Chet had been paying his mortgage on time for a long time, and given the equity in his home, Chet was able to refinance his loan to a lower interest rate with better terms and avoid foreclosure.

Constructive Contract/Promissory Estoppel

This defense is often used when a lender attempts to foreclose on your home while you are making payments pursuant to a trial or permanent loan modification agreement. As many homeowners who have tried to obtain a loan modification know, the loan modification process is often confusing and poorly managed. You may be offered a trial modification over the phone, begin making payments, and never receive the actual documents that memorialize the trial modification. The same thing often happens for borrowers who have been offered a permanent loan modification. Another common occurrence is being kept in a perpetual trial modification. A typical trial modification is supposed to last three months. If you have been in a trial modification for a longer period of time, you may be able to claim that the bank's failure to convert you to a permanent loan modification is a breach of your agreements with the bank.

Trial loan modifications do not typically guarantee that you will receive a permanent loan modification. They do not permanently change the terms of your loan. However, a bank's actions and the statements of its employees can potentially change this. For example, if you have been making trial loan modification payments for 18 months, and the bank's employees keep assuring you that your permanent modification is "coming soon," you may be able to claim that a contract exists between you and the bank.

Even if you do not have a written agreement, an oral agreement may be sufficient to modify your loan. If you relied on the bank's statements and fully performed your obligations, a contract exists by operation of law. This is what is known as a constructive contract or promissory estoppel. If you believe that this issue applies to your case, inform your attorney so that he or she can evaluate the issue.

Morgan Gibson, Plainfield, Illinois: A Constructive Contract Claim

As the financial crisis deepened, Morgan, a marketing executive, realized that he could no longer afford his adjustable rate mortgage loan. He contacted his lender and requested that he be considered for a HAMP loan modification. Morgan's lender informed him that he was not eligible for a HAMP modification, but that it would put him into an in-house trial loan modification program. If Morgan made three trial payments on time, and his financial status had remained stable, he would be offered a permanent loan modification. Morgan followed the lender's instructions and made his three timely trial payments. After he made his third payment, Morgan contacted his lender to find out whether he would be offered a permanent loan modification. His lender informed him that he would receive a permanent loan modification with payments beginning in the next month. Morgan was instructed to send a check for $50 to cover the cost of overnight delivery of his permanent modification documents.

Morgan sent his check to the lender, but never received his permanent loan modification documents. Morgan was afraid that if he didn't start making his new payments on time, he would not be offered another modification. His lender assured him that the documents were on their way. When the first payment became due, Morgan made it. Morgan continued to pay the modified loan payment for over a year. He was literally horrified when, 13 months after making his first payment, he received a foreclosure summons and complaint. The complaint alleged that Morgan was in default on his mortgage payments from the beginning of his trial modification some 16 months earlier. Morgan explained the situation to his attorney, who filed an answer to the complaint with affirmative defenses and counterclaims, asserting Morgan's constructive contract with his lender. Although Morgan had never executed his permanent modification documents, the fact that his lender continued to accept his payments without notifying him of a problem was evidence that Morgan and the lender had entered into an oral, yet permanent, loan modification agreement.

Rescission

This defense is based on the federal Truth In Lending Act (TILA). Under the Act, lenders are required to provide specific disclosures to borrowers either before the loan closes or at closing, or both, depending on the notice. For example, when you are refinancing the loan on your primary residence, you are entitled to receive two copies of a document called the "Notice of Right to Cancel." If you don't receive two copies, or if the notices do not comply with the suggested format, there has been a violation of TILA. Normally, you only have three days to rescind your loan. If your lender violates TILA, however, you have three years to rescind your loan.

So what is rescission? Quite simply, rescission is the process of unwinding the loan and returning the borrower and the lender to where they were before the loan was issued. In practice, the remedy is a bit different. The statute establishes an order of performance in a TILA rescission. Once the loan has been properly rescinded, the bank must release the mortgage and return any payments to the borrower. The borrower is then supposed to return the funds that the bank lent. A courts is free to modify this tender strategy if fairness dictates that it should. The effect of the broad equitable power to modify tender has been the subject of much of the case law related to TILA rescissions. As the law continues to evolve and develop, this remedy may be strengthened or weakened. In the meantime, it is always important to have your attorney evaluate your loan documents and determine whether you have a potential claim under TILA.

Rob and Linda Madison, Crystal Lake, Illinois: A Basis for Rescission

Rob and Linda are a married couple. Rob is a general contractor and Linda teaches high school English. They refinanced their home's mortgage two years ago. At the closing, Rob and Linda were provided with two copies of the Notice of Right to Cancel. The loan was taken out only in Rob's name, but Linda signed the mortgage to waive her homestead rights. In Illinois, homestead rights are created by statute and protect up to $15,000 of the value of a person's primary residence from liens. Most mortgage lenders require that borrowers waive these rights to make foreclosing on a mortgage easier. Based on these facts, Rob and Linda were not provided with the right number of copies of the Notice of Right to Cancel. TILA requires that every person with an interest in the property be provided with two copies of the Notice. Even though Linda was not personally obligated to repay the loan, the fact that she signed the mortgage entitled her to receive two copies of the Notice in addition to the two copies Rob should have received. Since their lender failed to provide enough copies, Rob and Linda have a three year right to rescind their loan. This provides Rob and Linda with a means of unwinding the loan, which can place them in a stronger bargaining position with their lender.

The Foreclosure Process In Illinois

Illinois homeowners are fortunate that Illinois is a judicial foreclosure state. In non-judicial foreclosure states, a lender does not have to file a lawsuit before foreclosing on a home. In those states, it is much more difficult to defend against a foreclosure action. The foreclosure process in Illinois is governed by the Illinois Mortgage Foreclosure Law (IMFL). The IMFL dictates the format of the complaint and provides homeowners with specific protections and remedies. This section describes the basic foreclosure timeline and specific time-sensitive remedies.

Title Theory States vs. Lien Theory States

Illinois is a lien theory state. Simply put, this means that when you take out a mortgage loan, the mortgage exists as a lien against your property. You have legal title to the property, and the bank merely asserts an interest in the property based on its loan. In other states, like Massachusetts, they subscribe to the title theory. In title theory states, the bank holds legal title to your home until you pay off the balance of your mortgage loan. Generally, states with a judicial foreclosure process tend to be lien theory states. The judicial foreclosure process serves as the mechanism for transferring title from the homeowner to the party that purchases the property at a sheriff's sale. States that subscribe to the title theory tend to be non-judicial foreclosure states. In those states, lenders are not required to engage in a lengthy court process before proceeding to a sale of the property. Since the lender owns legal title to the property, it can freely dispose of the property once it has complied with the terms of its own state's foreclosure laws.

Beginning the Case

A lender cannot begin a foreclosure case unless you are in default on your mortgage. The three most common events of default are failing to pay your property taxes, failing to maintain homeowner's insurance on the property, and failing to make principal and interest payments as set forth in the loan documents.

Assuming there is a default and that a lender has taken all of the proper pre-filing steps, such as providing written notice of acceleration to the borrower, the first step in beginning a foreclosure case is filing a foreclosure complaint and issuing a summons. Once a summons is issued, lenders will give the summons to either the county sheriff or a special process server to have the summons served on the borrower. If your home is currently subject to a foreclosure suit, but you were never served with a summons, your foreclosure defense attorney should file a motion to quash service. However, your attorney should verify that you were not served via publication. Service via publication is allowed when the lender is unable to serve you by traditional means. It is highly unlikely that you will actually read the published notice of the lawsuit in the newspaper. In a situation where service was obtained by publication, you may still be able to quash service if the lender made no attempt to obtain personal service, made defective attempts to obtain service, or otherwise violated the statute that governs service via publication. A defective attempt at obtaining service would be, for example, sending the sheriff's deputy or process server to the wrong address.

On January 9, 2012, the Illinois Appellate Court for the First Appellate District, which sits in Chicago, Illinois, clarified a previously unaddressed issue: can a foreclosing lender obtain a deficiency judgment against a borrower who was served with a summons via substitute service? Substitute service, also known as abode service, occurs when a process server serves a summons to a defendant's home address, but leaves the summons with a resident of the property who is over 13 years of age.

For example, Bank of America files a foreclosure lawsuit against Jack Stone related to his home in Wheaton, Illinois. Bank of America's attorneys attempt to serve a copy of the summons and complaint upon Jack via the DuPage County Sheriff. However, Jack is not home when the sheriff arrives. Instead, the deputy gives a copy of the summons and complaint to Jack's 15 year old son, Steve. The deputy explains to Steve what the summons is and also deposits a copy in the U.S. Mail, postage prepaid, which arrives at the Stone household a few days later. This would be proper abode or substitute service in Illinois.

According to the Illinois Appellate Court for the First Appellate District, this is proper personal service as "personal" is defined in the Illinois Mortgage Foreclosure Law. If the foreclosing lender obtains substitute/abode service on a defendant homeowner, the lender may pursue a deficiency judgment.[27] If the defendant homeowner never appears in court, and the lender obtains service by publication, the lender cannot obtain a personal deficiency judgment.

Assuming that you were properly served with the summons and a copy of the complaint, you have 30 days to file an appearance in the lawsuit and file a responsive pleading, which could be a motion to dismiss or an answer to the complaint, among others. Although judges generally allow defendants to respond to the complaint after the 30 day mark, the longer you wait to get involved in your case, the less likely it is that you will be allowed to respond. For example, if you ignore the summons and do nothing, the lender will eventually obtain a default judgment against you.

Thirty days after the default judgment is entered, it becomes extremely difficult to vacate the default judgment and fight the lawsuit. Although foreclosures are taking a long time to complete, doing nothing in court is the worst-possible plan. Keep in mind that even if you are attempting to obtain a loan modification, the bank will proceed forward with the foreclosure lawsuit. To fully protect your rights, you must defend against the foreclosure lawsuit. Simply applying for a loan modification is not enough. If a bank employee tells you that applying for a loan modification will delay the foreclosure case, then that person is lying to you. If the bank employee tells you that you do not have to hire an attorney or go to court during the pendency of your case, they are misleading you. Staying in touch with the bank and its employees will not stop a foreclosure lawsuit from progressing forward.

Responding to the Complaint

Once you or your attorney has filed an appearance in the case, you must respond to the complaint. In some cases, it may make sense to file a motion to dismiss the complaint. For example, if you are making payments on a permanent loan modification and are no longer in default, the case should be dismissed. Any permanent loan modification will provide for the repayment of your missed payments, which means that you are no longer in default. Depending on the preferences of the judge hearing your case, it may make more sense to file and answer with affirmative defenses and/or counterclaims.

An affirmative defense is a set of facts that either defeats the lender's claim or that mitigates the amount of money you owe to your lender. Affirmative defenses can range from claiming a lack of standing to sue to claiming a setoff to the loan balance. Counterclaims are claims that you can assert against the lender where you are generally seeking damages for the lender's misconduct. Counterclaims are a lawsuit-within-a-lawsuit and could just as easily be brought as a separate lawsuit against your lender. They set forth specific facts and apply those facts to an alleged violation of the law. Illinois courts require that all claims are pled with specific facts; general allegations are insufficient to support a counterclaim or an affirmative defense in Illinois. Although it is possible to handle this stage of litigation without an attorney, it is not advisable. The Illinois Code of Civil Procedure, the statute that sets forth the rules of engagement for any civil matter in Illinois, such as foreclosures, is technical and best administered by qualified professionals. However, some individuals have successfully defended their own matters before Illinois courts to varying degrees of success. To assist those who chose to go it alone, we have included in the appendices of this text critical definitions of the terms that a non-attorney needs to know to address a foreclosure action. However, relying on that alone is ill-advised.

An Example of an Affirmative Defense

Earlier in this section, we discussed some of the available defenses to a foreclosure lawsuit. Those defenses are normally brought as affirmative defenses and are included in conjunction with the answer to the complaint. One of the most common affirmative defenses is that the lender lacks the standing to bring the foreclosure lawsuit. This defense is most commonly used when the party suing is not the original lender. The defense will allege that, based on the face of the plaintiff's complaint and exhibits, the plaintiff has failed to establish that it has the power to enforce the mortgage and note against the homeowner. If the plaintiff cannot establish that it had the power to enforce the mortgage and note against the homeowner when the case was filed, then the case must be dismissed.

An Example of a Counterclaim

Earlier in this section, we discussed the idea of a constructive contract. In a situation like that of Morgan, the marketing executive from Plainfield, a wise attorney would file a counterclaim against the lender alleging that it is in breach of its contract with the homeowner. A counterclaim based on facts like Morgan's would establish the facts that gave rise to the constructive contract. A proper counterclaim would then lay out the applicable statutory or case law that creates the constructive contract. The counterclaim would then establish specifically how the lender breached the contract and plead a specific harm that the homeowner has suffered.

In the case of a constructive contract, the counterclaim would allege that by filing the lawsuit and failing to properly apply the modified loan payments to the loan balance, the lender breached the loan modification agreement. It would further establish that these breaches caused multiple injuries to the homeowner. For example, the damage to the homeowner's credit score caused by inaccurate reporting to the credit bureaus, the emotional distress caused by the lawsuit, and any fees or penalties charged by the lender would all be valid damages that a homeowner can assert against the lender. Morgan can even ask the court to order the lender to pay Morgan's attorney's fees.

Discovery

Soon after you have responded to the foreclosure complaint, you will want to issue discovery. Discovery is an orderly process that allows you to ask questions, request admissions of fact, and request the production of documents from the parties to a lawsuit. The lender is also entitled to discovery, and lenders will issue discovery requests in some cases. This is also the phase of litigation where you have the opportunity to depose live witnesses. Depositions in foreclosure cases are rare, but there are situations where they are appropriate. For example, if the lender is building its case based on the affidavit of one of its employees, you may want to depose that employee to ascertain whether the statements in the affidavit are accurate. Given the general disarray of most lender's files, it can take a significant amount of time to receive discovery responses from your lender. If a lender takes too long in responding to discovery, your attorney may file a motion to compel to obtain a court order directing the lender to respond.

The IMFL provides for a specific right of reinstatement.[28] In order to reinstate your loan, you must repay any missed payments and any costs and expenses required by the mortgage. You cannot be required to repay the amount of principal due as a result of the lender accelerating your loan. This right expires 90 days from the day you were served or from the date you voluntarily submitted to the court's jurisdiction (filing an appearance before being served). If you reinstate your loan within the 90 day period, the case against you must be dismissed because you are no longer in default. Although this option is available to every homeowner, not many many people are able to take advantage of it. Homeowners who receive large periodic bonuses at work or who have a family member willing to help can use this remedy to end their foreclosure and move on with their lives. Reinstatement is one of your rights under the law, but it can only be exercised once every 5 years. If you reinstate your loan in 2011, you cannot exercise the right again until 2016.

Andre Godwin, Hinsdale, Illinois: An Example of a Reinstatement

Andre works as an enterprise data solutions salesman for IBM. He fell behind on his mortgage in early 2011. His monthly mortgage payment is $1,500. After missing four payments, his lender filed a foreclosure lawsuit against him. At the time the lawsuit was filed, Andre owed $6,000 in missed payments, plus the fees and costs assessed to him pursuant to the terms of his note. His total reinstatement amount was $9,000. Fortunately for Andre, he is a salesman who receives periodic bonuses. Shortly after the foreclosure action was filed, Andre received a bonus payment of $11,000. Andre consulted with a foreclosure defense attorney who, based on the fact that his home was not underwater, advised him to exercise his right to reinstate his loan. Andre's attorney contacted the lender's attorneys and requested a current reinstatement figure. After making a payment of $9,350, which included interest and fees that had accrued since the suit was filed, Andre properly reinstated his loan. The lender then dismissed its lawsuit.

Motions for Summary Judgment

After discovery is completed and once the right to reinstate has expired, it is likely that the lender will file a motion for summary judgment. If you have outstanding affirmative defenses, this type of motion should generally fail. Some motions for summary judgment may be brought as a combined motion that attacks your defenses and then requests a judgment. A motion for summary judgment claims that, when all of the facts on the record are taken in the light most favorable to the non-moving party, there is no genuine issue of material fact left for the court to decide. The non-moving party is the party who has not filed the motion for summary judgment.

In some situations, the borrower may be able to file a motion for summary judgment. The most common reason for a homeowner to move for summary judgment is because the lender has failed to establish that it has the standing to sue. If you are being sued by a lender who is not your original lender and all of the documents presented to you in the complaint and via discovery do not indicate that the party suing you has the right to enforce the note against you, then you have a solid basis for summary judgment. This course of action is advisable for many reasons, but chief among them is securing a more predictable outcome for the borrower. If the party suing the borrower has no right to sue, or has failed to prove that it has the right to sue, then the issue is best resolved as soon as possible. This effort may assist in securing a swift settlement.

Melvin Gibbs, Chicago, Illinois: A Motion for Summary Judgment

Melvin Gibbs is a structural engineer and local musician who lives in the Wicker Park neighborhood of Chicago, Illinois. Melvin and his attorneys have been fighting his foreclosure case since early 2010. When the case was first filed, First Fidelity National Lending Association was the plaintiff. Attached to the complaint were a mortgage and note made in favor of Internet Lending Corp, Inc. The note and mortgage were not indorsed and there was no assignment of mortgage on file. After Melvin's attorneys issued their discovery requests, First Fidelity's attorneys filed an amended complaint. The amended complaint named National Country Servicing as the plaintiff. Attached to the amended complaint were the same copies of the mortgage and note that had been attached to the initial complaint.

Five months later, National Country Servicing's attorneys responded to Melvin's discovery requests. In their responses to Melvin's discovery requests, the bank's attorneys included the same copies of the mortgage and note that had been attached to both complaints. The bank refused to make the original mortgage and note available for viewing by Melvin's attorneys. After a lengthy battle in court, the judge ordered the bank to produce the original documents.

When Melvin's attorneys viewed the original mortgage and note, there was a major difference between the original documents produced outside of court and the copies that had been produced with National Country's complaint. The original documents included a blank indorsement signed by the now infamous Linda Green, Vice President of Internet Lending Corp, Inc. Melvin's attorneys filed a motion for summary judgment against National Country Servicing based on the bank's lack of standing to bring the lawsuit.

The bank argued that since it was in possession of a blank indorsed original note, it was the lawful holder of the note and had standing to sue. Melvin's attorneys argued that while the bank was *currently* in possession of a blank indorsed original note, there was no question of material fact that the bank was not in possession of the same document when the lawsuit was filed. After all, had the indorsed note been in the bank's hands when the lawsuit was filed, a copy of the indorsed note would have been attached to the original complaint. After both sides had submitted briefs supporting their positions, the court heard oral arguments on Melvin's motion for summary judgment. The court found in Melvin's favor and entered summary judgment against the bank. Shortly thereafter, Melvin was offered a permanent loan modification. Melvin accepted the permanent loan modification and achieved his goal.

Default Judgment

In most mortgage foreclosure cases, lenders obtain judgment by default. This is because most people do not defend against the lawsuit. In other cases, lenders will tend to obtain a judgment via a motion for summary judgment. It is extremely rare to see a foreclosure case go to trial. If your lender obtains a judgment against you, the case is still not over. In order to complete the foreclosure, your lender must conduct a valid sheriff's sale and have that sale confirmed by the court. By law, this cannot happen the day after a judgment is entered. The date that the judgment was entered is critical, as will be explained below.

The Right of Redemption

The Illinois Mortgage Foreclosure Law (IMFL) provides for a right of redemption.[29] This means that after a judgment is entered against you, you have 90 days to pay off the full balance of the judgment amount, which can include interest, court costs, and attorney's fees. The date of the judgment is critical; even if you file a bankruptcy or file a separate lawsuit against your lender, this 90 day period continues to run. The IMFL is very clear on this point.[30] Once the right of redemption has expired, it cannot be revived.

The redemption amount will consist of the full value of the loan, costs and penalties, as well as the lender's attorney's fees. Most borrowers don't have the funds to redeem – if they did, they likely would not be in foreclosure in the first place. However, fortunes can change. In the event that you find yourself with the ability to redeem your mortgage, you can exit the foreclosure lawsuit with your loan paid in full. For all practical purposes, the right of redemption provides some extra breathing room before the lender can proceed with a sheriff's sale. Until the right of redemption has run, a sale cannot be conducted.

After the right of redemption has expired, the lender is free to proceed with a sheriff's sale. A sheriff's sale is an auction typically held at the courthouse in the county where the property is located. For example, a piece of real estate located in Yorkville, Illinois would be subject to a sheriff's sale conducted at the Kendall County courthouse. At the auction, the winning bidder is generally required to pay 25% of its bid immediately, with the remaining balance due in 24 hours. The terms of the sale will vary depending on the company conducting the auction. The sale is not final until it is confirmed by a judge. Before the sale is confirmed, the winning bid is simply an irrevocable offer to buy the property.

Before the sale can be conducted, the lender must comply with the notice and advertisement provisions of the IMFL. The sale must be advertised in a newspaper in the county where the property is located. The advertisements must run for three consecutive weeks, not more than 45 days before the sale is scheduled, and not less than seven days before the scheduled sale. If the lender fails to meet this requirement, any sale that is held may be set aside by the court. However, unless the homeowner objects to the confirmation of sale, the judge may not notice the error and approve the sale.

If the sale was conducted properly, and there is no objection to the confirmation of the sale, the judge will confirm the sale of the property. After the sale is confirmed, there is a 30 day stay on the buyer's right to possess the property. Some judges will extend this period to 60 or 90 days if special circumstances warrant an extension. Judges will not extend this period without being asked, so it is important that you, at the very least, attend the confirmation hearing, even if you have had no involvement in the case up to that point. In the event that you need more time before being forced to vacate the property, you could ask the judge for more time. The judge does not have to grant your request. The judge can deny or approve your request in that judge's own discretion, but usually over the lender's objection.

There are four main grounds for objecting to the confirmation of a sheriff's sale. The first one is that the lender failed to properly provide notice of the sale. This could be based on a failure to advertise the sale for the proper period of time prior to the sale; it could also be based on a typographical error in the advertisement. Objections to the notice of sale can be highly technical, so it is advisable to consult with your defense attorney to determine whether you have grounds to object.

Another basis for denying the confirmation of sale is that the terms of the sale were unconscionable. For instance, if the fair market value of the property is $450,000, and the property is sold for $50,000, it is likely that the sale was unconscionable. This is even more likely when the only party bidding on the property is the lender. Unconscionability is a complex legal concept, and is another basis for objection that is best discussed with an attorney.

A third reason for denying the confirmation of sale is because the sale was conducted fraudulently. If the lender advertises the sale as taking place at the DuPage County Courthouse, knowing that it is going to conduct the sale in another location, this raises both an improper notice issue and a fraudulently conducted or defective sale issue. Another example is where the lender accepts a payoff amount from the homeowner but still proceeds to sale.

The fourth basis for denying confirmation of sale is that justice was not otherwise done. This catch-all provision can involve many different situations. Before the sale is conducted, it may be possible to find someone who is willing to purchase the property. If the buyer is willing to pay the full judgment amount, it may be possible to deny confirmation of sale, especially if the winning bid at auction would result in a potential deficiency against the homeowner. Some affirmative defenses may also be grounds for denying confirmation of sale. For instance, if you are paying on a permanent loan modification, and the lender proceeds to sale, there is a very solid basis for denying confirmation of the sale. Although it is set to expire at the end of 2012, the IMFL also contains a provision that requires denying the confirmation of a sheriff's sale if the homeowner is being considered for a loan modification under the federal HAMP program when the sale is conducted.

Augie Arnold, Yorkville, Illinois: An Objection to Confirmation of Sale

Augie Arnold is an experienced and successful carpenter who owned and operated a successful new home framing company. At some points during the boom years he had framing contracts scheduled out 12 to 18 months in the future. The downturn in new home construction left his business shaky. After obtaining a foreclosure judgment, Augie's lender took his home to a sheriff's sale in August of 2011. At the time, comparable homes in his neighborhood were selling for $300,000. His home was once valued over $600,000. When the sheriff's sale was conducted, the only bidding party was Augie's lender. The total balance of Augie's loan was $475,000. The lender bid a mere $175,000 for Augie's house. Augie's attorneys objected to confirmation on the basis that the sale price was unconscionable. Given that the fair market value of Augie's home was closer to $300,000, and given that the lender's bid would expose Augie to a $300,000 deficiency judgment, the court denied confirmation of the sale, forcing the lender to begin the sale process over from the beginning.

Post-Confirmation Remedies

Once a sale is confirmed, there is very little that a homeowner can do to unwind the sale. This is especially true because by the time a sale is conducted, the requirements for vacating a judgment are extremely difficult to meet. In general, the primary reason for undoing a confirmed sale is because the homeowner was never served with a summons at the outset of the foreclosure case. Because the constitution guarantees you the right to defend yourself in a lawsuit, if you are not served with a summons, you are being denied that right. While there may be other technicalities that can unwind a confirmed sale, they are few and far between.

The Special Right to Redeem

Once a sheriff's sale is confirmed, the special right to redeem may apply. The special right to redeem is a statutory remedy created by the Illinois Mortgage Foreclosure Law.[31] If the winning bidder at the sheriff's sale was the bank that initiated the foreclosure lawsuit, and if the purchase price of the property was less than the redemption value[32] (the amount needed to pay off the loan to the lender including all fees and costs), then the borrower has 30 days, from the date of confirmation, to exercise the special right to redeem. In order to exercise this right, the borrower must pay the sale price bid at the auction, all additional costs and expenses included in the final confirmation order, and interest from the date that the purchase price was paid. However, the difference remains as a lien on the title.

Much like the right to redemption, this right is very rarely exercised. Most homeowners will not have the funds to match the sale price plus the additional fees and costs. However, it is important to know that this right exists. A sudden financial windfall can turn this remedy into a reality.

Garrett Riley, Romeoville, Illinois: Exercising the Special Right to Redeem

Garrett, a disc jockey at a local radio station, purchased his home in Romeoville, Illinois for $350,000 in 2006. His home is currently worth approximately $200,000. Garrett had been seeking a loan modification to reduce his monthly mortgage payment. A customer service representative from his servicer told him that he had to be in default on his mortgage payments to qualify for the Home Affordable Modification Program.

Garrett did not know the statement was false, so he stopped making mortgage payments. Garrett's servicer filed a mortgage foreclosure action against Garrett while considering him for the loan modification. Garrett, still hopeful that he would receive his loan modification, did not fight the foreclosure action. The servicer obtained a default judgment against Garrett and took the property to a sheriff's sale. At the sheriff's sale, the only bidder was Garrett's servicer, which bid $200,000 for Garrett's property.

When the default judgment was entered against Garrett, the redemption value of his property was $325,000. This amount represented his unpaid loan balance plus other fees and costs. Since the servicer purchased the property from itself for less than this redemption amount, Garrett possessed the special right to redeem. Garrett had been saving his mortgage payments in a separate account since he stopped paying his mortgage. With those saved payments, plus a loan from a wealthy family member, Garrett was able to exercise his special right to redeem. As a result, Garrett's servicer assigned the bill of sale for Garrett's home back to him, with $125,000 remaining as a lien against Garrett's property. Although Garrett's home still has a lien against it, he now has $75,000 in equity in his property and the foreclosure case has been dismissed.

When a landlord's rental property enters foreclosure, the tenants may wonder what rights they have during and after the foreclosure process. On May 20, 2009, President Obama signed the "Protecting Tenants in Foreclosure Act of 2009" into law.[33] The Act provides protections for renters whose landlords are in foreclosure. Under the Act, leases are not terminated by the completion of a foreclosure. Instead, tenants are allowed to stay until at least the end of their leases. Month-to-month tenants must be given 90 days notice before terminating tenancy. However, an exception exists. If the party that buys the property after foreclosure intends to use it as a primary residence, the lease may be terminated with 90 days notice.

Bankruptcy – A Fresh Start

To many people, bankruptcy seems like a last resort or a major moral failing. Nothing can be further from the truth. People from all walks of life file bankruptcy every day. Major corporations enter into bankruptcies to cut loose bad investments and regain a strong financial footing. For the informed, such as corporations supported by their legions of attorneys and financial managers, it is a tactical maneuver to get on track. They use their attorneys to protect them from their creditors. The purpose of bankruptcy is to give the honest but unfortunate debtor a fresh start. You may have heard politicians or pundits talking about the "moral hazard" of letting people walk away from debts or giving people a break when a good investment becomes a bad investment. Don't be fooled. Corporations do this all of the time. Why should it be any different for you? Instead of throwing good money after bad, cut bad investments loose and move on with your life.

Financial freedom cannot be achieved by taking a casual approach to debt. Much like a game of chess, success goes not to the lucky, but to the informed individual who deliberately plans several moves ahead. There are no random moves, and no one move is more important than the other. A tactical approach to consumer debt is no different. By taking all available information into consideration and evaluating multiple strategies, the whole becomes greater than the sum of its parts.

Fear guides most financial decisions. Emotion and fear alone should never guide the economic decisions of consumers, but they all too often do. Financial decisions are best made rationally. Rational decisions take into account the various options presented by the U.S. Bankruptcy Code and the other powerful state and federal statutes enacted to level the playing field between the creditor and borrower. At the end of the process, the best choice is the one that is the most economically sound for the individual.

We should never discount the power of fear, as that is what ensures that we put our seat belts on every time we enter our cars for even short trips. However, the power of predictability can and will trump fear every time. Wearing a seat belt does not guarantee that you will never be in an auto accident. However, that same seat belt provides you with a more predictable outcome if an accident happens. A well-planned financial strategy is like a well-planned road trip. By charting the most effective and efficient route, one can reasonably predict when the destination will be reached. Even the most minor mistakes, repeated over time, can sidetrack the average person. Instead of working to fund their lives, most Americans are working to fund their debt. This lifestyle is utterly unsustainable, and is a major contributing factor to the erosion of the middle class.

The purpose of this section is to describe to the reader some of the tools at the informed's disposal. Achieving a goal always boils down to the quality of the information one has when formulating a plan and executing that plan. Informed decision-making is the difference between acting out of fear and taking focused actions reasonably calculated to achieve a goal. The luxury of the informed is twofold: possessing information and applying it strategically.

A Brief History of Bankruptcy Law

Anyone who has read Charles Dickens's *A Christmas Carol* may be familiar with the concept of debtor's prison. Originally, bankruptcy was a remedy that protected creditors, banks, and lenders under English law. A consumer's assets could be seized to pay back creditors. The individual was then imprisoned and his family was left to pay the remainder of his debts. It was not until the 1800s that the English system moved away from debtor's prison and towards a system even slightly resembling modern bankruptcy law.

In the United States, codifying bankruptcy law was a power granted to Congress by the U.S. Constitution. (*See* Article I, Section 8, clause 4.) It was not until 1800 that Congress enacted the first bankruptcy legislation, and not until the Bankruptcy Act of 1841 that voluntary bankruptcy was contemplated by Federal law. In 1938, the Chandler Act made amendments to existing bankruptcy law that tended to make voluntary bankruptcy more attractive to individual consumers.

In 1978, Congress enacted a major overhaul to the bankruptcy laws, known as the Bankruptcy Reform Act of 1978, or the Bankruptcy Code. It is from this legislation that we derive the names of the various forms of bankruptcy. In 2005, Congress enacted the Bankruptcy Abuse Prevention and Consumer

Protection Act. It changed several sections of the Code, including the addition of the means test to Chapter 7 filings. The means test was designed to prevent people with excess disposable income from filing a Chapter 7 bankruptcy. The intention was that more people would file Chapter 13 bankruptcies and repay their creditors at least a portion of what they owed. It is a myth that people with high incomes cannot file for Chapter 7 bankruptcy as a result of the 2005 amendments.

The Purpose of Bankruptcy: A New Opportunity in Life

In 1934, the Supreme Court explained bankruptcy's purpose: "[I]t gives to the honest but unfortunate debtor…a new opportunity in life and a clear field for future effort, unhampered by the pressure and discouragement of preexisting debt."[34] The point is this – bankruptcy is supposed to be a fresh start, not an albatross around your neck. If the process is followed properly, then many consumers can unburden their finances and get a fresh start. Bankruptcy is not a tool to be used again and again; the Bankruptcy Code limits the number of times an individual can file in a given period of time. The idea of resetting bad investments should be compelling to most. However, many get so caught up with social pressures that they write off this powerful remedy in favor of inaction.

The U.S. Bankruptcy Code contains provisions designed to prevent abuse of the bankruptcy process. For example, if you obtain a new credit card, max it out, and then file for bankruptcy, the creditor will likely object to the debt being discharged. This is because the behavior appears fraudulent – honest but unfortunate debtors don't generally obtain a credit card, max it out and then file a bankruptcy right away. If you've recently incurred large debts or made major purchases, it is always wise to advise your attorney of these facts up front. It may make more sense for you to wait a few months before filing.

A Bankruptcy Primer

Before filing for bankruptcy, it is important to know the different types of consumer bankruptcies that are available to you and how they function. Depending on your specific financial situation and long-term goals, one type of bankruptcy may be better for you than another. Also, different types of bankruptcy can be combined for the maximum possible effect. This section provides a brief overview of the various types of consumer bankruptcies and how the automatic stay and the bankruptcy discharge work.

The Different Types of Consumer Bankruptcies

Chapter 7

A Chapter 7 is an orderly, court-supervised procedure. A trustee takes over the assets of the consumer's estate, reduces them to cash, and makes distributions to creditors. This distribution is subject to the exemptions a consumer can claim.

In most chapter 7 cases, there may not be an actual liquidation of the consumer's assets. This is because there is little or no nonexempt property. In Illinois, state law establishes the exemptions you may claim. These exemptions are designed to protect some of your assets in a Chapter 7 bankruptcy. Most people have three primary assets: their homes, their cars, and retirement accounts. However, only the equity you have your assets is subject to liquidation. Your retirement accounts are completely immune from any creditor. Even when you have equity in your assets, your exemptions may protect them. If your home is underwater and your car is not paid off, you likely have no equity in these assets and they are exempt. When you don't have any nonexempt assets, your case is referred to as a "no asset" case. The vast majority of Chapter 7 filings are no asset cases. A creditor holding an unsecured claim will get a distribution from the bankruptcy estate only if the case is an asset case and the creditor files a proof of claim with the bankruptcy court. An unsecured claim may include credit card debt or medical bills. A secured claim is debt like a mortgage or an auto loan. Secured and unsecured claims are discussed in more detail below.

Even when exemptions do not completely protect an asset, other factors may prevent the asset from being liquidated. In some situations, like the sale of a house, the costs associated with selling the house may outweigh the amount of non-exempt equity. When a house is sold, realtors get paid their commissions, title companies collect certain fees, and other closing costs are applied. These commissions, fees and costs all take away from the bottom line at the closing table. In other situations, it may be possible to negotiate with the trustee to keep the asset by paying the trustee. The money paid will then be distributed to creditors. How the payment is made is up to the trustee, based on the guidelines set by the law, and may be a lump-sum payment or a payment made over time. In general, if the payment is made over time, the longest period of time allowed will be 6 months. Again, this is entirely at the trustee's discretion.

In most Chapter 7 cases, individual consumers receive a discharge that releases them from personal liability for certain dischargeable debts. The consumer normally receives a discharge just a few months after the petition is filed. The Bankruptcy Abuse Prevention and Consumer Protection Act of 2005 requires the application of a "means test" to determine whether individual consumers qualify for relief under chapter 7. If a consumer's income is in excess of certain thresholds, the consumer may not be eligible for chapter 7 relief. The means test will be discussed in more detail below, with examples that illustrate how it works.

Dean West, Bloomingdale, Illinois: Negotiating With a Trustee

Dean is a highly skilled auto mechanic who specializes in restoring classic cars. He bought expensive equipment and personally guaranteed hundreds of thousands of dollars worth of loans to pay for outfitting his business. That equipment is now worth a lot less than what he owes. The equipment is also economically obsolete because the value of the business that it generates is less than the cost of his monthly payments and operating expenses. He took a risk on buying the equipment and, for a long time, it paid off. However, during the economic downturn, his business suffered, and he ended up filing for bankruptcy relief under Chapter 7, severing the liability on the loans, allowing him to continue operating his business without the burden of the debt or the under-performing equipment.

Dean owns two cars. One is a Dodge Avenger, which has $6,000 in equity. The other is a 1962 Chevy II convertible, which he intends to restore and give to his son, Jack, on his 16th birthday. Dean can combine his $2,400 vehicle exemption with his $4,000 wild card exemption and protect the equity in his Dodge. However, the Chevy II is an unprotected asset. Although it needs considerable restoration work, the car itself is currently valued at $8,000. The trustee informs Dean that he intends to sell the Chevy II and use the sale proceeds to repay Dean's creditors. Dean explains to the trustee that an unrestored Chevy II will be difficult to sell, and that he is willing to pay to keep the vehicle. After some negotiations, Dean agrees to pay the trustee $1,500 up front, and make payments of $500 a month for three months. The trustee agrees to the payment schedule and Dean is able to keep and restore his Chevy II for his son. Remember, the purpose of bankruptcy is to give to "the honest but unfortunate debtor...a new opportunity in life and a clear field for future effort, unhampered by the pressure and discouragement of preexisting debt."[35] Dean has already built his business, and has taken the first steps towards a future that is not financed by debt. His stated goal is to be debt free and grow his firm without the chains of interest payments.

Chapter 13: Repayment

A Chapter 13, sometimes called a Wage Earner's Bankruptcy, may be available to consumers who do not meet the means test for a Chapter 7 filing. Chapter 13 allows consumers to keep their assets, because a Chapter 13 bankruptcy allows consumers to propose a plan to repay creditors over time. This plan will last 3 to 5 years or less, depending on individual income. As a general guideline, individuals whose income is below the state median income generally have 3-year plans or less, unless the

Bankruptcy Court finds "just cause" to extend the period. Those whose income exceeds the state median income typically have 5-year plans. Essentially, a shorter-term plan repays less money over time, allowing for portions of the preexisting debt to be extinguished. A Chapter 13 petition proposes a plan to repay your creditors; the plan lists all of the creditors and how they will be repaid.

Once the petition and plan are filed, a confirmation hearing takes place. At the confirmation hearing, the court either approves or disapproves the consumer's repayment plan, depending on whether it meets the Bankruptcy Code's requirements for confirmation. Unlike a Chapter 7 case, the Chapter 13 consumer generally remains in possession of his or her assets. Payments are made to creditors through the trustee, based on predicted income over the life of the plan.

A Chapter 13 bankruptcy is not resolved in a matter of months like a Chapter 7 bankruptcy. Before a consumer can receive a discharge in a Chapter 13, he or she must make all of the payments in the plan. Once the plan is completed, the Chapter 13 discharge eliminates all personal liability for most debts. Long-term debts like mortgages are not necessarily eliminated in a Chapter 13 bankruptcy. The consumer is protected from lawsuits, garnishments, and other creditor actions while the plan is in effect. More kinds of debts are eliminated by the Chapter 13 discharge than the Chapter 7 discharge. This is because the Chapter 13 plan repays creditors, so certain types of judgments and other debts can be discharged. In most circumstances the Chapter 7 bankruptcy is the more advisable and attractive option because most individuals have limited assets. Make no mistake, all assets in retirement accounts are immune and not considered assets of the bankruptcy estate. Most people really only have three assets; the equity in their home which is usually protected, cars which are almost always underwater, and the cash and other commodities held in retirement accounts, which are completely protected from any creditor.

Chapter 11

Many consumers are unaware that they can use a Chapter 11 bankruptcy to reorganize their debts. Most people are aware of Chapter 11 as a means of reorganizing a corporation that is insolvent. Since the 2005 amendments to the Bankruptcy Code, individual Chapter 11 bankruptcies function much like Chapter 13 bankruptcies. If your secured debts exceed $1,081,400.00 or your unsecured debts exceed $360,475.00, you cannot file a Chapter 13 bankruptcy.[36] For individuals whose debt exceeds these limits, a Chapter 11 bankruptcy can provide similar relief. Individuals can use their post-petition earnings to fund their plan; those earnings are protected as property of the bankruptcy estate. The bankruptcy estate is created when you file your petition and includes your assets. Post-petition earnings are money you earn after you file your Chapter 11 case. Since these funds came into existence after you filed, they are not subject to liquidation. Although most people think of Chapter 11 as being used solely by corporations, individuals who do not operate businesses can still use Chapter 11 for relief.

There are significant differences between a Chapter 13 and a Chapter 11. When an individual Chapter 11 is filed, a new entity is formed – the debtor in possession. The debtor in possession has all of the rights and powers of a Chapter 11 trustee, and must perform the duties of a Chapter 11 trustee. These duties include accounting for property, examining and objecting to claims, and filing informational reports as required by the court and the U.S. trustee or bankruptcy administrator, such as monthly operating reports. The debtor in possession also has many of the powers of a Chapter 11 trustee, such as employing, with the court's approval, attorneys, accountants, appraisers and other professionals necessary to assist the debtor during its bankruptcy case. The debtor in possession must also file tax returns and any necessary or court-ordered reports, such as a final accounting. The Chapter 11 trustee oversees the debtor in possession's compliance with the reporting requirements. All current funds and post-petition earnings are deposited into a special account. All insured assets (homes, cars, other property insurance) are changed to name the debtor in possession as the beneficiary. Also, depending on the amount of total disbursements under the plan, a quarterly fee must be paid to the U.S. Trustee's office, as this is how the system is funded.

So why would you want to file an individual Chapter 11? Unlike a Chapter 13 filing, there are no limits on secured debts in a Chapter 11. A person who holds several investment properties may not qualify for relief under Chapter 13. A person who wishes to liquidate assets without losing control of the process may also want to file an individual Chapter 11. There are also more opportunities to cram down debt on assets like real property in a Chapter 11. While this bankruptcy remedy is not right for everyone, it may be a good option for an individual in the right financial situation.

The Automatic Stay

The automatic stay is one of the more powerful protections available to a person who has filed a bankruptcy. As soon as your case is filed, the automatic stay goes into effect. The automatic stay puts an immediate stop to any and all collection activity. This means that creditors cannot continue or begin lawsuits against you, cannot make collection calls, cannot repossess cars, cannot proceed with foreclosures, cannot continue to garnish your wages, and cannot continue to freeze your bank accounts. In general, the automatic stay remains in effect until a discharge is received.

Keith is a private high school teacher who lives in Aurora, Illinois. Keith has a PhD in Education, and has been teaching for 15 years. As a result, he makes in excess of $95,000 a year. Keith also has $45,000 in credit card debt, which was used to finance some unexpected expense throughout the years. He also has a second mortgage on his home that is no longer secured by the property's value, meaning the first mortgage exceeds the current value of the home leaving the entire second mortgage completely unsecured. Although Keith makes the minimum payments on all of his credit cards each month, he has realized that he will never pay off the balances. After consulting with an attorney, Keith makes the informed decision to file a Chapter 13 bankruptcy to resolve his credit card debt and strip the second mortgage from his home, paying back only a portion of the credit card balances and the second mortgage. This is because all of Keith's unsecured debt is treated the same way in a Chapter 13 bankruptcy. The amount of debt he repays is based on his disposable monthly income. At the end of the plan, Keith should have equity in the home that he wants to keep and he will have no credit card debt. The moment Keith files his bankruptcy case, the automatic stay goes into effect. Roughly two weeks after filing, one of Keith's credit card companies begins calling him to demand that he make a full payment on his account balance, or face the account being closed. Keith notifies his bankruptcy lawyer of the phone calls. Keith's attorney then files an adversary proceeding against the creditor, seeking damages for its violation of the automatic stay, the Fair Debt Collection Practices Act, and the Illinois Consumer Fraud and Unfair Practices Act.

There are some limits to the automatic stay's protection that will vary from case to case. For example, while the automatic stay can put the brakes on a foreclosure lawsuit, if the house has already gone to sale and the sale has been confirmed, then the automatic stay may not provide much protection if the goal was to keep the home. A creditor in that situation will likely file a motion for relief from the stay and will generally win because these motions are rarely challenged. Also, if you filed a bankruptcy within the last year that was dismissed, the stay only lasts for 30 days. This shortened stay can be modified if there is good reason. If you filed two or more dismissed bankruptcies in the last year, then the stay will not apply until you obtain a court order extending the automatic stay. More informed attorneys are aware of this and will generally file a motion requesting the extension of the automatic stay when they file your bankruptcy petition.

The automatic stay does not protect you from criminal proceedings, child support/spousal support-related actions, actions that collect from property that is not included in the bankruptcy estate, and tax audits. If you have issues like these, you'll want to consult with your attorney before you file to address how those liabilities will be handled. In some cases, it may be possible to work out a solution with the creditor. However, unless you disclose these concerns to your attorney as early as possible, the attorney's ability to plan will be seriously limited.

The Bankruptcy Discharge

The goal of a successful bankruptcy filing is the discharge. It is the discharge order that truly puts you on the path towards securing financial freedom. It not only represents a fresh start, but it is also a powerful protection against your creditors. Once a debt is discharged, the creditor can never try to collect the debt again. The discharge is a court ordered injunction authored by a federal judge. This means that the Bankruptcy Court orders your creditors to cease collecting on your debts and considers them to be completely zeroed-out. Creditors who violate the protection of the discharge injunction can be sued for damages, much like with a violation of the automatic stay.

When you receive your discharge, the effect of the discharge order depends on which chapter you file under. For example, you can discharge more types of debt in a Chapter 13 bankruptcy than you can in a Chapter 7. This is because a Chapter 13 plan repays creditors over time; certain kinds of judgments and other debts can be discharged if they are partially repaid. For example, some debts related to fraud or personal injury judgments can be discharged in a Chapter 13 bankruptcy.[37] However, a Chapter 7 discharge is generally obtained 45 to 60 days after the first meeting of the creditors. This meeting is also known as a 341 hearing and is discussed in depth below. In a Chapter 13, you will not receive your discharge until after you have completed your plan payments. This can take up to five years, but depending on your income, it can be accomplished in as little as three years, or even less depending on the strategy employed.

A discharge order utterly obliterates any and all personal obligations to repay a discharged debt. Once your debts are discharged, creditors are barred from attempting to collect the debt from you. Discharged debt must be reflected on your credit report as a $0 balance. Although creditors can inform the credit reporting agencies that the debt was discharged in bankruptcy, they cannot list the debt as "charged off," "settled" or any other status. If a creditor violates the bankruptcy discharge, you can sue that creditor. If a creditor continues to attempt to collect a discharged debt, consult your bankruptcy attorney.

The Bankruptcy Process

Filing a bankruptcy is generally not something that you do overnight. In order to make sure that you fully benefit from a bankruptcy filing, your attorney needs to collect important information about your finances and long-term financial goals. A good attorney will examine your life goals and use his experience to help you achieve those goals. In some situations, you may wish to delay your filing to account for specific financial events that occurred before you decided to take advantage of this powerful consumer protection. This is why it is important to plan your bankruptcy around your goals and specific financial situation. A good attorney will also ask questions designed to identify potential issues before they become a problem. Like any other process, there is always a starting point.

Initial Steps of Filing for Bankruptcy Protection

Once you have decided to explore bankruptcy as an option, the first step is to contact a bankruptcy attorney and set up a consultation. At Sulaiman Law Group, our consultations can take an hour or longer. This is to ensure that we fully explain the various types of bankruptcy and what effect they will have on you achieving your goals. We also seek to obtain as much information as we can in order to help you make a more informed choice. Being a fiduciary for someone means that you would act in the manner described if you were your own client. We cannot advise a client on a course of action unless we know certain critical pieces of information regarding that client. The initial consultation is also a time for you to determine whether our firm is a good fit for you. Even if you are filing a Chapter 7 bankruptcy, which has a very short time line, you want to make sure that you trust and are comfortable with your attorney before deciding to file bankruptcy.

At the initial consultation, you will be given some documents to fill out. For instance, the initial intake form helps us prepare your bankruptcy petition and provides us with a snapshot of your financial situation. Some clients are candidates for both a Chapter 7 bankruptcy and a Chapter 13 bankruptcy. By attending the initial consultation and filling out the intake forms, you help us determine which type of bankruptcy best serves your long-term financial goals as well as your short-term financial goals. In order for bankruptcy to be a truly fresh start, it helps to make sure that you file under the right chapter and that filing sets you up for financial success in the future. We also need your financial information in order to determine whether you pass the means test. This is an essential part of filing a Chapter 7 bankruptcy and has implications for the other chapters as well.

We will also give you some discount codes for a few credit counseling agencies. Credit counseling teaches you how to manage credit, set a budget, and keep your debt under control. Credit counseling is now required by the Bankruptcy Code. This requirement went into effect with the 2005 amendments to the Code. The 2005 amendments to the Bankruptcy Code are also known as the Bankruptcy Abuse Prevention and Consumer Protection Act. Mandatory credit counseling was introduced to help prevent repeat filings. While the information provided in the counseling is rather remedial, taking the courses is now required by the law. The classes can be taken online via a computer and will take approximately 45 – 60 minutes to complete. If you do not take the pre-filing credit counseling, your case will be dismissed. If you do not take the pre-discharge credit counseling, you will not receive your discharge and you may have to pay an additional filing fee to reopen the case and get your discharge. Although it may seem boring or time consuming, credit counseling is a necessary step towards achieving your goal.

Choosing the Right Chapter

Whether you file a Chapter 7 or a Chapter 13 may depend on more than whether you pass the means test. For example, if you own a home and want to keep it, you aren't automatically forced into a Chapter 13 filing. Here are some hypothetical clients and their results.

Sam earns $4,100 a month as a retail sales associate. He occasionally receives bonus checks from his employer, but his monthly income is never higher than $4,500 a month. Sam rents an apartment in the Lakeview neighborhood on Chicago's North Side, owns a late-model Toyota, and has a rather large record collection. Sam has a 401k account through his employer with $75,000 in mutual fund assets, but does not own any stocks or other easily liquidated assets outside of his retirement accounts. Sam also has $50,000 in credit card debts. One of Sam's credit card providers recently filed a lawsuit against him to collect the balance due on his account. Sam is a perfect candidate for a Chapter 7 bankruptcy. He is likely to pass the means test, and his personal possessions are protected by exemptions. Although Sam assigns a lot of value to his collection of obscure vinyl records, a Chapter 7 trustee likely will not. Filing a Chapter 7 bankruptcy will allow Sam to obliterate his credit card debts while keeping all of his belongings. It will also stop the pending lawsuit, preventing his creditor from obtaining a judgment against him and moving on to collection methods like wage garnishment. He will also only have to wait two years after his discharge to qualify for an FHA-sponsored home loan. He can reduce the two year waiting period to one year if he can show that he filed his bankruptcy due to extenuating circumstances beyond his control and that he has since exhibited a documented ability to manage his finances responsibly.[38]

Dave earns $5,000 a month and is an associate attorney at a family law firm located in Chicago. He is married and has one child. Dave's wife is a stay-at-home mother and does not work outside the home. Dave and his wife own a house in Riverside, Illinois, a suburb located in Cook County. Unlike many home owners, Dave's home is not underwater – he purchased it in 1999 and has always been current on his mortgage. His home has $50,000 in equity. In 2005, Dave was in a car accident. As a result of the accident, both of Dave's legs were broken in several places, requiring two surgeries to repair them. Dave also underwent eighteen months of physical therapy. Although Dave's savings covered his living expenses while he was in the hospital, his insurance did not cover all of the cost of his surgeries or his physical therapy.

Dave still owes $45,000 in medical bills. He also has amassed $25,000 in credit card debt, much of which was used to pay for his physical therapy. Dave and his wife own their cars free and clear, but both have high mileage and are worth less than $2,000 each. Like Sam, Dave is likely to pass the means test. Although it is possible that the Chapter 7 trustee could object to Dave's Chapter 7 filing as abusive, Dave's expenses and overall financial picture indicate that his case is likely to survive that challenge. Because the majority of Dave's assets are protected by his exemptions and those of his wife, it is unlikely that the trustee will seek to liquidate his assets. Additionally, although Dave cannot exempt the entire value of his home's equity, his $15,000 exemption and the closing costs associated with a property sale will likely make his home unattractive to the Chapter 7 trustee, whose goal is to quickly liquidate assets to repay creditors. A Chapter 7 filing will allow Dave to discharge his medical bills and credit card debt. It will also sever his personal liability on his home loan. So long as Dave continues to make his mortgage payments on time, his home is secure. If Dave is ever forced to default on his mortgage, and his home enters foreclosure, he will not be liable for a deficiency judgment. If the home is sold for less than the loan balance, Dave will not have to repay the difference.

Sarah Miller, Chicago, Illinois: Chapter 13 Lien Strip

Sarah earns $12,000 a month and is a commodities trader at the Chicago Board of Trade. Her house in Lincoln Park is worth $500,000, but is subject to two mortgages. The first mortgage is $500,000 and the second is $100,000. Sarah's home is deeply underwater, but she is determined to keep her home. Sarah also has $10,000 in credit card debt. Sarah earns too much money to qualify for a Chapter 7 bankruptcy, and a Chapter 7 bankruptcy won't allow her to recover any value in her home. On the other hand, a Chapter 13 bankruptcy can help Sarah eliminate her credit card debts and also partially restore some equity in her home. Since her first mortgage exceeds the value of her home, Sarah's second mortgage can be treated as an unsecured asset. Depending on her allowable expenses, Sarah's Chapter 13 plan will repay her creditors over five years, allocating all of her disposable income towards repaying her debts. Sarah's goal is to come up with a plan that repays 10% of her debt over those five years. If successful, she will discharge her $10,000 in credit card debt for $1,000 and her second mortgage for $10,000. Throughout the plan, she will also continue making payments on her first mortgage. By removing the second mortgage, she may see her home return to positive equity over the term of her plan. At very least, Sarah will be at the break-even point, which is much better than being $100,000 underwater.

Nancy and Mike Smith, Naperville, Illinois: Chapter 13
Severance/Surrender

Nancy and Mike are a married couple with a household income of $100,000 a year. Their income exceeds the median income for their area, so they are unlikely to pass the means test, even after deducting their expenses. They purchased a home in Naperville, Illinois at the height of the real estate boom. Nancy and Mike love that they are within walking distance of the Riverwalk and Downtown Naperville. However, their home is now underwater by $200,000. They have two car loans, each with a balance of $15,000. The cars are three years old and have depreciated significantly. Both Nancy and Mike drive extensively for work and the mileage on their cars is the main factor in their reduced value. The couple also has several credit cards carrying a total balance of $30,000. Nancy and Mike feel that their mortgage and car payments are unsustainable investments. Although their car payments are current, they are two months behind on their mortgage payments.

A Chapter 13 bankruptcy provides powerful remedies for Nancy and Mike. If Nancy and Mike are willing to cut their losses and surrender their home to the lender, they can surrender the home in full satisfaction of the secured portion of their mortgage. While many lenders do not file a proof of claim for the unsecured portion (roughly $200,000 in this fact pattern), this is not a guarantee. If their mortgage lender manages to prove how much unsecured debt that Nancy and Mike owe, it can file a proof of claim, which means that Nancy and Mike would have to repay the unsecured portion as part of their Chapter 13 plan. Since they have had their cars for longer than 910 days, Nancy and Mike can also use their Chapter 13 to cram down their car loans to the current value of their cars. When they receive their discharge, they will own the cars free and clear of the loans, while only paying back a portion of the loan balances. This is an extremely attractive option for the informed.

Alex filed a Chapter 7 bankruptcy ten months ago with a different attorney. He received a discharge and no longer has any personal liability on his mortgage. Since Alex already discharged his credit card debts and other debts in his Chapter 7 filing, it may seem that he cannot benefit from another bankruptcy filing. After all, he is not eligible for a discharge for another 4 years due to his recent Chapter 7 filing. However, Alex owns a home in Montgomery, Illinois. He is committed to keeping his home, even though his second mortgage puts him underwater by $100,000. He is currently four months behind on his mortgage, but his lender has not yet filed a foreclosure action. Alex is a good candidate for what is sometimes called a Chapter 20 bankruptcy.

Even though he cannot receive a discharge from a Chapter 13 filing, Alex can use the Chapter 13 filing for two main purposes: he can get his mortgage current and strip his second mortgage. Since he is only four months behind on his mortgage, and given that he will be attempting a 10% payback plan, Alex's plan may be very short, depending on his disposable monthly income. At the end of the plan, he will be current on his mortgage and no longer underwater because his second lien will be stripped in the Chapter 13 bankruptcy.

Chapter 7 Bankruptcy in Detail

Chapter 7 Overview

A Chapter 7 bankruptcy is an orderly, court-supervised procedure. A trustee takes over the assets of the consumer's estate, reduces them to cash, and makes distributions to creditors. This distribution is subject to the exemptions a consumer can claim. Most people do not have the kinds of assets that a trustee is interested in liquidating. Trustees are interested in liquidating things like cash, stocks, bonds, and precious metals. Assets that are difficult to value or sell are not as attractive. Assets that cost money to liquidate are not as attractive.

In many cases, there may not be an actual liquidation of the consumer's assets. This is because there is little or no nonexempt property. These cases are called "no-asset cases." A creditor holding an unsecured claim will get a distribution from the bankruptcy estate only if the case is an asset case and the creditor files a proof of claim with the bankruptcy court.

In most Chapter 7 cases, individual consumers receive a discharge that releases them from personal liability for dischargeable debts. The consumer normally receives a discharge just a few months after the petition is filed. The Bankruptcy Abuse Prevention and Consumer Protection Act of 2005 requires the application of a "means test" to determine whether individual consumers qualify for relief under Chapter 7. If such a consumer's income is in excess of certain thresholds, the consumer may not be eligible for Chapter 7 relief.

Chapter 7 Eligibility – The Means Test and Abuse

The 2005 amendments to the U.S. Bankruptcy Code established a means test to determine an individual's eligibility for filing a Chapter 7 bankruptcy. The means test is designed to prevent abuses of the Bankruptcy Code, although many attorneys find that it has done very little to prevent people from filing bankruptcies, and even less to prevent abuse of the system. The means test looks at the median income for a specific family size in a specific geographic area. For instance, the median income for a three person family in the 60618 zip code, which includes Chicago's North Center and Ravenswood neighborhoods, was $66,758 a year in December of 2011. If your family's income meets or falls below the median, you may be eligible to file a Chapter 7 bankruptcy. If it exceeds the median, a presumption of abuse arises. This presumption can be rebutted, in particular if you can demonstrate that special circumstances and expenses make your actual income lower than your paystubs may indicate. In fact, people who make more than the median income for their area can qualify for Chapter 7 protection.

Keep in mind that passing the means test is not necessarily a guarantee that you are eligible for a Chapter 7 bankruptcy. If your income suddenly changes or if it appears that you have a significant amount of net income, a bankruptcy judge can apply what is known as the "totality of the circumstances" test and determine that a Chapter 7 filing is abusive. If abuse is found, the case is either converted to a Chapter 13 or it is dismissed. How you have conducted your financial affairs prior to filing your bankruptcy can also have an effect on this analysis. For example, spending large amounts of money on luxury items in the months preceding your bankruptcy filing is generally considered abusive. This is why it is especially important that you disclose all of your financial affairs to your attorney. In some cases, it may be wise to postpone a bankruptcy filing.

Post-Holiday Filing Issues

The winter holiday season is a time when people generally spend money on gifts for friends and family. Many people also take advantage of the sales retailers offer to obtain new creature comforts for their homes. If you use your credit cards to purchase gifts and non-essential consumer goods during the holiday season and file for bankruptcy at the beginning of the year, it may appear to be an abuse of the Bankruptcy Code. This can be overcome by waiting to file your bankruptcy petition. When a person runs up a large amount of credit card debt on luxury items and then immediately files for bankruptcy, it appears abusive. By waiting to file and attempting to pay down some of the balances, you can avoid this appearance of abuse.

Ron Pullman, Chicago, Illinois: An Example of A Bad Faith Filing

Ron lives in Chicago, Illinois. He is a librarian at a nearby public library. Instead of being laid off, Ron chose to take a salary cut when the library's budget was slashed. With his $45,000 salary, Ron qualifies for a Chapter 7 bankruptcy, but only has one credit card, which he uses to purchase gas. Ron pays this account monthly and has a great credit score. Ron also wishes he could afford to transform his condo into a true "man cave," with leather recliners, flat-screen TV's, a premium sound system, and other creature comforts. Ron applies for several credit cards with high limits. He then proceeds to outfit his man cave to his heart's content. Once he is finished with his shopping spree, Ron realizes that he cannot possibly pay off his new debts. Ron decides to file a Chapter 7 bankruptcy. Ron's creditors object to their debts being discharged as an abuse of the Bankruptcy Code. After a hearing on his creditors' objections, Ron is granted a discharge, but none of the objecting creditors' debts are included in the discharge. Ron is now on the hook for all of the debt he just incurred. Ron could have withdrawn his filing as well to avoid the uncertainty of fighting the creditors' objections. An experienced attorney would not have let Ron file on these facts.

The Chapter 7 Process

A Chapter 7 case begins when you file a petition with the bankruptcy court. Before you file, it is important that you have assembled all of the documents that you will need in order to file your petition. For example, you will need to provide your last two tax returns as well as your last six months of pay stubs. If you are self-employed, you will need to provide your bank statements for the past six months. You must also complete the pre-filing credit counseling and provide your attorney with a certificate indicating that you completed the course.

In order to complete the forms that make up the petition, statement of financial affairs, and schedules, you must provide the following information:

1. A list of all creditors and the amount and nature of their claims;

2. The source, amount, and frequency of the your income;

3. A list of all of your property; and

4. A detailed list of your monthly living expenses, i.e., food, clothing, shelter, utilities, taxes, transportation, medicine, etc.

Your attorney will work with you to gather this information. It is very important that you list all of your creditors. Not every creditor will necessarily report your debts to the various credit reporting agencies, so simply providing a copy of your credit report may not be sufficient. Anyone to whom you owe money qualifies as a creditor. If your Aunt Sally lent you $30,000 as a down payment on your house, and you have a plan to pay her back, she is one of your creditors.

Married individuals must gather this information for their spouse regardless of whether they are filing a joint petition, separate individual petitions, or even if only one spouse is filing. If only one spouse files, the income and expenses of the non-filing spouse are required so that the court, the trustee and creditors can evaluate the household's financial position. All of your financial information is organized into "schedules." These schedules are lists of your assets and debts that are organized by type.

Among the schedules that an individual will file is a schedule of "exempt" property. The Bankruptcy Code allows an individual to protect some property from the claims of creditors because it is exempt under federal bankruptcy law or under the laws of the consumer's home state. If you have recently moved from another state, inform your bankruptcy attorney as you may be eligible to use your prior state's exemptions. Since exemptions vary from state to state, you may discover that your old state's exemptions cover more or less than the Illinois exemptions. If your old state's exemptions provide you more protection, you may want to file before you are no longer eligible to use them. For example, if the Illinois exemptions provide you with more protection, you may want to wait to file until you are eligible to use the Illinois exemptions.

Filing a petition under chapter 7 creates an "automatic stay" that stops most collection actions against you and your property. The stay arises by operation of law and requires no judicial action. This means that as soon as you file, with a few exceptions, the stay goes into effect immediately. As long as the stay is in effect, creditors generally may not initiate or continue lawsuits, wage garnishments, or even telephone calls demanding payments. The bankruptcy clerk gives notice of the bankruptcy case to all creditors whose names and addresses are provided by the consumer. If you have specific creditors who are about to move forward with a lawsuit, your attorney should also directly notify those creditors and their counsel of your bankruptcy filing. For example, if you file a bankruptcy petition on a Friday and your home is scheduled for a sheriff's sale the following Tuesday, you or your attorney should provide notice to that creditor. The extra layer of documentation may make the difference between a successful stay violation claim and an unsuccessful one.

This extra layer of documentation is exceptionally powerful. When you have taken extra steps to provide notice of your bankruptcy filing, creditors who violate the automatic stay expose themselves to significant legal liability. The law makes a distinction between an "inadvertent" or "accidental" violation of the stay and a "willful" or "knowing" violation of the stay. If a creditor did not have proper notice of the bankruptcy filing, then the relief available to you is limited to actual damages and attorney's fees. However, if the creditor has been provided with added notices, it is easier to categorize a violation of the stay as willful or knowing. These types of violations can entitle you to punitive damages, which are a powerful remedy designed to punish willful violations of the automatic stay.

Between 20 and 40 days after you file your petition, the bankruptcy trustee will hold a meeting of creditors. This is also referred to as the 341 meeting. 341 refers to the section of the Bankruptcy Code which requires that the meeting be held. During this meeting, you are put under oath, and both the trustee and creditors may ask questions. You **must** attend the meeting and answer questions regarding your financial affairs and property. Failing to attend your 341 meeting can result in your case being dismissed. If a husband and wife have filed a joint petition, they both must attend the creditors' meeting and answer questions. These meetings are generally very short and last typically no more than 5 to 15 minutes. There is a set of general questions that the trustee will ask. These questions are primarily designed to ensure that you listed all of your assets and debts in your petition. A set of sample 341 meeting questions can be found in Appendix 1. Within 10 days of the creditors' meeting, the U.S. trustee will report to the court whether the case should be presumed to be an abuse under the means test described here. It is very important that you cooperate with the trustee and provide any financial records or documents that the trustee requests.

The Bankruptcy Code requires the trustee to ask questions at the meeting of creditors to ensure that you are aware of the potential consequences of seeking a discharge in bankruptcy, the ability to file a petition under a different chapter, the effect of receiving a discharge, and the effect of reaffirming a debt. Some trustees provide written information on these topics at or before the meeting to ensure that you are aware of this information. If this is the case, be sure you have read the information before your 341 meeting begins.

Who Is The Trustee? What Does A Trustee Do?

When a Chapter 7 petition is filed, an impartial case trustee is appointed to administer the case and liquidate your nonexempt assets. A trustee is generally an attorney, although non attorneys may qualify to serve as a Chapter 7 trustee if they meet the requirements set forth in the Code of Federal Regulations.[39] Your specific trustee is randomly assigned to your case when it is filed. Sometimes a trustee will be substituted for another trustee if a scheduling conflict or other conflict arises. For example, if your first cousin is a Chapter 7 trustee, and is assigned to your case, you will be assigned a new trustee.

If all of your assets are exempt or subject to valid liens, the trustee will normally file a "no asset" report with the court, and there will be no distribution to unsecured creditors. Most Chapter 7 cases involving individual consumers are no asset cases. You may be surprised to learn that even though your personal belongings have sentimental value, it is very rare that they have any true resale value. Trustees are concerned with assets that can be easily sold. Precious metals, cash, stocks, bonds, houses and vehicles are most attractive to trustees. Trustees are paid a flat fee for each case they handle. They also receive a percentage of the value of any liquidated assets. If an asset is difficult to sell, then a trustee likely won't be interested in it. If the trustee is interested in a specific asset, it is possible to purchase those assets back from the trustee.

If the case appears to be an "asset" case at the outset, unsecured creditors must file their claims with the court within 90 days after the meeting of creditors. A typical claim establishes the amount owed and provides documentation to support the claim. In some situations, your attorney may want to object to the claim if it is improperly filed or if it is otherwise defective. A governmental unit, like the IRS, has 180 days from the date the case is filed to file a claim. In the typical no asset Chapter 7 case, creditors do not file proofs of claim because there will be no distribution, meaning that there are no assets to liquidate. If the trustee later recovers assets for distribution to unsecured creditors, the Bankruptcy Court will provide notice to creditors and will allow additional time to file proofs of claim. This rarely occurs in practice and can be prevented by fully disclosing your financial affairs to your attorney. Before filing a case, your attorney will already know if yours is an "asset" case or a "no asset" case. Typically, this is disclosed at the time of filing.

When you file your bankruptcy case, it creates an "estate." The estate technically becomes the temporary legal owner of all of your property. It consists of all legal or equitable interests you have in property at the time of filing; this includes property in which you share ownership. Your creditors are paid from non-exempt property of the estate. If the Chapter 7 trustee determines that yours is an asset case, the trustee's job is to liquidate your nonexempt assets. The trustee will sell your nonexempt property and distribute that money to your unsecured creditors.

The trustee also has the power to "look back" and try to recover money or property you may have spent or transferred 90 days prior to filing your case. If you paid some creditors and not others within the 90 days before you filed, the trustee can attempt to recover that money. This is called a "preference." A good example is money paid to a family member to settle an outstanding debt while other creditors go unpaid. Remember Aunt Sally? If you paid back her $30,000 loan shortly before filing bankruptcy, odds are that your trustee would expect her to return those funds to the bankruptcy estate for distribution to all of your unsecured creditors.

The trustee can also undo transactions where you borrowed money against your assets prior to filing. A good example would be a consumer that took out a home equity line of credit prior to filing bankruptcy. The trustee also has the power to undo sales or other transfers of property. For example, if you have a boat and a "weekend driver" car and sell those to your friend prior to filing for a Chapter 7 bankruptcy, the trustee can undo that sale, bringing the property back into the bankruptcy estate.

What Happens When My Case Is Discharged?

A discharge releases you from personal liability for most debts and prevents the creditors owed those debts from taking any collection actions against you. This powerful injunction provides you with absolute personal protection from your creditors. Creditors who violate the discharge injunction can be sued and you may be able to recover damages from them. In most Chapter 7 cases, the Bankruptcy Court will issue a discharge order relatively early in the case. This is usually 60 to 90 days after the meeting of creditors.

The court may deny you a discharge if it finds that you failed to keep or produce adequate financial records; did not explain, satisfactorily, any loss of assets; committed a bankruptcy crime like perjury; failed to obey a lawful order of the bankruptcy court; fraudulently transferred, concealed, or destroyed property; or failed to complete an approved instructional course concerning financial management. These situations rarely occur, but they highlight the importance of full disclosure to both your attorney and the bankruptcy court.

Secured vs. Unsecured Debt

Unsecured debt, like credit cards, is generally paid from your bankruptcy estate. If your case is an asset case, the assets will be sold to pay these debts. Secured debt is tied to a piece of property. The most common secured debts are mortgages and automobile loans. Real estate is known as real property. Cars, boats, paintings, etc. are known as personal property.

Secured creditors may retain some rights to seize property even after a discharge is granted. This is because the discharge only removes your personal liability for your debts. Debts tied to property will still be tied to the property. For example, if you have a mortgage on your home, even though your personal obligation to pay your debt is discharged, the bank can still take your home to satisfy the debt. This is because your bankruptcy discharges your personal obligation to repay the money lent to you. This obligation is described in the promissory note you signed at the real estate closing. The mortgage on your home is a separate obligation that ties the physical property to the debt. The Chapter 7 discharge cannot remove this obligation because it is not your personal obligation, but one that is linked to the property itself. If you stop making your mortgage payments, then the lender can proceed forward with a foreclosure. However, if you continue to make your payments, it is likely that the lender will happily accept them.

Reaffirming Debts

It is possible to "reaffirm" debts. Reaffirming a debt involves an agreement between you and your secured creditor. You agree to pay all or a part of your debt; the creditor agrees to not take back the property as long as you continue to make payments. Before you reaffirm any debts, you should consider your ability to make the payments required by your agreement.

Before deciding to reaffirm a debt, discuss it with your attorney first. You should never enter into a reaffirmation agreement before consulting with your attorney. If, after talking to your attorney, you decide to reaffirm a debt, you will be required to file a signed reaffirmation agreement with the court. Your reaffirmation agreement must include disclosures. These disclosures are required by the Bankruptcy Code. Among other things, the disclosures must advise you of the amount of the debt being reaffirmed, how it is calculated, and that reaffirmation means that your personal liability for that debt will not be discharged in the bankruptcy. It is highly unlikely that a competent attorney would ever advise a client to reaffirm a debt on an underwater asset because there is no financial benefit to the client.

You are also required to file a signed statement of your current income and expenses. The statement must show that you can afford to pay the reaffirmed debt. If your statement shows that you cannot afford to pay the debt, the court may presume that the debt is an undue hardship. In that case, it would deny the reaffirmation agreement.

If you are represented by an attorney in connection with the reaffirmation agreement, your attorney must certify in writing that he or she advised you of the legal effect and consequences of the agreement, including the result of defaults under the agreement. Your attorney must also certify that you gave informed consent to the debt and that repaying it will not be an undue hardship on you or your dependents. Even if you don't have a reaffirmation agreement, you may repay a debt voluntarily without reestablishing personal liability for the debt. This is almost always a better position than reaffirming.

In general, it is a bad idea to reaffirm debts as part of your Chapter 7 bankruptcy, especially on underwater assets. Reaffirmation agreements generally contain clauses that force you to accept personal liability for the reaffirmed debt. This means that your discharge will not apply to the reaffirmed debt. If your goal was to obtain a fresh start with absolute freedom from your debts, reaffirming a debt defeats the purpose of filing a bankruptcy in the first place. Remember, a discharge represents absolute freedom from your existing dischargeable debts.

Once your debts are discharged in your Chapter 7 bankruptcy, your creditors cannot initiate or continue any attempts to collect the discharged debts from you. Some debts cannot be discharged in a Chapter 7 bankruptcy.

They include:

- Alimony and child support
- Certain tax obligations, although it may be possible to discharge tax obligations that are greater than 3 years old.
- Student loans, unless you can demonstrate that repaying the loan would be an undue hardship on you and your dependents.
- Personal injury judgments
- Debts related to DUI or DWI damages
- Criminal restitution orders such as an order to pay restitution to the victim of a battery you committed.

If these types of debts are not paid as part of your Chapter 7 bankruptcy, you will still be personally liable for them.

It is very important that your filing be 100% truthful. The bankruptcy court may revoke your Chapter 7 discharge if the trustee, a creditor or the U.S. trustee requests it and demonstrates a valid basis for revoking the discharge. The request will be granted if the discharge was obtained through fraud, if you acquired property that is property of the estate and knowingly and fraudulently failed to report or to surrender it to the trustee, or if you made a material misstatement or failed to provide documents or other information in connection with an audit of your case.

Sam Jackson, Schaumburg, Illinois: A Revoked Discharge

When Sam filed his Chapter 7 bankruptcy petition, his wealthy Uncle Larry was terminally ill. A week before Sam was to attend the 341 meeting of the creditors, his uncle passed away. Uncle Larry's will stated that Sam would receive a cash inheritance of $500,000.00. At the 341 meeting, the Chapter 7 trustee asked Sam if he had acquired any new assets since he filed his bankruptcy case. Sam said that he had not. The Chapter 7 trustee declares Sam's case to be a no-asset case and recommends discharge. Sam is granted his discharge, and begins to spend his inheritance. One of Sam's creditors discovers Sam's inheritance and files a motion to revoke the discharge. Given that Sam lied to the trustee during the 341 meeting, and given that he failed to disclose the inheritance as required by the Bankruptcy Code, the Bankruptcy Court grants the motion to revoke Sam's discharge. He may have also exposed himself to liability for bankruptcy fraud. If Sam's uncle died months after the completion of his bankruptcy, this would have not been a problem. Assets acquired after a discharge is received are the property of the individual, not the bankruptcy estate. Again, the underlying principal behind the

Bankruptcy Code is a fresh start, allowing people like Sam to spend and invest money again.

Chapter 13 Bankruptcy In Detail

Chapter 13 Overview

A Chapter 13 bankruptcy is available to consumers who do not meet the means test for a Chapter 7 filing because they make too much money or who have valuable assets they intend on keeping. The definition of valuable varies from person to person. A home with negative equity in pure economic terms is valueless. A car that is constantly depreciating in value is a liability when one takes maintenance into consideration. You must treat your decisions in pure economic terms to truly achieve your goal of perfect financial freedom. Chapter 13 filings also offer more flexibility for people who want to keep their homes or for those who have assets that they cannot protect with exemptions. For example, if you own several fully-restored classic cars, you risk losing them in a Chapter 7 filing. A Chapter 13 filing allows you to keep those assets. Chapter 13 allows consumers to keep all of their assets because a Chapter 13 bankruptcy allows consumers to propose a plan to repay creditors over time. This plan will generally last three to five years, depending on individual income. As a general guideline, individuals whose income is below the state median income generally have three-year plans unless the Bankruptcy Court finds "just cause" to extend the plan period.

Once the petition and plan are drafted and filed, a confirmation hearing takes place. At the confirmation hearing, the court either approves or disapproves the consumer's repayment plan, depending on whether it meets the Bankruptcy Code's requirements for confirmation. If a proof of claim has been filed, they may also be challenged during the confirmation process. In that event, confirming a Chapter 13 plan may require multiple hearings. Unlike Chapter 7, the Chapter 13 consumer remains in possession of his or her assets and makes payments through the trustee based on predicted income over the life of the plan. The trustee then distributes the plan payments to the creditors. If income goes down during the plan, the payments can be adjusted. Conversely, if an individual's income increases substantially, the amount repaid can go up if you were paying less than 100% of the amount owed to your creditors. This only happens if a creditor or the trustee files a motion to increase the plan payments. You have to be notified of the motion and must be given an opportunity to object to it.

A Chapter 13 bankruptcy is not resolved in a matter of months like a Chapter 7 bankruptcy. Before a consumer can receive a discharge in a Chapter 13, he or she must make all of the payments in the plan. The consumer is protected from lawsuits, garnishments, and other creditor actions while the plan is in effect. More types debts are eliminated by the Chapter 13 discharge than the Chapter 7 discharge. For example, debts related to property or money obtained under false pretenses or fraud can be discharged in a Chapter 13 because they are being repaid.

What Are The Advantages of Filing A Chapter 13 Bankruptcy?

Chapter 13 offers individuals a number of advantages when compared to liquidation under Chapter 7. One major difference is that a Chapter 13 plan allows consumers to keep their homes, even if they are in foreclosure. By filing under this chapter, individuals can stop foreclosure proceedings and may cure delinquent mortgage payments over time. They must still make all mortgage payments that come due during the Chapter 13 plan on time, however. Homeowners also have another powerful tool at their disposal. A Chapter 13 bankruptcy allows consumers to strip unsecured mortgages. A mortgage is unsecured when its value is not supported by the value of the house.

Allen Adams, Lombard, Illinois: Secured vs. Unsecured Debt and Chapter 13 Lien Strips

For example, Allen owns a house with two mortgages in Lombard, Illinois. The house is worth $300,000, but his first and second mortgages total $450,000. The second mortgage is $125,000 and is completely unsecured by the property's value. Allen can strip the second mortgage from his home and treat it as an unsecured debt, paying back a portion of the debt over the lifetime of his plan. As a result, Allen will have put himself in a position where he is only $25,000 underwater, as opposed to $150,000. During the course of his Chapter 13 plan, Allen will be paying down the balance on his first mortgage. Once he receives his discharge, his home may be approaching the break-even point on its equity.

Chapter 13 Eligibility

Even if you are self-employed, you are eligible for Chapter 13 relief as long as you are a human being (corporations cannot file for Chapter 13 relief) and your debts are below certain limits. For example, if your secured debts exceed $1,081,400 you cannot file a

Chapter 13 bankruptcy. A secured debt is one that is tied to property. The most common secured debts are mortgage loans and auto loans. Also, your unsecured debts cannot exceed $360,475. Most debts are unsecured and include debts like credit card debts, medical bills, utility bills and store credit cards.

In order to have your Chapter 13 repayment plan confirmed, it must be feasible. This means that you have to have regular income, as well as enough disposable income to fund your repayment plan. If you don't have enough money left over after paying for your monthly expenses, then you cannot fund your plan. Fortunately, you can use many sources of income to fund your plan. In addition to regular wages or salary, you can use income from self-employment, commissions from sales or other work, pension payments, Social Security benefits, disability and worker's compensation benefits, unemployment payments, welfare payments, child support, alimony, royalties, rents, proceeds from selling property, and contributions from other sources.

The Chapter 13 Bankruptcy Process

A Chapter 13 case begins by filing a petition with the bankruptcy court. Unless the court orders otherwise, you must also file with the court schedules of assets and liabilities, a schedule of current income and expenditures, a schedule of executory contracts and unexpired leases, and a statement of financial affairs. An executory contract is a contract where both parties still owe each other specific obligations such as a lease. You must also file: a certificate of credit counseling and a copy of any debt repayment plan developed through credit counseling, evidence of payment from employers received 60 days before filing, a statement of monthly net income and any anticipated increase in income or expenses after filing, and a record of any interest you have in federal or state qualified education or tuition accounts. A qualified attorney knows what documents are needed and when they are needed.

You must also provide the Chapter 13 case trustee with a copy of the tax return or transcripts for the most recent tax year, as well as tax returns filed during the case. A husband and wife may file a joint petition or individual petitions. The petition is the initial document filed to open your case. There are many reasons why a couple would choose to file jointly or separately. Your attorney should be able to advise you as to the best choice for your circumstances.

In order to complete the official bankruptcy forms that make up the petition, statement of financial affairs, and schedules, you must compile a list of all creditors and the amounts and nature of their claims, the source, amount, and frequency of the your income, a list of all of your property, and a detailed list of your monthly living expenses, i.e., food, clothing, shelter, utilities, taxes, transportation, medicine, etc. Again, a qualified attorney will guide you through this process.

Married individuals must gather this information for their spouse regardless of whether they are filing a joint petition, separate individual petitions, or even if only one spouse is filing. In a situation where only one spouse files, the income and expenses of the non-filing spouse is required so that the court, the trustee, and creditors can evaluate the household's financial position. If you are unemployed, you can use your employed spouse's income to fund your plan. If only one spouse files, it does not affect the credit of the non-filing spouse.

Chapter 13:
The Automatic Stay – Protecting You from Creditor Harassment

When you file your Chapter 13 petition, a trustee is appointed to administer the case. The Chapter 13 trustee both evaluates the case and serves as a disbursing agent, collecting your payments and making distributions to creditors. The trustee does this for a fee, which is built into your monthly plan payment. The fee is based on a percentage of the money to be paid to your unsecured creditors over the lifetime of your Chapter 13 plan. The percentage will vary from trustee to trustee.

Steve Johnson is a Chapter 13 trustee who handles bankruptcy cases filed in Cook County. He charges a fee of 4%. Sue Smith files a Chapter 13 plan that will repay her unsecured creditors 10% of what they are owed over the course of the plan. Sue's total unsecured debt is $100,000. Her plan will repay $10,000 to her secured creditors. This means that Steve's fee will be $400.

The automatic stay is one of the most attractive protections provided by law. Filing the bankruptcy petition under chapter 13 "automatically stays" (stops) most collection efforts against you and your property. Filing the petition does not stay certain types of actions. For instance, the stay does not stop:

- Criminal proceedings
- Paternity suits
- Domestic support obligations
- Child custody proceedings
- Divorce proceedings
- License suspension proceedings

The stay may be in effect for only a short time in some situations. For example, previously dismissed bankruptcy cases may limit the duration of the stay. The stay happens automatically and usually does not require the involvement of the bankruptcy court. As long as the stay is in effect, creditors generally may not initiate or continue lawsuits, wage garnishments, or even make telephone calls demanding payments. The bankruptcy clerk gives notice of the bankruptcy case to all creditors whose names and addresses are provided in your petition.

Chapter 13 also contains a special automatic stay provision that protects co-signers. Unless the bankruptcy court authorizes otherwise, a creditor may not seek to collect a "consumer debt" from any individual who is liable along with the consumer filing the Chapter 13 bankruptcy. Consumer debts are those incurred by an individual primarily for a personal, family, or household purpose. An example of a non-consumer debt would be a small business loan.

Individuals may use a Chapter 13 proceeding to save their home from foreclosure. The automatic stay stops the foreclosure proceeding as soon as you file the Chapter 13 petition. You may then bring the past-due payments current over a reasonable period of time. However, your case must be on file before a foreclosure auction takes place. If the mortgage company completes the sale of your home before you file, the stay will not protect your property. You may also lose the home if you fail to make the regular mortgage payments that come due after the Chapter 13 filing.

Between 20 and 50 days after you file the Chapter 13 petition, the Chapter 13 trustee will hold a meeting of creditors. The meeting generally lasts no more than 20 or 30 minutes. During this meeting, the trustee will place you under oath. Both the trustee and creditors may ask you questions. You must attend the meeting and answer questions regarding your financial affairs and the proposed terms of the plan. If a husband and wife file a joint petition, they both must attend the creditors' meeting and answer questions. The parties typically resolve problems with the plan either during or shortly after the creditors' meeting. Generally, you can avoid problems by making sure that the petition and plan are complete and accurate, and by consulting with the trustee prior to the meeting. Your attorney will handle these kinds of matters.

In a Chapter 13 case, to participate in distributions from the bankruptcy estate, unsecured creditors must file their proofs of claim with the court within 90 days after the first meeting of creditors. A governmental unit, like IRS, has 180 days from the date the case is filed to file a proof of claim. After the meeting of creditors, you, the Chapter 13 trustee, and those creditors who wish to attend will come to court for a hearing on your Chapter 13 repayment plan.

The Chapter 13 Plan:
Your Roadmap to a Brighter Financial Future

You must file a repayment plan with the Chapter 13 petition or within 14 days after the petition is filed.[40] A plan must be submitted for court approval and must provide for payments of fixed amounts to the trustee on a regular basis, usually every other week or once a month. The trustee then distributes the funds to creditors according to the terms of the plan, which may offer creditors less than full payment on their claims.

There are three types of claims: priority, secured, and unsecured. Priority claims are those granted special status by the bankruptcy law, such as most taxes and the costs of the bankruptcy proceeding. Secured claims are those that are tied to property and allow the creditor to take the property if you do not pay the underlying debt. Unsecured claims are generally not tied to property that you own. Credit cards are an example of an unsecured claim, and are given the lowest priority for repayment. This means that they will be the last debts satisfied by the plan.

If you want to keep property that secures a debt, your plan must provide for the regularly scheduled payments on the debt. In some situations, you may be able to "cram down" a debt to the actual value of the property. Generally, a cramdown is only available for investment property and vehicles. You cannot use a cramdown on your primary residence. For example, if your car loan balance is $10,000, but your car is only worth $6,000, you may be able to repay the actual value of the car in full satisfaction of the debt. Your plan must still repay the unsecured portion of the debt, but it receives the lowest priority of payment. This means that most people using cramdown to their advantage only pay a portion of the unsecured claim. Payments to secured creditors may follow the original payment schedule, which is often longer than the duration of the plan. If you have past-due payments, they must be made up as part of your plan.

Your plan is not required to pay your unsecured creditors in full. If your unsecured creditors receive at least as much money as they would in a Chapter 7 case, and you agree to pay all "projected disposable income" to them over the course of the plan, you can make partial repayments. In some cases, you may repay as little as 10% of the amount owed, or even less. In a Chapter 13 bankruptcy, "disposable income" is defined as your income minus your reasonable living expenses and any charitable contributions up to 15% of your gross income.

Within 30 days after filing the bankruptcy case, even if the plan has not yet been approved by the court, you must start making plan payments to the trustee. If you have secured loan payments or lease payments that are due before your plan is confirmed, you must make payments directly to your lender or landlord. Before you begin making payments, consult with your attorney. Your attorney will be able to tell you to whom and when to make payments.

Within approximately 45 days after the meeting of creditors, the bankruptcy judge must hold a confirmation hearing and decide whether your plan will work and whether it meets the requirements of the Bankruptcy Code. Creditors will receive 28 days' notice of the hearing and may object to confirmation.[41] The most common objections revolve around the amount of compensation the creditor is to receive or how much of your income is committed to the plan.

If the court confirms the plan, the Chapter 13 trustee will begin distributing the funds paid into the plan. If the court does not confirm the plan, you may file a modified plan. You may also convert the case to a liquidation case under Chapter 7. If the court does not confirm the plan or the modified plan and dismisses the case, the trustee must return all remaining funds to you, less what the trustee is allowed to keep for costs.

Sometimes a plan will need to be modified because a creditor was left out or because a creditor threatens to object to the plan. In these cases, modification can take place before or after confirmation of the plan. This modification is sometimes done at the request of the trustee or an unsecured creditor. The consumer may also request a modification to the plan based on a change in financial circumstances, such as a loss of income which would reduce the disposable monthly income paid into the plan. The consumer may also convert to a Chapter 7 filing.

Making Your Plan Work

In order to receive a discharge, you must complete your plan. This means that you must make all of your payments and make them on time. Because your plan is supposed to include all of your disposable income, you will be living on a fixed budget for the duration of the plan. Keep in mind that you cannot take on any new debt during the lifetime of your plan without first speaking to your trustee and obtaining the court's approval.

Keep in mind that no two Chapter 13 filings are alike. Because they are based on the specific financial circumstances of the person filing, each plan is crafted to specifically address the individual's financial liabilities and to achieve the individual's specific goals.

If you fail to make timely payments, your plan can be dismissed or converted to a Chapter 7 liquidation. If your circumstances change during your plan, you can modify the plan to fit those circumstances, so long as the plan is still feasible.

The Chapter 13 Discharge

Under Chapter 13, you are entitled to a discharge upon completion of all payments under the Chapter 13 plan so long as you certify that all domestic support obligations that came due prior to making such certification have been paid, that you have not received a discharge in a prior Chapter 13 case filed within two years or a prior Chapter 7, 11, or 12 case within four years, and that you have completed an approved financial management course.[42]

The discharge releases you from all debts provided for by the plan or disallowed, with limited exceptions. Creditors provided for in full or in part under the Chapter 13 plan may no longer initiate or continue any legal or other action against you to collect the discharged obligations.

Debts not discharged in Chapter 13 include:
- Certain long term obligations (such as a home mortgage)
- Debts for alimony or child support
- Certain taxes
- Debts for most government funded or guaranteed educational loans or benefit overpayments
- Debts arising from death or personal injury caused by driving while intoxicated or under the influence of drugs

- Debts for restitution or a criminal fine included in a sentence on conviction of a crime.

You will be responsible for these debts after the Chapter 13 plan ends if you do not pay them as part of your Chapter 13 plan.

The discharge in a Chapter 13 case is somewhat broader than in a Chapter 7 case. Debts dischargeable in a Chapter 13, but not in Chapter 7, include debts for willful and malicious injury to property, debts incurred to pay nondischargeable tax obligations, and debts arising from property settlements in divorce or separation proceedings.[43] These debts can be discharged in a Chapter 13 because the creditor receives some compensation. This balances the creditor's interest in being made whole with society's interest in having as many consumers as possible participating in the economy.

After confirmation of a plan, circumstances may arise that prevent you from completing the plan. In such situations, you may ask the court to grant a "hardship discharge."

Generally, such a discharge is available only if your failure to complete plan payments is due to circumstances beyond your control and through no fault of your own, if your creditors have received at least as much as they would have received in a Chapter 7 liquidation case, and if modification of the plan is not possible.

Injury or illness that precludes employment sufficient to fund even a modified plan may serve as the basis for a hardship discharge. The hardship discharge is more limited than the discharge described above and does not apply to any debts that cannot be discharged in a Chapter 7 case.[44]

Life During and After Bankruptcy

Filing bankruptcy does not eliminate your rights. In fact, it puts you in a much stronger position in relationship to your creditors. Consumer laws like those provided for in the Bankruptcy Code serve to level the playing field between creditors and borrowers. The automatic stay and the discharge injunction are powerful protections that give you rights in addition to other state and federal consumer protection laws. If you think that one of your creditors is violating the automatic stay or your discharge, you should inform your attorney immediately.

Stay Violations

When creditors attempt to collect a debt while the automatic stay is in place, they are in violation of the automatic stay. The most common stay violations are collection calls and letters, but there are many ways that creditors can violate the automatic stay. These are serious violations of the law for which you may collect your actual damages, your attorney's fees and, in some cases, punitive damages. This is because the automatic stay is designed to protect you from your creditors during the pendency of your bankruptcy case. It is one of the most powerful consumer protections available under the law.[45]

Proceeding With a Sheriff's Sale

Sometimes, especially when a bankruptcy is filed shortly before a scheduled sheriff's sale of a property, lenders will conduct the sale even though the automatic stay is in effect. So long as you provided proper notice of the bankruptcy filing to the creditor, proceeding with the sale violates the stay, even if it was an "honest" mistake. If you are filing at the eleventh hour before the sale, your bankruptcy attorney will want to provide notice directly to the creditor's attorneys as well as the creditor.

If the sale is held, your bankruptcy attorney will need to file an adversary proceeding against the creditor to address the stay violation. In addition to unwinding the sale, you can receive the value of your actual damages and your attorney's fees. If the violation was willful and knowing, it is possible to recover punitive damages. Punitive damages are damages in excess of your actual damages; they are designed to severely punish bad behavior.

Repossessing Your Car/Ignition Kill Switches

If the automatic stay is in effect and the owner of your auto loan repossesses your car, it is a stay violation. Some auto dealers, especially the "buy here-pay here" dealers install devices in their cars that can remotely shut the car's ignition off. This makes it easier for the dealer to locate and repossess the car. If the automatic stay is in effect and the dealer's disabling device is triggered, this behavior violates the automatic stay. The automatic stay protects anything that is property of the bankruptcy estate. Disabling your car is prohibited because it is both a constructive repossession and an attempt to collect a debt.

Collection Calls and Letters

The automatic stay protects you from attempts to collect on your debts. If your creditors continue to call you after you file your bankruptcy case, they are in violation of the automatic stay. Keep in mind that some correspondence is permissible even if the automatic stay is in place. For example, a creditor can send you an account statement without attempting to collect the debt. If you feel that your creditors are harassing you in violation of the automatic stay, contact your attorney to determine whether the behavior violates the automatic stay. In addition to the damages you can collect for a stay violation, you may be able to collect damages for violations of other state and federal laws, such as the Fair Debt Collection Practices Act.

Lawsuits

The automatic stay protects you from your creditors filing lawsuits against you and halts lawsuits that have already been filed. If the automatic stay is in effect and one of your creditors files a collection lawsuit against you, your creditor has violated the automatic stay. If there is a lawsuit pending against you and your creditor moves for judgment or otherwise tries to advance the case without first lifting the stay, then your creditor has violated the automatic stay.

Enforcing Judgments

The automatic stay protects you from attempts to enforce judgments already entered against you. This includes actions like filing a judgment lien against your home. A judgment lien is a lien filed against real property that you own. If a judgment lien is filed against a piece of property that you own, you will not be able to sell that property without first satisfying the judgment lien. Other attempts to enforce a judgment include garnishing your wages or bank accounts. Even a letter from the judgment creditor can violate the stay if the creditor demands a payment or requests that you contact the creditor to work out a repayment plan.

Other Offensive Conduct

The automatic stay provides broad protections. Any action that attempts to collect on claims that existed before your case was filed may be a stay violation. If creditors take actions against the property of the bankruptcy estate, there is also a likely stay violation. As with most situations, if you believe that a creditor is violating the automatic stay, you should immediately contact your attorney to determine if a violation has occurred.

Discharge Violations

Once you have received your discharge, creditors whose debts were discharged are prohibited from attempting to collect the discharged debt. However, you can voluntarily repay your debts after your discharge. Do not be fooled. If a discharged creditor contacts you requesting payment, hinting at the possibility of paying, or merely referencing the discharged debt, it is likely a discharge violation. If you believe that a creditor is violating the discharge injunction, you should contact your bankruptcy attorney.

A violation of the discharge entitles you to recover damages and attorney's fees from the creditor who is violating the discharge.

Debt Buyers

Believe it or not, there is a market for discharged debts. Companies purchase discharged debts from creditors for a fraction of the value of the discharged debt. They then attempt to collect those debts. In most cases, the debt buyer will report the debt on your credit report. If you are not monitoring your credit report, you may be completely unaware that the debt buyer has been reporting your discharged debt to the credit bureaus. Many consumers discover the trade line on their credit report when they are trying to obtain credit elsewhere, like when purchasing a car or a new home.

In many cases, the debt buyer's entry on the credit report is the only factor preventing you from obtaining credit. Debt buyers do this in the hopes that you will voluntarily make a payment on the debt in order to obtain the credit you need. This is a violation of the discharge and other state and federal laws. If a debt buyer is reporting discharged debt on your credit report, contact your bankruptcy attorney. You are not without a legal remedy and should aggressively protect your credit and your rights under the law.

Two years ago, Emmet, a production assistant for a local television news program, filed a Chapter 7 Bankruptcy to discharge his credit card debts. Since his Chapter 7 discharge, Emmet has been using his credit responsibly. He has been under the impression that his credit score has been steadily improving. Emmet decides that it is time to get rid of his 2004 Toyota Corolla, as it has finally hit the 75,000 mile mark. When he goes to the car dealership to purchase a new car, he is denied a loan because there is an outstanding $3,000 unpaid account reflected on his credit. The car salesman informs Emmet that if he pays off the debt, he will qualify for a loan. Emmet checks his credit report and sees that a company called Account Reconciliation Specialists has reported a past-due account on his credit report. In his Chapter 7 bankruptcy, Emmet discharged a $3,000 credit card debt payable to Mastercard. Emmet contacts Account Reconciliation Specialists and inquires as to the nature of the debt. They inform him that they will remove the negative report and close the account if he pays them $300. Instead of paying the money, Emmet contacts his bankruptcy attorney, who files an adversarial proceeding against Account Reconciliation Specialists for a violation of Emmet's discharge, a violation of the Fair Debt Collection Practices Act, the Illinois Collection Agency Act, and the Illinois Consumer Fraud and Unfair Business Practices Act. Emmet has provable damages

174

that he may collect on these facts and his attorney's fees will be paid as well.

You would think that discharge violations are the exception, but they are not. Even inaccurate credit reporting that remains uncorrected after being disputed can be a discharge violation. In some cases, creditors are aware that their computers do not properly report discharged debt to the credit bureaus. Given that many people are unaware of their rights, these creditors will maintain a cash fund for paying out settlements to the few individuals who fight them because it is cheaper than fixing their software. Some creditors may continue to send you statements after your discharge. This may be a computer error, or it may be a purposeful attempt to collect a debt. In either case, it is a violation of your discharge. If you believe that a creditor is violating your bankruptcy discharge, contact your bankruptcy attorney.

Complaints about debt collectors have dramatically increased in recent years. Illinois Attorney General Lisa Madigan has reportedly seen a rise in aggressive and illegal collection techniques. For example, Attorney General Madigan filed a lawsuit against a debt collector called PN Financial in early 2012.[46] The company is accused of trying to collect debts that it could not legally collect, revealing information about debts to employers and people's family members, and for threatening borrowers with fake case numbers. Attorney General Madigan's office received 52 complaints about PN Financial before filing suit. In 2010, the Federal Trade Commission received 140,036 complaints about debt collectors.[47] Harassing borrowers and violating the law is a cottage industry in the United States.

Credit Score Recovery

Many people think that filing for bankruptcy will ruin their credit for the rest of their lives. This is 100% false. Although your bankruptcy filing will remain on your credit report for several years after your discharge, it is not the only factor that determines your credit score. After you receive your discharge, you will start to receive credit card offers from creditors. The cards are generally high-interest, annual fee, low-limit cards. Because the Bankruptcy Code prevents you from receiving back-to-back discharges, creditors know that offering you credit after your discharge is somewhat low risk. Essentially, credit card companies perceive you to be a better credit risk because you cannot get another discharge in bankruptcy for 4 years after a Chapter 13 discharge and if you filed a Chapter 7 Bankruptcy, you are precluded from filing for another 8 years.[48] If you continue to run up large credit card debts after your discharge, you cannot discharge them before the creditor can sue you and obtain a judgment. A smart consumer will take advantage of this cynical attitude and use the offers of credit to his advantage by using the credit and paying it off on time with the goal of rebuilding credit. Practically speaking, it is often the best idea to avoid consumer credit as much as possible. Unless it is used for housing, education, or a vehicle that you can't pay cash for, using consumer credit is almost always a bad investment.

One of the easiest ways to improve your credit score after receiving your discharge is to accept 1 credit card offer and use the card responsibly. Since most cards will have a very low limit, it's difficult to get in too deep at first. However, if you are paying on time every month, many card providers will raise your credit limit without being asked. So long as you are keeping your balance low, and making more than the minimum payment each month, you will see your credit score rise in short order and dramatically. Do not be fooled by this. Creditors live off of lending and the interest payments it generates. The higher the limit and the more you use, the more the creditor makes. If have graduated out of the debt, never get pulled back in.

It is also important to monitor your credit reports. You are entitled to a free credit report each year, and it is a good idea to check it yearly. You can obtain a free credit report from AnnualCreditReport.com. You may discover that creditors are incorrectly reporting your discharged debts. If they are, you should dispute the trade line with the credit reporting bureaus. Make sure to attach a copy of your discharge order to your dispute letter. You should also notify the creditor of the inaccurate reporting. By providing notice to the reporting bureaus and the creditor, you are building a stronger case for yourself if you have to bring an action against the creditor in the future. If you are having difficulty disputing an inaccurate entry on your credit report, contact your attorney.

The three credit reporting bureaus can be contacted at the following numbers:

- Experian (800) 392-1122
- Equifax (800) 685-1111
- Trans Union (216) 779-7200

If you have other recurring debts, make sure that you prioritize your payments. If you have a credit card and a student loan, and you have extra cash you can use to pay down one debt or the other, pay the credit card first. Credit cards tend to have much higher interest rates than student loans, and paying down your revolving credit has a higher bang-for-your-buck factor than paying extra towards a student loan. This doesn't mean that you should fail to pay your student loan. However, directing extra funds in a way that helps improve your credit score is always a good idea.

Choosing a Bankruptcy Attorney

If you have decided that filing for bankruptcy is right for you, you will want to carefully choose your bankruptcy attorney. Filing for bankruptcy can be stressful for many people; you want to select an attorney with whom you are comfortable and can trust. Some firms offer more access to your attorney than others. If you are thinking of filing a Chapter 13 bankruptcy, you may be working with your attorney for several years. Is the attorney a person you can work with? Is the attorney someone who will answer your questions and take some of the worry off of your shoulders? At large bankruptcy "mills," you may only interact with paralegals and other office staff. If you are comfortable with that approach, make sure that you are aware of what services the office will provide for the fee that it charges. What a great firm offers may be very different.

This is particularly important because you should shop around for the attorney that is best for you. You may discover that the inexpensive bankruptcy attorney only wants to handle simple cases that do not require extra effort or work. Even more expensive attorneys will only include certain tasks in their initial retainer. Other work like adversarial proceedings or disputing a creditor's proof of claim may require a separate retainer with either an hourly fee or a contingency fee. Knowing what you're getting up front will allow you to make an informed decision when choosing the attorney that you want to hire.

You may also want to ask your friends and family if they know of a reputable attorney. Keep in mind that not every attorney is experienced in handling bankruptcy cases, and simply because someone is recommended by a person that you know does not mean that attorney is a good fit for a bankruptcy case. Even if you meet someone who is willing to learn about bankruptcy law in order to take your case, consider whether you want to be someone's first case. If you have a case that is more complex than a simple no-asset Chapter 7 filing, you may want to hire an attorney who has some experience with bankruptcy law. Remember, more experienced does not necessarily mean more expensive.

The Initial Consultation – What to Expect

Assuming that you are meeting with an attorney who wants to help you make an informed decision about your financial future, you can expect the initial consultation to take approximately an hour of your time. Be prepared to candidly discuss your financial affairs with the attorney. If you don't provide accurate information, the advice you receive may not be the best possible advice. Every case is different. Your attorney can only base his or her opinion on the information that you provide. The attorney's experience also influences his or her opinion.

The attorney will want to collect some basic information about you to determine how you are financially situated. For instance, where you live, how much money you make, and the size of your family are all important pieces of information that can help determine your eligibility to file for a Chapter 7 bankruptcy. Although you likely will not need to provide documents to your attorney until you have signed a retainer and are ready to begin the process of assembling your bankruptcy petition, it may be helpful to bring copies of collection letters, pay stubs from the last six months, a copy of your most recent mortgage statement or car loan statement, and the summons for any lawsuits to which you are a party. This will give the attorney a broad view of your financial situation. Not every person who may file bankruptcy is financially distressed. An underwater home may be the event that triggers the bankruptcy filing.

If you own a property that is $80,000 underwater, meaning the mortgage exceeds the value of the property by $80,000, do you really own the property? A home that you owe $330,000 is not likely to recover in the next five years to even what you currently owe on it. If you pay $3,000 a month between principal, interest, taxes, insurance and maintenance payments, over a course of 5 years, you would have paid $180,000 on a property currently worth $250,000. Essentially, you are merely maintaining the property on behalf of the lender.

During the same period you likely would not have paid down the mortgage significantly, considering that the vast majority of your monthly mortgage payment is just interest. Economically speaking, housing has two purposes: shelter or investment. Shelter is much easier to come by than something with investment value. Value is the main theme of conversations we have with our clients regarding their goals. Start with identifying the value of assets you own. Once you establish value, use that value to guide your decisions.

The initial consultation is a time for you to explore your options, get to know the attorney, and determine whether bankruptcy can help you achieve your long-term goals. Before attending your consultation, spend some time thinking about your goals and where you want to be in a few years. If you feel pressured or rushed to sign a retainer, odds are that the attorney is not a good fit for you. Ask lots of questions. Great attorneys are hard to come by. You will know them by their ability to not only answer your thorniest questions, but also by their ability to answer the questions that you have not thought to ask. That is the definition of experience. Find out how many cases the attorney has handled. Ask whether the retainer covers court appearances beyond the creditor's meeting and the plan confirmation hearing (if you are filing Chapter 13). Before you sign a retainer, make sure that all of your questions have been answered.

Adversary Proceedings

What is an Adversary Proceeding?

An adversary proceeding is a lawsuit filed within your bankruptcy case. They are initiated by filing a complaint with the bankruptcy court. Only a creditor, a trustee, or the bankruptcy filer can bring an adversary proceeding. Only certain kinds of matters may be brought as an adversary proceeding. One major benefit to filing an adversary proceeding as a consumer is that no additional filing fee is required. On the other hand, filing a similar claim in a

Federal District Court would require paying another filing fee in addition to the bankruptcy filing fee.

Creditors and Adversary Proceedings

For example, a creditor may bring an adversary proceeding to object to its debt being discharged. This is generally done if the debt falls within one of the exceptions to a discharge or when the creditor believes that the bankruptcy was filed in bad faith. If a bankruptcy is filed for honest purposes, it is very rare that a case will be dismissed as a bad faith filing. Bad faith filings are those that attempt to manipulate the Bankruptcy Code for less-than-savory purposes, not those that attempt to use the Bankruptcy Code to obtain a fresh start on the best possible terms. Remember that the Bankruptcy Code was enacted to give the honest but unfortunate debtor a fresh start, unencumbered by the weight of previous debts.

Trustees and Adversary Proceedings

When a trustee files an adversary proceeding, it is generally because the trustee wants to dismiss the case as a bad faith bankruptcy filing or because the trustee wants to convert the case from a Chapter 7 to a Chapter 13 bankruptcy. Trustees may also use adversary proceedings to claw back payments made to creditors before your bankruptcy case was filed. A Chapter 7 trustee may use an adversary proceeding to return property to the bankruptcy estate. In general, so long as you are honest with your bankruptcy attorney, and disclose all of your financial affairs, you will not see an adversary proceeding filed in your bankruptcy case by a creditor or trustee.

Consumers and Adversary Proceedings

People filing for bankruptcy can also bring adversary proceedings. These are almost always brought against creditors for violations of the automatic stay or the discharge injunction. Generally, an adversary proceeding brought for a stay or discharge violation will also contain other claims based on federal and state law. Your attorney can tell you which claims are available to you. If your creditors are harassing you during or after your bankruptcy case, you have the right to file an adversary proceeding. Doing so protects your rights and can result in your collecting damages for the creditor's misconduct.

In particular, discharge violations tend to create more claims than the violation itself. For example, if a creditor continues to report a discharged debt as delinquent and continues collection attempts on that debt, the creditor has likely violated both the Fair Credit Reporting Act[49] and the Fair Debt Collection Practices Act.[50] In such a situation, it is possible to recover damages for the discharge violation, the fair credit reporting violation, and the fair debt collection violation in the same case. Although these kinds of claims can go to trial, it is common to see creditors settle these claims before substantial litigation takes place. This is because most creditors have funds set aside specifically for satisfying judgments and settlement agreements.

Miranda Baker, Orland Park, Illinois: A Discharge Violation

Miranda, a former United States Marine Captain, filed a Chapter 7 bankruptcy in August 2010 and received her discharge at the end of October 2010. In her bankruptcy filing, she named Mastercharge as one of her creditors. Her balance due on her Mastercharge account was $30,000. Mastercharge received notice of both the bankruptcy filing and the discharge. It did not object to her discharge. In early 2011, Miranda checked her credit report. Although Mastercharge was properly reporting her debt as discharged, there was a $30,000 debt being reported by a company called Stride Credit Solutions. Miranda had never heard of the company, and filed a dispute with each of the three credit reporting bureaus.

All three credit bureaus reported to Miranda that Stride Credit Solutions was claiming her debt was past-due and owing to Stride Credit Solutions. Miranda, through her attorney, provided each bureau with a copy of her bankruptcy discharge and list of creditors from her Chapter 7 petition. She assumed that doing so would clear up the problem. About a month later, Miranda received a collections notice from Stride Credit Solutions. It stated that her account was several months past-due and offered her a one-time payoff amount of $10,000. Instead of paying off the account, Miranda contacted her attorney again. Miranda's attorney informed her that debt purchasers are common in the industry. Because so many people aren't aware of their rights, debt purchasers will buy discharged debts from other creditors and attempt to collect on those debts. The debts are purchased for a fraction of the balance due, which means that even collecting a small amount of money is profitable. Miranda's attorney also informed her that in addition to being a discharge violation, he had identified several other claims based on the Fair Debt Collection Practices Act (FDCPA), the Fair Credit Reporting Act (FCRA) and the Illinois Consumer Fraud and Deceptive Practices Act (ICFA).

Miranda signed a contingency fee retainer with her attorney.. A contingency fee retainer is an agreement between an attorney and his or her client that the attorney will only be paid if the client's lawsuit ends in the client's favor. The attorney drafted an adversary proceeding complaint and filed it with the U.S. Bankruptcy Court for the Northern District of Illinois, Eastern Division. In the complaint, her attorney alleged a violation of the bankruptcy discharge as well as violations of the FDCPA, the FCRA and ICFA. About two weeks after Stride Credit Solutions was served with the adversary proceeding complaint, Stride's attorney filed a motion to dismiss the adversary proceeding. Miranda, through her attorney, responded to the motion. After oral argument on the motion, the bankruptcy judge denied Stride's motion. The next day, Miranda's attorney sent a settlement offer to Stride, requesting $25,000 in damages and his attorney's fees. After some negotiations between Stride's attorneys and Miranda's attorney, Stride agreed to pay a total of $30,000 to settle Miranda's claims. It also agreed to cease all collection and credit reporting activities on the debt.

Objecting To Proofs of Claim

It is not necessary to file an adversary proceeding to object to a proof of claim. However, an adversary proceeding can be used to object to a proof of claim where other claims can be asserted against the party filing the claim. This means of objecting to a proof of claim is similar to filing a counterclaim in a state court foreclosure action.

Leroy Williams, Frankfort, Illinois: Objecting to a Proof of Claim

Leroy filed a Chapter 13 bankruptcy in order to strip the second mortgage from his property and rebuild some equity in his home. American Bank Corp., the entity that services Leroy's second mortgage, has filed a proof of claim in Leroy's case. Leroy feels that the amount of the claim is high and asks his attorney to dispute the bank's proof of claim. Before filing the objection, Leroy's attorney asks Leroy for his most current mortgage statements. He notices that in the months immediately before Leroy filed for bankruptcy, Leroy's mortgage payment increased significantly. Itemized on the statements were charges for property insurance. Leroy has always maintained his own property insurance. His lender had improperly "force-placed" insurance on the property. This force-placed insurance was being billed at a rate three times that of normal homeowner's insurance. Instead of filing a typical objection to the proof of claim, Leroy's attorney drafted an adversary proceeding complaint alleging breach of contract and filed it as his objection to the proof of claim. The adversary proceeding ultimately settled with the bank agreeing to remove the charges for the force-placed insurance from its claim and paying Leroy's attorney's fees.

Consumer Rights Statutes

In addition to foreclosure defense and consumer bankruptcy, state and federal law both include other powerful consumer protections. Many of these laws are also violated when creditors violate the automatic stay or the bankruptcy discharge. You may have already experienced violations of certain consumer protection statutes and been utterly unaware of the violation. This section discusses two consumer rights statutes that Sulaiman Law Group has used to protect the rights of its clients.

The Fair Debt Collection Practices Act[51]

Who Is A Debt Collector?

The Fair Debt Collection Practices Act (FDCPA) protects consumers from the unfair and harassing conduct of debt collectors. While many people are under the impression that the FDCPA covers all debt collection activity, this is not necessarily the case. The FDCPA regulates the conduct of debt collectors. A debt collector is defined by the statute,[52] and does not include creditors who collect their own debts while using their own name. For example, if Bob's Electronics Hut is collecting a debt and is collecting in its own name, then Bob's Electronics Hut is not a debt collector as defined by the FDCPA. However, if Bob's Electronics Hut collects under the name, "Bob's Collections," then it is likely that Bob's is acting as a debt collector. If Bob's Electronics Hut hires Dewey, Collectem, & Howe, P.C. to collect on debts owed to Bob's, Dewey, Collectem & Howe, P.C. is absolutely acting as a debt collector as defined by the FDCPA.

What Conduct Does The Fair Debt Collection Practices Act Prohibit?

The Fair Debt Collection Practices Act prohibits a wide range of conduct. Among other things, it dictates when debt collectors may contact you, whom debt collectors may contact, and what debt collectors may say to you.

Debt collectors are prohibited from calling you before 8 am or after 9 pm. This calling window is deemed to be reasonable by Congress. Anything outside that window is technically a violation of the Act. Debt collectors cannot contact you directly once they are informed that you are represented by an attorney. Keep in mind that being represented by an attorney doesn't require you to be involved in a lawsuit or a bankruptcy filing. Plenty of people retain attorneys to advise them in their financial affairs. More probably would if they knew about this provision of the Act. Once a debt collector receives a written notice of representation from your attorney, all collection calls must stop.

Debt collectors cannot communicate with third parties about your debt without your consent. If a debt collector calls your employer and tells the receptionist that you are being contacted regarding a debt, then that is a violation of the Act. Debt collectors may attempt to confirm specific information about you, such as your contact information or address, but they cannot inform others of your debts. This includes your family. If a debt collector calls your mother and threatens a lawsuit if your debt is not paid, it is a violation of the Act.

If you tell the debt collector to stop contacting you, or if you dispute the debt, the debt collector may not call you. The only exceptions that allow a debt collector to contact you are to confirm that it will no longer contact you, to inform you of the remedies available to the creditor, and to give you notice that the creditor has elected to pursue a remedy. This means that once you tell a debt collector to stop contacting you, you may receive a letter confirming the request, and the debt collector may still contact you to inform you that it has decided to pursue a lawsuit against you. However, the attempts to collect the debt must stop.

Harassment and Abuse Is Prohibited

Debt collectors are prohibited from using violence or the threat of violence to collect a debt. This means that if the local auto title loan shop sends a thug with a baseball bat to your home to collect a debt, then it is in violation of the FDCPA, in addition to the many criminal statutes such an action would violate. It also means that a debt collector cannot say things like, "I will come to your house and force you to pay." Debt collectors are also prohibited from using profanity or insulting language when they contact you. If a debt collector said, "You f**king deadbeat, you had better pay up or I'll send someone to your house to beat the money out of you!" that statement would include three violations of the FDCPA.

Debt collectors are prohibited from making excessive phone calls in one day. The Act does not set a specific limit, but clearly persistence becomes harassment at some point. Two phone calls in one day are within the limits defined by the Act. Twenty calls in one day are a clear violation. The Act specifically states that debt collectors are engaging in harassment by "causing a telephone to ring or engaging any person in telephone conversation repeatedly or continuously with intent to annoy, abuse, or harass any person at the called number."[53] If you receive three calls a day for one week, it is difficult to establish that the conduct violates this provision. However, if you receive 99 calls in one week, it is much more obvious that a violation has occurred.

False or Misleading Representations Are Prohibited

Debt collectors are prohibited from lying to collect a debt. The Act provides a list of the types of false and misleading representations that are prohibited.[54] For example, a debt collector cannot claim to be backed by or vouched for by the U.S. government or any state government. They cannot lie about the amount of debt owed, why the debt is owed, or about any services or compensation that they have provided to you. Debt collectors cannot pose as attorneys.

They cannot claim that failure to pay will result in imprisonment, arrest, garnishment, or other remedies unless those remedies are available and the creditor intends to use them. One example of this behavior is a debt collector telling a person that the police are outside her home waiting to arrest her and take her children into protective custody. Under no circumstances is such a remedy available to any debt collector, and such a statement is a clear and blatant violation of the Act.

Debt collectors are also not allowed to threaten consumers. This includes threatening illegal actions like violence. Even an "idle" threat is prohibited; debt collectors cannot threaten to take an action that they do not intend to take. This means that a statement like, "If you don't pay this credit card off, I'm going to buy a full-page ad in the Chicago Tribune so that everyone knows you're a deadbeat," violates the Act. Given that taking out the ad would also violate the Act, one can assume that the statement is an "idle" threat. Debt collectors also cannot claim that you are committing a crime by not paying your debts. Debtor's prison was abolished centuries ago.

Anyone who has received a call from a debt collector has likely heard the following statement, "This is an attempt to collect a debt. Any information obtained may be used to assist in collection efforts." This statement is required by the Act. A debt collector that does not identify itself as a debt collector is breaking the law. This statement must appear on any correspondence you receive and must appear on any lawsuit filed against you as well.

Debt collectors cannot engage in unfair or unconscionable behavior.[55] For instance, making up false fees is prohibited. Disguising one fee as another is prohibited. Debt collectors cannot collect fees that are not allowed by law or described in the agreement that created the debt. For example, if your car loan provides for a late payment fee of $50, the debt collector cannot try to increase that fee. Consumers who are currently making payments on a Chapter 13 plan should closely monitor how their creditors are applying the plan payments. In particular, many mortgage servicers will improperly add fees onto the loan balance during a bankruptcy. This not only violates the FDCPA, it also violates the U.S. Bankruptcy Code.

This section of the Act also prohibits debt collectors from sending post cards or other mail that identifies the sender as a debt collector. The Act jealously protects the privacy of consumers in this regard. If a debt collector sends you a post card, and someone else reads it, the debt collector has violated the Act twice: once for sending the post card and once for communicating with a third party about your debt. Even though the person reading the post card wasn't necessarily intended by the debt collector, it counts as a communication to a third party.

Violations of the Act expose debt collectors to legal liability. For each violation of the Act, creditors are liable for actual damages suffered by the debtor, statutory damages of $1,000, and attorney's fees. Actual damages are damages that can be proven at trial. For instance, if the harassing behavior of a debt collector causes you to lose sleep and experience emotional distress, you may be able to recover actual damages. The Act also provides for class actions, which are lawsuits where a specific group of consumers claim to have been harmed in the same way by the same debt collector. Class actions are particularly dangerous for debt collectors because they magnify the impact of one small claim by multiplying that claim many times over. It is important to note that the Act has a one-year statute of limitations. This means that you must file a lawsuit against a debt collector within a year of it violating the Act.

The Illinois Consumer Fraud and Deceptive Business Practices Act[56]

The Illinois Consumer Fraud and Deceptive Business Practices Act (ICFA) is a broad piece of legislation that gives Illinois citizens powerful protections against a wide range of behavior. At its most broad level, the Act prohibits unfair methods of competition and unfair acts and practices in the conduct of commerce.[57] The language of the Act incorporates elements of the Federal Trade Commission Act[58], which also prohibits unfair and deceptive business practices. In addition to this very broad language, the Act contains specific provisions that regulate 64 different commercial activities.[59] For all practical purposes, most consumers rely on the Act's prohibition of unfair and deceptive practices to make their case.

This is particularly true when consumers bring adversary proceedings against their creditors in a bankruptcy case, or when a consumer files a Fair Debt Collection Practices Act lawsuit against a debt collector. When a creditor attempts to collect a debt in violation of the automatic stay, it may also be violating ICFA. Consumers who have valid ICFA claims may seek their actual damages and punitive damages, with a few exceptions.[60]

Sue runs a very successful online retail business selling hand-crafted soaps, candles, and other items. She filed a Chapter 13 bankruptcy to strip the second mortgage from her home and to cram down the loan on her 3 year old car. Shortly after she filed her case, Sue received a letter from a debt collection agency hired by her auto loan lender. The letter informed her that due to her bankruptcy filing, she was in breach of her loan agreement and the car would be repossessed unless she paid the loan balance in full within 30 days. This behavior clearly violates the automatic stay, which went into effect when Sue filed her bankruptcy case. It also violates the Fair Debt Collection Practices Act. The debt collector is impermissibly contacting her, is making false representations, and is engaged in an unfair practice (violating the automatic stay). This behavior also violates ICFA because the debt collector is misrepresenting a material fact (that she is in breach of her loan agreement) in the hopes that she will rely on the statement and pay the money. Sue contacts her attorney, and ultimately files an adversary proceeding in the Bankruptcy Court based on the debt collector's conduct. Sue can attempt to recover damages for each statutory violation.

The Real Estate Settlement Procedures Act

The Real Estate Settlement Procedures Act (RESPA)[61] was enacted by the U.S. Congress in 1974. RESPA prohibits kickbacks and fee-sharing between lenders and third-party agents (like mortgage brokers). It also requires that lenders provide specific disclosures to borrowers, including a Good Faith Estimate of what the credit offered by the lender will cost and a settlement statement that itemizes the costs of closing the loan. This settlement statement is commonly called a HUD-1 statement.

Qualified Written Requests

RESPA also requires that lenders respond in a timely fashion to disputes and requests regarding a specific mortgage loan. These requests are also called qualified written requests or QWRs. The Dodd-Frank Act contains provisions that accelerate the timeframe in which lenders must respond to such a request. However, there is some confusion as to when the Dodd-Frank changes become live. As of June 2012, the changes are not reflected in the current version of the statute,[62] but they may become effective as early as July 21, 2012. Given that the changes are not yet incorporated into the current version of the statute, this section will discuss QWRs based on the pre-Dodd-Frank version of the statute.

QWR Basics

Typically, a qualified written request will request a complete transactional history of the loan including all payments and charges. It is also useful to request a key or glossary of the transaction codes the lender uses. This will make it possible to interpret the loan's transaction history. In general, these documents are largely unreadable without knowing what the various transaction codes mean.

Other requested documents can include the Pooling and Servicing Agreement (if any) for your loan; the name, address, and contact information for the current holder of your mortgage and note; and copies of all correspondence, notes, and other records related to your account. These documents should demonstrate who owns your loan. More importantly, the lender cannot later deny the validity or accuracy of those documents because they were voluntarily produced from their own records.

Most lenders have a specific address to which your QWR should be sent. Make sure to send the QWR to the right address, or the lender may deny receiving it. The lender may also claim that any delays in responding to the QWR are due to the letter being sent to the wrong address. It is also important to send your QWR via certified mail. The return receipt, or "green card," that you receive will be proof of when the QWR was received by your lender.

Time to Respond

Currently, lenders are required to acknowledge receipt of a QWR within 20 days of receiving the letter.[63] 60 days after receiving the QWR, the lender must respond to the QWR with the requested documents. However, the Dodd-Frank Act has changed these time frames. There has been some debate among consumer defense attorneys as to when those changes take effect. Based on the text of the Dodd-Frank Act, it would appear that the changes will take effect between July 21, 2012 and July 21, 2013. [64] Once the changes have taken effect, lenders will have 5 days to acknowledge receipt of the QWR and 30 days to respond to it.

Failing To Respond

As the law currently stands, lenders that fail to comply with RESPA's QWR provisions can be pursued for actual damages sustained by the borrower, additional damages up to $1,000.00 if the lender has a pattern of non-compliance with RESPA, as well as attorney's costs and fees.[65] Once the Dodd-Frank changes take effect, the additional damages available will be increased to $2,000.00.[66]

The Department of Housing and Urban Development has made a sample QWR available at:
http://portal.hud.gov/hudportal/HUD?src=/program_offices/housing/ramh/res/reslettr

How You Can Help Protect Your Rights

Why You Should Hold Creditors Accountable

There are many powerful consumer protection laws that protect you from unfair lending practices, unfair debt collection practices, unfair credit reporting practices, and other abuses. However, most of those protections are worthless unless you use them to your advantage. Your state's Attorney General and the U.S. Attorney General cannot prosecute every abusive creditor. They simply do not have the resources. This is why most consumer protection statutes give you the right to sue when creditors violate the law. However, you cannot be an effective private attorney general if you do not have the evidence to make your case.

Creditor harassment is best documented by the person being harassed. While an experienced and effective attorney can build a strong case, it is up to you to provide the materials. Without those materials, your case is generally little more than a game of he-said, she-said.

A well-planned consumer defense strategy will have you working closely with your attorneys and their staff. For instance, if you are planning to file for protection under the U.S. Bankruptcy Code, you may want to plan ahead. A creditor who inadvertently violates the automatic stay is treated differently under the law than a creditor who knowingly and willfully violates the automatic stay. Similarly, playing a recording of a phone call from a creditor is more powerful than simply describing the phone call to a judge or a jury. Learning to document creditor harassment is essential to the success of a well-planned consumer defense strategy. This section describes some best practices for building your case.

Always Provide Written Notices

Never rely on a phone call or an email to provide notice to your creditors. This is true at every stage in any consumer defense strategy. When you retain an attorney, that attorney should notify your creditors in writing that they are to no longer contact you. This no-contact letter is invaluable for building claims against your creditors. Once a creditor is notified that a consumer is represented by an attorney, the creditor should cease direct contact with the consumer. If a creditor continues to contact the consumer, the creditor is in violation of the Fair Debt Collection Practices Act. Consumers considering filing a Chapter 13 bankruptcy may want to provide this notice to creditors prior to filing the case. This way, any contacts from creditors can be brought as an adversary proceeding within the bankruptcy case.

The importance of written notices is especially relevant in a bankruptcy context. Relying on the clerk of courts to provide notice to each creditor is not enough. If a bankruptcy is being filed to prevent a home from going to a sheriff's sale, it is vital that the creditor and its attorneys be notified in writing. This notification should be provided via fax or certified mail. Without the additional layer of notice, it may be more difficult to pursue a stay violation claim if the creditor holds the sale. Written notice to each creditor also verifies that the creditor is aware of the bankruptcy filing. This notice can make or break a claim for punitive damages.

Documenting Violations Is Important

When creditor harassment goes undocumented, it is very difficult to bring successful claims against creditors who are violating the law. It is one thing to claim that a specific creditor called you 1,000 times in one month. It is another to document the time and date of each call and to record some of the phone calls.

Similarly, simply throwing away collection letters prevents them from being used as evidence in an adversary proceeding or a federal lawsuit brought pursuant to the Fair Debt Collection Practices Act. Although creditor calls and letters are stressful and annoying, properly documenting a creditor's behavior can help build a strong case.

Learn To Record Phone Calls

As long as you give notice to the person on the other end of the line, you can legally record a phone call. Recording phone calls is one of the most powerful tools available for fighting back against creditor harassment. Here is how to record a call:

1. Start your tape recorder.
2. Put the call on speaker phone.
3. Say the following: "I am recording this phone call. If you continue talking, that means that you consent to being recorded."
4. Record the entire call.
5. State the date and time of the call and who you spoke to before you stop recording.
6. Stop recording.

If the creditor's agent doesn't stop talking, then the agent has consented to being recorded. By recording the call, it is possible to document violations of federal and state law that would otherwise resolve in a "he said-she said" battle in court. For instance, if a debt collector calls you an offensive name or swears at you, then that is a violation of the Fair Debt Collection Practices Act. That violation can be pursued in addition to other potential violations. Although it is possible to win based on the strength of your testimony alone, having a recording is always the best means of proving your claims.

Mark Jones, Rosemont, Illinois: Recording A Phone Call

As part of his consumer defense strategy, Mark has been advised to record phone calls from his creditors. Mark is preparing to file a Chapter 13 bankruptcy, and his attorney has already notified his creditors that they are to cease calling Mark. One of Mark's creditors has continued to call Mark at least three times a day. Mark always records the date and time of the calls on his phone call log. When Mark has time to answer the calls, he waits to get a live person on the phone, turns on his microcassette recorder, and says, "I am recording this phone call. If you continue to speak to me, you consent to being recorded." Sometimes the caller hangs up. Other times the caller continues to speak to Mark. On one such occasion, the caller replied, "Do whatever the f**k you want, deadbeat. We're going to have the sheriff come out to your house and arrest you if you don't pay this debt today." Mark informs the debt collector that he is only to contact Mark's attorney. Mark then politely ends the phone call. Mark notes the date and time of the call, as well as the collector's name before he stops recording. He writes the details of the call on his phone log and stores the tape in a safe place. Based on these facts, Mark has 4 valid claims against the debt collection company for violations of the Fair Debt Collection Practices Act. He also has a claim based on the Illinois Consumer Fraud and Deceptive Business Practices Act.

It is very important to keep a written log of every call. If you have recorded a call, it is always best to write the date of the call on the tape and document that call on your log. It will help you keep your tapes organized, and will make it easier to find a specific tape when you need it.

Keep your tapes in a safe place. Do not record over your tapes. This is important because the tapes may become evidence at a future trial. In order for them to be admitted as evidence, you must be able to account for their location at all times from the time you make the tape to the time it is presented to the court. Careful documentation and storage is one of the most important practices. Each time you document a potential violation, you are adding to your potential future cash recovery.

Learn to Ask the Right Questions

When a creditor calls, record that call. In addition to recording the call, ask questions. If the person on the phone provides what turns out to be false or misleading information, then that is yet another valuable violation of the Fair Debt Collection Practices Act. If the creditors are going to take your time, then you should make the best possible use of that time.

Ask questions like:

1. What is your name?
2. What is your operator identification number?
3. Who do you represent?
4. What alleged debt is this regarding?
5. When did you purchase this debt?
6. Who did you purchase it from?
7. Based on your records, what is the balance due?

The key is to always ask questions using the W's – who, what, when, where, why. You want to make the person answer in as much detail as possible. If the person cannot answer, ask to speak to someone who can answer your questions. Always keep the creditor's agents talking. The more they say, the more potential claims you may discover.

If you ask no other questions, always be sure to find out to whom you are speaking. Get a name and an operator ID number.

These are crucial pieces of evidence that help build a foundation for introducing that phone call at trial.

Learn To Properly Open and Store Letters

If you don't have a letter opener, get one. When creditors send you letters, it is important to save each and every letter, including the envelope. The most important thing about the envelope is the postmark. That postmark is valuable evidence. This is why using a letter opener is so important. You want postmarks to be 100% legible and undamaged.

If you don't have a file box, get one. The money spent on a file storage box and folders is an investment in your financial future. Make a folder for each creditor. As you receive correspondence, store the letters in the appropriate folder. Properly stored letters can help establish claims for stay violations, discharge violations, and other violations of state and federal law. Without the letters and postmarked envelopes, these kinds of claims are much more difficult to prove.

Learn To Read Your Credit Report and Store Copies of Previous Reports

When a bankruptcy discharge is issued, creditors are obligated to report discharged debts as having a zero balance. They are allowed to report them as discharged in bankruptcy, but can no longer report them as anything else. Reporting the debt as "charged off," "settled," or anything else violates the Fair Credit Reporting Act as well as the Fair Debt Collection Practices Act. The best way to prove these violations is to engage in the dispute process with the three major credit reporting bureaus. When disputing an improperly reported debt, it is essential that you provide the credit reporting bureau with documentation to support your dispute. If a debt is being reported as "past due" when it has been discharged in a bankruptcy, a proper dispute letter would include a copy of the bankruptcy discharge.

You will need to obtain and store copies of your credit report. You will also need to learn to identify old debts masquerading as new debts. This will often happen because your creditors sold your discharged debt to a third party. If a debt suddenly pops up on your credit report, and you don't recognize the name of the creditor, pay close attention to the balance due. Does it match a debt you discharged in bankruptcy? If it does, you are likely looking at an entry created by a debt-buyer. Armed with that knowledge, it is possible to pursue violations *and* have the discharged debt removed from your credit report.

Conclusion

Consumer defense is the luxury of the informed. While nothing in life is guaranteed, having predictability on your side can make a big difference. For too long, our society has frowned on those who choose to live free from the debts that would otherwise hold them back. This attitude towards debt makes absolutely no logical sense. Achieving financial freedom is impossible when we consider debts to be moral obligations. Debt should not be a tool for maintaining a specific lifestyle. The road to serfdom is paved with consumer debt. In order to survive and thrive, consumers must begin making informed decisions about their debts.

Imagine a life where debt is a fading memory, not the elephant in the room. You have the power to leave your bad investments behind and build the financial future you desire. However, you must take the first steps on the road to financial freedom. Think long and hard about your current financial position and your future goals. Those who are truly wealthy are those with the tools and information necessary to protect themselves from the pitfalls of consumer debt and the bad behavior of debt collectors.

Appendix 1

Sample 341 Meeting Questions

Attending the 341 Meeting or the Meeting of the Creditors can be a nerve-wracking experience for someone who doesn't know what to expect. Below is a list of questions that the Trustee will likely ask. They are designed to make sure that there are no inaccuracies in your petition and to determine if there are any assets or liabilities that are not listed in your petition.

1. State your name and current address for the record.

2. Please provide your picture ID and Social Security number card for review.

3. Did you sign the petition, schedules, statements, and related documents and is the signature your own? Did you read the petition, schedules, statements, and related documents before you signed them?

4. Are you personally familiar with the information contained in the petition, schedules, statements and related documents? To the best of your knowledge, is the information contained in the petition, schedules, statements, and related documents true and correct? Are there any errors or omissions to bring to my attention at this time?

5. Are all of your assets identified on the schedules? Have you listed all of your creditors on the schedules?

6. Have you previously filed bankruptcy? (If so, the trustee must obtain the case number and the discharge information to determine your discharge eligibility.)

7. What is the address of your current employer?

8. Is the copy of the tax return you provided a true copy of the most recent tax return you filed?

9. Do you have a domestic support obligation? To whom? Please provide to me the claimant's address and telephone number, but do not state it on the record.

10. Have you read the Bankruptcy Information Sheet provided by the United States Trustee?

Other Sample Questions

These questions will only be asked if the Trustee thinks it is necessary. This is not an exhaustive list of every other question that the Trustee may ask, but a collection of some of the most common.

1. Do you own or have any interest whatsoever in any real estate?

If you own a house:
When did you purchase the property? How much did the property cost? What are the mortgages encumbering it? What do you estimate the present value of the property to be? Is that the whole value or your share? How did you arrive at that value?

If you rent a house:
Have you ever owned the property in which you live and/or is its owner in
any way related to you?

2. Have you made any transfers of any property or given any property away within the
last one year period?
If yes:
What did you transfer? To whom was it transferred? What did you receive in exchange? What did you do with the funds?

3. Do you have a claim against anyone or any business? If there are large medical debts, are the medical bills from injury? Are you the plaintiff in any lawsuit? What is the status of each case and who is representing you?

4. Are you entitled to life insurance proceeds or an inheritance as a result of someone's
death?

If you become a beneficiary of anyone's estate within six months of the date your
bankruptcy petition was filed, the trustee must be advised within ten days through your
counsel of the nature and extent of the property you will receive.

5. Does anyone owe you money?

If yes:
 Is the money collectible? Why haven't you collected it? Who owes the money and where are they?

6. Have you made any large payments, over $600, to anyone in the past year?

7. Were federal income tax returns filed on a timely basis? When was the last return

filed? Do you have copies of the federal income tax returns? At the time of the filing of your

petition, were you entitled to a tax refund from the federal or state government ?

8. Do you have a bank account, either checking or savings?

If yes:

In what banks and what were the balances as of the date you filed your petition?

9. When you filed your petition, did you have:

a. any cash on hand?

b. any U.S. Savings Bonds?

c. any other stocks or bonds?

d. any Certificates of Deposit?

e. a safe deposit box in your name or in anyone else's name?

10. Do you own an automobile?

If yes:

What is the year, make, and value? Do you owe any money on it?

Is it insured?

11. Are you the owner of any cash value life insurance policies?

If yes:

State the name of the company, face amount of the policy, cash surrender value, if

any, and the beneficiaries.

Appendix 2

Glossary

\#

341 meeting

The meeting of creditors required by section 341 of the Bankruptcy Code at which the consumer is questioned under oath by creditors, a trustee, examiner, or the U.S. trustee about his/her financial affairs. Also called creditors' meeting.

A

ab initio

A Latin term generally used to describe how something relates back to its beginning or inception. For instance, a contract may be declared void *ab initio*, which means that, effectively, the contract never existed because it was void from the time of its formation.

acceleration

In lending terms, acceleration is the process by which a lender declares the entire balance of the loan to be payable immediately. This process is governed by the terms of the loan documents. In general, acceleration can only occur after a default by the borrower. Defaults are defined in the loan documents. One example of a default would be failing to make a scheduled loan payment.

actual damages

Actual damages are damages which directly relate to a tortious act or breach of duty. They are damages that can be readily proven to have occurred. For example, medical bills incurred as a result of another person's negligence (e.g. in an auto accident) are actual damages.

adversary proceeding

A lawsuit arising in or related to a bankruptcy case that is commenced by filing a complaint with the court.

adverse possession

A means of obtaining title to real property, even against the record owner. This method is defined by statute. In general, in order to claim title to real property via adverse possession, a person must demonstrate possession of a piece of real property that is actual, visible, open, and notorious. Also referred to as "squatter's rights." The period of time required to assert adverse possession varies from state-to-state. In Illinois, an individual must make open and notorious use of a piece of real property for a period of 20 years before asserting a claim for adverse possession.

Affidavit of title

An affidavit of title is given by a seller of property to a buyer of property. The affidavit of title explicitly states the potential legal issues involving the property or the seller. In a real estate transaction, an affidavit of title would state that the seller actually owns the property, is not selling the property to anyone else, that there are no liens against the property, and that the seller is not involved in a bankruptcy.

affirmative defense

An argument advanced by a defendant that seeks to introduce new facts that would mitigate or defeat the plaintiff's claim against the defendant.

ALTA survey

A land survey drawn to the specifications of the American Land Title Association (ALTA). ALTA specifies the data to be shown on the survey and this includes boundary lines, location of the main building including improvements, location of ancillary buildings, the identification of easements (access rights by service companies such as water, gas, telephone, railways and other utilities).

amortization

The paying off of debt in regular installments over time. The amortization schedule for a mortgage loan will display the monthly payment over the lifetime of the loan and will often display how payments are applied to principal and interest over the lifetime of the loan.

answer

An answer is a legal document submitted in a lawsuit. It is part of the pleadings and is submitted by a defendant in response to a plaintiff's complaint. In the answer, the defendant either admits or denies the allegations in the plaintiff's complaint. The defendant also asserts its affirmative defenses in its answer.

appellate court

Although the name of appellate courts may vary from jurisdiction to jurisdiction, they all serve the same function in our judicial system. Appellate courts review the rulings of lower courts and determine whether those rulings should be upheld, overturned, or remanded back to the lower court with instructions regarding the application of the law.

APR

APR stands for annual percentage rate. It represents the interest rate for a whole year as applied to loans, mortgage loans, credit cards, etc. Methods of calculating APR vary. In the United States, the calculation and disclosure of APR is governed by the Truth In Lending Act. In general, APR in the United States is expressed as the periodic interest rate times the number of compounding periods in a year, and also includes fees. The Office of the Comptroller of the Currency has made an APR calculator available at: http://www.occ.gov/tools-forms/tools/compliance-bsa/aprwin-software.html (last visited May 9, 2012).

ARM

Adjustable Rate Mortgage. This type of mortgage begins with a low interest rate (also known as a "teaser rate"). After a period of time (typically 3, 5, or 7 years), the interest rate adjusts to a new interest rate. The method of calculating the adjusted interest rate is defined in the loan documents. In general, the adjusted rate is calculated by adding a fixed percentage to an industry-recognized standard, such as the London Inter-Bank Offer Rate (LIBOR).

arrears

Arrears are the past-due payments on a loan, including late fees and other charges. If a borrower is behind $100 on his loan payments, and there are late fees of $25 also due, the total arrears would be $125.

Article 3

Article 3 of the Uniform Commercial Code is the section of the Code that establishes the law regarding negotiable instruments like promissory notes and personal checks.

Article 9

Article 9 of the Uniform Commercial Code is the section of the Code that establishes the law regarding the sale of security interests.

attorney-client privilege

Attorney-client privilege is a fundamental legal concept that allows clients to communicate with their lawyers without fear that their statements will later be used against them. This privilege generally only applies if the communication between the attorney and client is truly private. A statement made by the client to the attorney in a closed room with nobody else present is covered by the privilege. A statement made by the client to the attorney in a crowded train station is likely not covered by the privilege.

assignment

A legal document that transfers an interest in a right or property from one to another.

automatic stay

An injunction that automatically stops lawsuits, foreclosures, garnishments, and all collection activity against the consumer the moment a bankruptcy petition is filed.

B

balloon payment

A balloon payment is a large final payment due on a loan. This payment tends to be much larger than the monthly loan payment. Many modern loan modifications include a balloon payment at the end of the loan. This is because the past-due payments (arrears) are tacked on to the end of the modified loan's payment schedule.

bankruptcy

A legal procedure for dealing with debt problems of individuals and businesses.

Bankruptcy Code

The informal name for title 11 of the United States Code, the federal bankruptcy law.

bankruptcy court

The bankruptcy judges in regular active service in each district; a unit of the district court.

bankruptcy estate

All legal or equitable interests of the consumer in property at the time of the bankruptcy filing. (The estate includes all property in which the consumer has an interest, even if it is owned or held by another person.)

bankruptcy fraud

Bankruptcy fraud is a federal crime. The most common type of bankruptcy fraud is the concealment of assets. When a consumer files a bankruptcy petition, he certifies that the information in the petition is accurate and complete. Concealment of assets occurs when the consumer knowingly omits assets from his petition to avoid their inclusion in the bankruptcy estate.

bankruptcy judge

A judicial officer of the United States district court who is the court official with decision-making power over federal bankruptcy cases.

bankruptcy petition

The document filed by the individual that begins the bankruptcy case.

binding authority/precedent

Legal precedent is binding when the court issuing a written ruling is "superior" to another court. For example, rulings issued by the United States Supreme Court are binding authority nationwide. However, a ruling issued by the Illinois Appellate Court is only binding on courts in the issuing court's district and is not binding on the Illinois Supreme Court.

blank indorsement

A blank indorsement is an indorsement on a negotiable instrument that does not specify an individual or entity to who the instrument is being transferred. In a foreclosure context, foreclosing lenders will frequently present blank indorsed promissory notes to demonstrate that they are the proper owner of the debt. An individual or entity in possession of a blank indorsed instrument is known as a "holder."

bundle of rights

A term used to help explain the complexity of real property ownership. A person who owns a piece of real property is described as having a bundle of rights or a "bundle of sticks." This concept is designed to demonstrate that there are many rights which attach to real property. It is also used to illustrate the idea that a specific action against a piece of real property may only involve some of the rights in the bundle. For example, if a land owner leases his land to another person, the lessee has been granted specific rights from the bundle (e.g. the right to be in possession of the property), but not all of the rights (e.g. the right to sell or otherwise encumber the property).

C

certified mail

Certified mail is a service offered by the United States Postal Service. It requires that the recipient sign a green card that acknowledges receipt of the letter or package. Certified mail generally cannot be delivered to a post office box.

chancery

In Illinois, courts of equity are part of the Chancery Division of Illinois's Circuit Courts. Mortgage foreclosures, mechanic's lien foreclosures, and other cases that invoke the court's equitable powers are heard in the Chancery Division.

chapter 7

The chapter of the Bankruptcy Code providing for "liquidation,"(i.e., the sale of a consumer's nonexempt property and the distribution of the proceeds to creditors.)

chapter 13

The chapter of the Bankruptcy Code providing for adjustment of debts of an individual with regular income. (Chapter 13 allows a consumer to keep property and pay debts over time, usually three to five years.)

chain of title

In a real property context, chain of title is a fundamental concept that makes our system of real property ownership work. Quite simply, it describes the succession of ownership to a specific piece of real property. In the context of negotiable instruments, chain of title is often used to refer to each individual or entity that has held a possessory interest in the negotiable instrument.

claim

A creditor's assertion of a right to payment from the consumer or the consumer's property.

closing

In real estate terms, a closing is the last step in a real estate transaction. At a closing a buyer executes a mortgage, note, and other documents and disclosures as required by state and federal law. This generally takes place at a title company. Loan refinances and home purchases both require a closing to complete the transaction.

closing costs

In real estate terms, closing costs are the costs associated with completing a real estate transaction. Depending on how the transaction is structured, a buyer or seller may have to bring cash to the closing to satisfy the closing costs. In some transactions, the closing costs are built into the loan's principal balance.

common law

Common law refers to the English and American systems of law that is developed over time by the court system. Common law, by its nature, is not defined by a statute, but may be defined in various treatises like the Restatements of Law. The common law of contracts, for example, is compiled in the Restatement of the Law of Contracts, Second.

compensatory damages

See **actual damages.**

complaint

The document filed to begin a lawsuit. A complaint sets forth facts and legal claims supported by those facts. It is also referred to as a pleading.

concealment

In a bankruptcy context, concealment is generally a debtor's purposeful omission of assets and liabilities from the bankruptcy petition's schedules. In general, concealment is an effort to make more difficult the discovery of something that one is legally obligated to reveal.

condition precedent

A legal term of art that describes an action or event that must occur before a lawsuit can be filed. In a mortgage foreclosure context, lenders must notify borrowers that their loan is in default, that the lender intends to accelerate the debt, and that the lender may choose to proceed with a foreclosure before the lender can file a foreclosure lawsuit.

confirmation of plan

Bankruptcy judge's approval of a payment plan in chapter 13.

confirmation of sheriff's sale

In Illinois, a sheriff's sale is not final, and a foreclosure case is not closed until the sheriff's sale is confirmed by a judge. This is codified in the Illinois Mortgage Foreclosure Law at 735 ILCS 5/15-1508.

consent foreclosure

In Illinois, a consent foreclosure is a statutory remedy codified at 735 ILCS 5/15-1402. In a consent foreclosure, the homeowner consents to a judgment of foreclosure being entered against him, and to title vesting immediately in the foreclosing lender. In exchange, the lender agrees to waive any deficiency judgment to which it may be entitled.

consumer

We avoid using the term "debtor." You can find out why here. In our use, a consumer is any individual citizen who is seeking assistance with debt.

consumer debts

Debts incurred for personal needs. These cannot be debts incurred for business needs.

Consumer Financial Protection Bureau

The Consumer Financial Protection Bureau is a federal agency established by the Dodd-Frank Act. It has primary responsibility for promulgating rules and regulations that implement the nation's consumer protection laws.

consumer fraud

Consumer fraud is the use of unfair or deceptive business practices. In Illinois, consumer fraud is prohibited by the Illinois Consumer Fraud and Deceptive Business Practices Act. At the federal level, the Fair Trade Commission Act prohibits the same conduct.

contested matter

Those matters, other than objections to claims, that are disputed but are not within the definition of adversary proceeding.

contract

A contract is an agreement between two or more parties where the parties exchange mutual obligations. A contract is a promise or set of promises for which there is a remedy at law in case of a breach of those promises. Contracts can be both written and oral.

co-signer

An individual who signs a legal instrument along with one or more individuals. For example, when a parent and child both sign student loan documents, the parent is generally referred to as the co-signer.

counterclaim

A counterclaim is a lawsuit brought by a party to an existing lawsuit within that lawsuit. For example, If A sues B, and B then asserts claims against A, B's claims are referred to as counterclaims. In Illinois, a counterclaim may also be brought by two parties on the same side of the lawsuit. For example if A sues B and C, and then B asserts claims against C, it is called a counterclaim even though B and C are both defendants relative to A.

credit bureau

This term generally refers to the three major credit reporting bureaus, Equifax, TransUnion, and Experian. Their credit reporting behavior is regulated by the Fair Credit Reporting Act (FCRA).

credit counseling

Generally refers to two events in individual bankruptcy cases: (1) the "individual or group briefing" from a nonprofit budget and credit counseling agency that individual consumers must attend prior to filing under any chapter of the Bankruptcy Code; and (2) the "instructional course in personal financial management" in chapters 7 and 13 that an individual consumer must complete before a discharge is entered. There are exceptions to both requirements for certain categories of consumers, exigent circumstances, or if the U.S. trustee or bankruptcy administrator have determined that there are insufficient approved credit counseling agencies available to provide the necessary counseling.

creditor

One to whom the consumer owes money or who claims to be owed money by the consumer.

creditors' meeting

This is the "meeting of the creditors" and is also known as the 341 meeting

credit report

A credit report is a report generated by a credit reporting bureau. It lists positive, negative, and neutral accounts held by a specific individual. Credit reports are generally used in determining whether a lender will extend a loan to a specific borrower.

current monthly income

The average monthly income received by the consumer over the six calendar months before filing of the bankruptcy case, including regular contributions to household expenses from other individuals and income from the consumer's spouse if the petition is a joint petition. This does not include social security income and certain other payments made because the consumer is the victim of certain crimes.

D

debt collector

As defined by the Fair Debt Collection Practices Act (FDCPA), a debt collector is an individual or entity that attempts to collect debts on behalf of a creditor, but does not identify itself as the creditor. For example, if Bob's Discount Stereo Hut hires Kneecapper's Collection Agency to collect its delinquent store accounts, then Kneecapper's is a debt collector under the FDCPA. If Bob's attempts to collect its debts directly, it is not a debt collector under the FDCPA.

debtor

A person who has filed a petition for relief under the Bankruptcy Code. We do not like to use this term. We explain why here.

deceptive act or practice

In a consumer fraud context, a deceptive act or practice is any undertaking which has a likelihood to confuse or deceive a reasonable person. The Federal Trade Commission defines a deceptive act or practice as "a representation, omission, or practice that is likely to mislead the consumer."[67]

deed

A deed is a written instrument that transfers an interest in land from the grantor to the grantee. The main function of a deed is to pass title to land.

deed in lieu of foreclosure

A deed in lieu of foreclosure is a specialized transfer of property from a borrower to a lender. In Illinois, it is a statutory remedy codified at 735 ILCS 5/15-1401. In Illinois, the deed in lieu of foreclosure allows a borrower to deed his home to the lender. In turn, the lender agrees to waive any deficiency judgment it may be entitled to collect from the borrower.

deed of trust

In title-theory states, a deed of trust is used in place of a mortgage. A deed of trust vests title in a piece of land in the name of a third-party trustee.

default order

A default order is entered when a defendant fails to file an appearance or answer within a specific amount of time. A default order merely finds the defendant in default and does not function as an enforceable judgment against the defendant.

default judgment

A default judgment is entered after, and sometimes in conjunction with, a default order. In Illinois, a default judgment cannot be obtained without the plaintiff first proving its damages. A default judgment is a final judgment and can be enforced against the defaulted defendant.

defendant

An individual (or business) against whom a lawsuit is filed.

deficiency

A deficiency is the difference between the balance of a mortgage loan and the price for which the property sells at a sheriff's sale. In some states, like Illinois, lenders may pursue borrowers for this deficiency. When this is done, the deficiency amount is reduced to a deficiency judgment.

discharge

A release of a consumer from personal liability for certain dischargeable debts set forth in the Bankruptcy Code. A discharge releases a consumer from personal liability for certain debts and prevents the creditors owed those debts from taking any action against the consumer to collect the debts. The discharge also prohibits creditors from communicating with the consumer regarding the debt, including telephone calls, letters, and personal contact.

dischargeable debt

A debt for which the Bankruptcy Code allows the consumer's personal liability to be eliminated.

discovery

Discovery is an orderly, court-supervised process that allows parties to a lawsuit to request the production of documents, admissions of fact, and responses to interrogatories. Anything that may lead to relevant evidence supporting a claim is discoverable.

down payment

In a real estate context, a down payment is the amount of money that a purchaser pays up front to secure a contract for the purchase of a piece of property. Traditionally, a down payment on a home is 20% of the home's purchase price.

E

eminent domain

Eminent domain is the power of the state or other governmental body to take private property for public use. The state must compensate the land owner for any land taken. Obtaining the land needed for airports and interstate highways is often done via eminent domain.

Equal Credit Opportunity Act

The Equal Credit Opportunity Act (ECOA) is codified at 15 U.S.C. §1691 and makes it unlawful for any creditor to discriminate against any applicant, with respect to any aspect of a credit transaction, on the basis of race, color, religion, national origin, sex, marital status, or age.

equitable contract

An equitable contract is created when an individual or entity relies on the representations of another individual or entity to its detriment, and that reliance is reasonably foreseeable by the other party. This is also known as a quasi-contract or promissory estoppel. In a consumer defense context, this is most often seen when a home owner is placed into multiple, successive trial loan modifications, with a promise that a permanent offer will be made if certain conditions are met.

equitable mortgage

In Illinois, an equitable mortgage is created when a deed appears to secure a debt, even if no actual mortgage is executed. Illinois courts look to many factors to determine whether an equitable or constructive mortgage exists, but one of the main factors is the intention of the parties.

equity

1. The value of a consumer's interest in property that remains after liens and other creditors' interests are considered. (Example: If a house valued at $100,000 is subject to a $80,000 mortgage, there is $20,000 of equity.)

2. *See* **chancery.**

escrow

A fund of money held in a specific account for a specific purpose. In a real estate context, some home owners choose to make monthly payments into an escrow account in order to save funds to pay property taxes and insurance premiums.

eviction

Also known as forcible entry and detainer, an eviction is a legal proceeding where a land owner seeks to terminate an individual's possession of a piece of real property. In Illinois, landlords are not allowed to perform "self-help" evictions. This means that a landlord seeking to evict a tenant must file a lawsuit and obtain a court order to do so.

exemptions, exempt property

Certain property owned by an individual consumer that the Bankruptcy Code or applicable state law permits the consumer to keep from unsecured creditors. The availability and amount of property the consumer may exempt depends on the state the consumer lives in.

F

Fair Credit Reporting Act

The Fair Credit Reporting Act (FCRA) regulates the activities of creditors and the credit reporting bureaus. Entities like Equifax, Experian, and TransUnion are examples of credit reporting bureaus governed by the FCRA. It is codified at 15 U.S.C. §1681 et. seq.

Fair Debt Collection Practices Act

The Fair Debt Collection Practices Act (FDCPA) is a federal law that regulates debt collectors and their debt collection activities. It was designed to protect consumers from abusive and deceptive debt collection practices. It is codified at 15 U.S.C. §1692 et. seq.

Federal Deposit Insurance Corporation

The Federal Deposit Insurance Corporation (FDIC) was created by the Glass-Steagall Act of 1933. It is a government corporation that provides deposit insurance, guaranteeing the safety of deposits in member banks, up to $250,000.00 per depositor. The FDIC has regulatory authority over banks and takes failed banks into receivership. An FDIC receivership typically results in either the liquidation of the failed bank or in the purchase and assumption of the failed bank by another bank.

Federal Trade Commission

The Federal Trade Commission (FTC) was established in 1914 by the Federal Trade Commission Act. Its primary purpose is to protect consumers from unfair and deceptive business practices. It also regulates corporations, and is designed to prevent harmfully anti-competitive business practices such as monopolies. When the FTC identifies a business or industry that is behaving badly, it will often force that business or industry into a consent decree. FTC consent decrees generally last for tens of years and require the subject business or industry to submit to heavy regulatory scrutiny.

fee simple

Fee simple is a type of an estate in land. In the United States, the vast majority of deeds convey a fee simple interest in the land. Generally, a fee simple interest in land allows the owner to convey the land to another person with no restrictions.

force-placed insurance

Force-placed insurance is a practice where a mortgage lender or servicer purchases insurance for a property when the borrower fails to maintain homeowner's insurance or does not have adequate homeowner's insurance. There has been a large amount of concern related to banks abusing this ability, in particular because force-placed insurance is generally more expensive than regular homeowner's insurance. The cost of the force-placed insurance is passed along to the borrower, which can cause a monthly mortgage payment to skyrocket.

foreclosure

Foreclosure is the process by which a bank repossesses a piece of real property due to a borrower's default on a loan secured by the property. In Illinois, this process is governed by the courts and is known as a judicial foreclosure. In some states, there is no judicial process. In those states, the process is called non-judicial foreclosure.

fraud

At common law, fraud is the false representation of an existing, material fact, with the speaker's knowledge of the falsity and his intention that the statement be relied upon by others who are unaware of the falsity and are subsequently injured by that reliance. For example, if Bob tells Anna that his car is in 100% working order (knowing that its engine will require extensive repairs to run) in order to convince Anna to purchase the car, then if Anna relies on Bob's statement and purchases the car, Bob has likely committed fraud.

free house

There is no such thing as a free house. This term is often used by creditors and their attorneys to describe a person who is defending his home against foreclosure. "All he wants is a free house." There are no free houses – if someone tells you they can get you a free house based on mortgage irregularities or any other theory, that person is either seriously misguided or lying.

G

good faith and fair dealing

This phrase is a legal concept associated with contracts and business relationships. The implied covenant of good faith and fair dealing applies to all parties to a contract and assumes that they will be honest and fair to each other so that all parties can enjoy their rights under the contract.

Good Faith Estimate

A good faith estimate (GFE) is a disclosure required by the Real Estate Settlement Procedures Act. It is to be given to a borrower by a mortgage lender or broker when a borrower is purchasing a home or refinancing a loan. The GFE includes an itemized list of the costs and fees associated with the loan and must be provided within three days of the borrower applying for the loan.

guarantor

A person or entity that has provided a guarantee. In a real estate context, guarantor refers to a person or entity that has guaranteed a loan's repayment on behalf of a corporation or another person. This is most often seen in commercial real estate loans, where a corporation is purchasing a piece of property.

H

Hardest Hit Fund

The Hardest Hit Fund was established by the United States Treasury in February 2010. It is designed to provide targeted relief to the states most affected by the economic crisis.

holder

A holder is an individual or entity that is in lawful possession of a negotiable instrument or other commercial paper, like a check, and who is entitled to payment on the instrument. A promissory note is another kind of negotiable instrument, and only the lawful holder of the promissory note may demand payment on the note.

holder in due course

A holder in due course is a holder who has taken lawful ownership of commercial paper who has taken it for value (e.g. paid cash) in good faith, and without notice of any claim against the instrument or that it has been dishonored (e.g. payment refused).

Home Affordable Modification Program

The Home Affordable Modification Program (HAMP) is likely the best-known and most-maligned program included in the Making Home Affordable program. It is designed to encourage lenders to enter into loan modifications with borrowers, thus preventing foreclosures. The program has undergone significant modifications since its inception, but is generally viewed as an underperforming program.

home equity line of credit

A home equity line of credit (HELOC) is a very common form of second or third mortgage taken out against residential real estate. Instead of taking a large sum of money against the home's equity up front, a HELOC operates as a line of credit upon which the homeowner can draw up to a set limit. These loans tend to have a variable interest rate. Homeowners may draw funds from the line of credit during the loan's draw period (usually 5 to 25 years). There are generally monthly payments that may be "interest only" payments. This means that the monthly payment only pays the accrued interest and does not reduce the principal balance. During the real estate boom of the early 2000's, some borrowers purchased homes with 100% financing, where 80% of the purchase price was supported by a mortgage and the other 20% was supported by a HELOC that was already drawn to its limit.

homestead rights/homestead exemption

In Illinois, the homestead right or exemption is a statutory right that was originally designed to protect spousal rights to a piece of land. It currently functions as an exemption to which a judgment lien cannot attach. Each spouse is entitled to a specific exemption amount which cannot be pursued by a judgment creditor. The amount is currently $15,000.00 per person.

Housing and Urban Development, Department of

The Department of Housing and Urban Development (HUD) became a Cabinet department in the Executive branch of the federal government in 1965. HUD's mission is to create strong, sustainable communities, and to prevent discrimination in the housing and rental markets. HUD also engages in community planning and development activities. It also oversees the Government National Mortgage Association (Ginnie Mae).

HUD-1

The HUD-1 is the standard settlement statement form used in real estate closings. The HUD-1 itemizes all closing costs and fees. Borrowers can compare their Good Faith Estimate to the HUD-1 and ask for an explanation of any changes.

I

Illinois Mortgage Foreclosure Law

The Illinois Mortgage Foreclosure Law (IMFL) is the section of the Illinois Code of Civil Procedure which governs the mortgage foreclosure process in Illinois. It is codified at 735 ILCS 5/15-1101 et. seq.

indorsement

An indorsement is a signature placed on an instrument or piece of commercial paper. To be a valid indorsement, the indorsement must be effective to transfer the entire instrument.

in personam

A Latin phrase meaning "against the person." It is used to define specific types of claims that are brought against a person in a lawsuit. It is also used to describe a court's jurisdiction over the person.

in rem

A Latin phrase meaning "against the thing." It is used to define claims that are brought against things like cars, houses, tracts of land, sums of money, etc. When a state seeks to seize an asset pursuant to its drug-related forfeiture laws, it must file an in rem claim against the asset it wishes to seize.

insolvent

A financial condition wherein a person or entity is unable to pay debts as they come due in the ordinary course of business, or a person or entity whose liabilities exceed assets at a given time.

interest rate

A loan's interest rate is the amount charged, reflected as a percentage of the principal balance, by a lender to a borrower for the use of assets. Borrowers who are considered to be a lower risk are generally charged a lower interest rate than those considered to be higher risk.

insider (of individual consumer)

Any relative of the consumer or of a general partner of the consumer; partnership in which the consumer is a general partner; general partner of the consumer; or a corporation of which the consumer is a director, officer, or person in control. In a bankruptcy context, debt repayments to insiders made shortly before a bankruptcy filing may be unwound by the bankruptcy trustee.

interrogatories

Interrogatories are a type of discovery request. They are used to ask questions of a party to a lawsuit. For example, "State the date on which you came into possession of the subject note," may be a useful interrogatory in a mortgage foreclosure lawsuit where the plaintiff is not the original lender, but an entity asserting its right to sue because it is the holder of an indorsed note.

investment property

An investment property is generally a piece of real estate that is not the owner's primary residence. Many investment properties contain multiple dwelling units, which the investor will rent out to support the property's mortgage and ultimately make a profit. Investment properties may be treated differently by various state and federal laws regulating mortgage lending and foreclosures.

J

joint petition

One bankruptcy petition filed by a husband and wife together.

Joint tenants

A joint tenancy is a means of holding title to land. It vests title in two or more persons who have co-equal rights and interests in the property. A joint tenancy includes a right of survivorship. When one joint tenant dies, his or her interest in the property fully vests in the other joint tenant or tenants. If one joint tenant sells or conveys his or her interest in the property, the joint tenancy is destroyed and the remaining joint tenants become tenants in common with the new party.

judgment creditor

A judgment creditor is any individual or entity with a money judgment against another individual or entity. If Steve sues Alice for breach of contract and obtains a $5,000.00 judgment against her, then Steve becomes Alice's judgment creditor.

judgment lien

In Illinois, a judgment lien is a lien that can be placed on a piece of real property. This lien will most likely be a junior lien to any mortgages or other liens already filed against the property. However, in order for the lien to be extinguished, the judgment must be satisfied and the lien released. This means that before the property can be sold, the judgment lien must be satisfied.

judgment proof

This phrase describes an individual or entity that is financially insolvent. If a judgment is obtained against such an individual or entity, collecting the judgment will be extremely difficult, if not impossible.

judicial foreclosure

In Illinois, the foreclosure process is handled by the court system. A judicial foreclosure is one that is handled by the court system. States that do not have a judicial process for foreclosures are called non-judicial foreclosure states.

junior mortgage/lien

This term is used to describe mortgages or other liens that are "next in line" after the primary or senior mortgage or lien. For example, if Bob purchases a home by taking out a mortgage loan against the property, that mortgage is the senior mortgage. When Bob then takes out a home equity line of credit to pay for roof repairs, the line of credit becomes a junior mortgage, subject and subordinate to the senior mortgage.

jurisdiction

Jurisdiction is a court's power to hear cases and assert its authority over people, entities, and things.

L

laches

Laches is an equitable defense to a claim that argues an undue lapse of time has passed since the claim arose and that the plaintiff was negligent in not pursuing the claim earlier.

legal description

A legal description is a specialized way of describing a specific parcel of land. They are often based on metes and bounds, lot and block surveys, or other systems. A legal description is the written statement that identifies the property.

lien

The right to take and hold or sell the property of a consumer as security or payment for a debt or duty. Common liens include automobile loans, mortgages, and mechanic's liens.

Lien theory

Lien theory describes states where a mortgage exists as a lien against a piece of real property. The borrower/homeowner retains legal title to the property. In general, lien theory states are also judicial foreclosure states.

liquidation

A sale of a consumer's property with the proceeds to be used for the benefit of creditors.

liquidated claim

A creditor's claim for a fixed amount of money.

liquidated damages

Liquidated damages are an amount stipulated in a contract which the parties agree are a reasonable estimation of the damages owed from one party to another in the event of a breach of the contract.

loan application

A loan application is the document a prospective borrower submits to a lender to be considered for a loan. It generally lists the borrower's income, assets, and liabilities.

loan modification

A loan modification is an agreement between a borrower and a lender which modifies the terms of the loan. Lenders are under no obligation to modify loans. Since the beginning of the financial crisis, the federal government has made efforts to encourage loan modifications as an alternative to foreclosures.

loan to value ratio

The loan to value ratio (LTV) is a useful tool for determining whether equity exists in a piece of real property. It is also useful for evaluating whether saving a specific piece of property makes financial sense. If a property has a loan balance of $300,000.00 and it has a market value of $200,000.00, then it has an LTV of 1.5.

London Interbank Offered Rate

The London Interbank Offered Rate (LIBOR) is the average interest rate that leading banks in London charge when lending to other banks. This is a common index used for calculating the interest rate of adjustable rate mortgages.

loss mitigation

Loss mitigation is a phrase used to describe attempts to avoid foreclosure or to minimize the impact of a foreclosure. Loan modifications, consent foreclosures, deeds in lieu of foreclosure, and short sales are all types of loss mitigation.

M

maker

In a commercial law context, a maker is an individual or entity who executes a promissory note and thus promises to repay the amount due under the note.

Making Home Affordable

Making Home Affordable (MHA) is a program created by the Financial Stability Act of 2009. It is an official program of the Department of the Treasury and the Department of Housing and Urban Development. MHA includes many sub-programs, the most famous of which is the Home Affordable Modification Program (HAMP).

means test

Section 707(b)(2) of the Bankruptcy Code applies a "means test" to determine whether an individual consumer's chapter 7 filing is presumed to be an abuse of the Bankruptcy Code. Abusive filings are either dismissed or converted to Chapter 13 cases (with the consumer's consent.) If a consumer fails the means test, other factors are considered to determine whether the filing is abusive. The consumer may rebut a presumption of abuse only by a showing of special circumstances that justify additional expenses or adjustments of current monthly income.

motion

A motion is a specialized application to the court that requests an order or rule to be issued in the moving party's favor. Most motions are founded on a specific section of the state or federal rules of civil procedure. Typical types of motions are motions to dismiss, motions for summary judgment, and motions to compel discovery.

mortgage

A legal instrument that secures a loan against a piece of real property. In Illinois, this interest is represented as a lien against the title of a piece of real property.

mortgage-backed security

A mortgage-backed security (MBS) is a specialized financial instrument. A MBS is a pool of mortgage loans that has been placed into a trust and then sold in "strips" as securities. Traditionally, a MBS was a safe, long-term investment vehicle that was used by pension funds and other investment funds for stable, long-term growth.

mortgagee

The mortgagee is the party lending money in a mortgage loan transaction.

mortgage insurance

An insurance policy that protects a mortgage lender or title holder in the event that the borrower defaults on payments, dies, or is otherwise unable to meet the contractual obligations of the mortgage.

mortgagor

The mortgagor is the party borrowing money in a mortgage loan transaction.

motion to lift the automatic stay

A request by a creditor to allow the creditor to take action against the consumer or the consumer's property that would otherwise be prohibited by the automatic stay.

N

Negotiable instrument

A specific type of commercial paper that is a writing, signed by the maker, which contains an unconditional promise to pay a sum certain in money, is payable on demand or at a definite time, and is payable to order of a named party or bearer. Personal checks and promissory notes are two types of negotiable instruments.

negotiation

In commercial law, negotiation is the process by which a negotiable instrument is passed from one owner to the next. For promissory notes, this involves indorsement and delivery of the original instrument.

nemo dat, rule of

The rule of nemo dat is based on the Latin phrase, "nemo dat non quod habet," which means, "no one gives what he doesn't have." It is used to express the concept that a person who does not have title to a piece of property cannot convey anything to another person, leaving the purchaser without any title to the piece of property.

no-asset case

A chapter 7 case where there are no assets available to satisfy any portion of the creditors' unsecured claims.

No income no asset

A no income no asset loan (NINA) is a type of loan that was very popular during the housing bubble of the early 2000's. Mortgage brokers would submit loan applications based solely on the borrower's credit score and not disclose any income or assets to the lender. These loans are no longer allowed and have become to be known as "liar loans."

nondischargeable debt

A debt that cannot be eliminated in bankruptcy. Examples include a home mortgage, debts for alimony or child support, certain taxes, debts for most government funded or guaranteed educational loans or benefit overpayments, debts arising from death or personal injury caused by driving while intoxicated or under the influence of drugs, and debts for restitution or a criminal fine included in a sentence on the consumer's conviction of a crime.

non-judicial foreclosure

States that do not require a lender to file a lawsuit to foreclose on a mortgage are called non-judicial foreclosure states.

note

See also **promissory note**

nunc pro tunc

A Latin phrase which means "now for then." In a legal context, courts will sometimes issue orders nunc pro tunc. These orders correct the court record and operate as if the correction had always been operative.

O

objection to dischargeability

A trustee's or creditor's objection to the consumer being released from personal liability for certain dischargeable debts. Common reasons include allegations that the debt to be discharged was incurred by false pretenses or that debt arose because of the consumer's fraud while acting as a fiduciary.

objection to exemptions

A trustee's or creditor's objection to the consumer's attempt to claim certain property as exempt from liquidation by the trustee to creditors.

obligor

One who has promised to perform a specific act or pay a sum of money pursuant to a contract.

Office of the Comptroller of the Currency

The Office of the Comptroller of the Currency (OCC) is an independent bureau within the United States Treasury that was established by the National Currency Act of 1863. It charters, regulates, and supervises all national banks as well as the federal branches and agencies of foreign banks in the United States.

order

An order is issued by a judge and can have many operative effects. Some orders merely set cases over to a new date, others may dismiss a case, impose sanctions, or otherwise direct parties to act.

originator

In a mortgage lending context, the originator is the entity that works with a borrower to complete a mortgage transaction. A mortgage originator can be a mortgage broker or a mortgage banker. Either party would be considered the original lender on the mortgage.

P

party in interest

A party who has standing to be heard by the court in a matter to be decided in the bankruptcy case. The consumer, the U.S. trustee or bankruptcy administrator, the case trustee and creditors are parties in interest for most matters.

payday loan

Payday loans are loans designed to be short-term loans, often being paid off in a matter of days or weeks. However, these loans also charge amazingly high interest rates. Many consumers are unaware of this fact because the interest rate is not disclosed and is expressed as a flat fee due at the time of repayment. These loans are often self-perpetuating. A borrower will pay back a loan on his or her next payday, then need another payday loan to have money until the next paycheck arrives. These loans are best avoided.

payee

A payee is the person or entity to whom a promissory note is payable. If Bob writes a personal check to Steve, then Steve is the payee of that check.

payment shock

Payment shock is a term used to describe the risks associated with adjustable-rate loans. While some adjustable rate mortgages have low initial payments, these payments can skyrocket when the loan's interest rate adjusts.

personal guarantee

A personal guarantee is often used in commercial lending. For example, if Dave has a company and wants to have a loan issued to his company, then he may be required to sign a personal guarantee on that loan. This means that if Dave's company defaults on the loan, Dave will be personally liable for repaying the loan.

persuasive authority

Persuasive authority is a term used to describe legal precedents that are not binding on a specific court. Persuasive authority is often used when a specific jurisdiction does not have similar case law on an issue, or when an attorney seeks to have a court adopt a rule from a different jurisdiction.

Pick A Payment Loans

Pick a payment loans are a specialized type of loan often offered to individuals with bad credit, or to individuals who have non-standard income, like those who are self-employed. They allow borrowers to pick various payment schedules. However, they are also dangerous for the unaware borrower. By only making the minimum payment, many borrowers are surprised when their loan balance begins to climb. This is because many pick a payment loans roll interest into the loan's principal balance.

PITI

PITI is an acronym that stands for Principal Interest Taxes Insurance. PITI is the total monthly cost of owning real property with a mortgage loan attached to it. Most borrowers have escrow accounts designed to cover property taxes and insurance payments, so most borrowers' monthly mortgage payments can be expressed as PITI.

plaintiff

A person or business that files a formal complaint with the court.

plan

A consumer's detailed description of how the consumer proposes to pay creditors' claims over a fixed period of time. In an consumer context, these are used in Chapter 13 filings.

points

In a mortgage lending context, points (also known as discount points) represent money paid at loan origination to lower the interest rate on a loan. This means that, in exchange for an up-front payment, the borrower will have lower payments on the loan over its lifetime due to the lower interest rate.

Pooling and Servicing Agreement

A Pooling and Servicing Agreement (PSA) is the legal document that creates a mortgage-backed security trust. It governs how loans become part of the trust, how they are serviced, and what kinds of bonds are issued to investors in the trust.

postpetition transfer

A transfer of the consumer's property made after the commencement of the case.

precedent

A precedent is a rule of law established by a court for the first time in a type of case which is then applied to future cases of the same type. It is a foundational concept of Anglo-American common law.

predatory lending

Predatory lending is a term used to describe deceptive, unlawful, abusive, and discriminatory practices used by some lenders in the loan origination process. There is no official legal definition of the term in the United States, but it is generally defined as the practice of imposing unfair and abusive loan terms on consumers.

preference or preferential debt payment

A debt payment made to a creditor in the 90-day period before a consumer files bankruptcy (or within one year if the creditor was an insider) that gives the creditor more than the creditor would receive in the consumer's chapter 7 case.

primary residence

A person's primary residence is the place where the person normally lives. A vacation home used a few months out of the year is generally not a primary residence. Similarly, an investment property is generally not a primary residence.

principal

In a lending context, principal is the amount borrowed or still owed on a loan, separate from interest. Since interest is calculated from a loan's principal balance, paying down principal is a good way to save money over the lifetime of a loan.

priority

The Bankruptcy Code's statutory ranking of unsecured claims that determines the order in which unsecured claims will be paid if there is not enough money to pay all unsecured claims in full.

priority claim

An unsecured claim that is entitled to be paid ahead of other unsecured claims that are not entitled to priority status. Priority refers to the order in which these unsecured claims are to be paid.

private mortgage insurance

Private mortgage insurance (PMI) is often required when a borrower seeks to obtain a mortgage with less than a 20% down payment. It serves to protect lenders in the event that borrowers default on their mortgage payments.

promissory estoppel

Promissory estoppel is an equitable theory also referred to as a quasi-contract theory. Under promissory estoppel, an individual argues that although there was no true contract between two parties, the actions and representations of one party to the other has created a contract. A party claiming promissory estoppel must demonstrate that he or she reasonably relied on the promise made by the other party and that he or she was harmed by that reliance.

promissory note

A type of negotiable instrument where the maker (borrower) agrees to pay a certain sum of money at a specific time.

proof of claim

A written statement and verifying documentation filed by a creditor that describes the reason the consumer owes the creditor money.

property index number

A property index number (PIN) is used to identify a specific parcel of real property.

property of the estate

All legal or equitable interests of the consumer in property as of the commencement of the bankruptcy case.

pro se

Pro se is a Latin phrase meaning "for oneself." It is used in the law to describe a person who is representing himself or herself in a legal proceeding without the assistance of an attorney. In some states, the term "pro per" is used.

Punitive damages

Punitive damages are a type of damages awarded in some lawsuits. They are not related to actual harm, but are designed to punish a pattern or practice of bad behavior. Punitive damages are rarely awarded by U.S. courts but are available in some situations.

Q

quasi in rem

Quasi in rem is a legal term used to describe specific types of lawsuits and the power or jurisdiction that a court exercises over the case. Actions against a person are "in personam" actions. Actions against property are "in rem" actions. In Illinois, a mortgage foreclosure lawsuit is a quasi in rem action because the action is brought against the homeowner *and* against the mortgaged property.

quiet title

Quiet title is a specific kind of legal action brought to establish a party's clear title to a piece of land against all other claimants. It is generally brought to remove liens or other "clouds on title" which may exist in relation to a specific piece of land.

quit claim deed

A quit claim deed conveys property to a person or entity subject to any liens that may exist on the property. Unlike a warranty deed, a quit claim deed contains no guarantees regarding the grantor's title to the property. When purchasing real estate, it is an immensely bad idea to accept a quit claim deed without fully investigating the title to the land.

R

reaffirmation agreement

An agreement by a chapter 7 consumer to continue paying a dischargeable debt (such as an auto loan) after the bankruptcy, usually for the purpose of keeping collateral (i.e. the car) that would otherwise be subject to repossession.

Real Estate Mortgage Investment Conduit

A Real Estate Mortgage Investment Conduit (REMIC) is a specialized type of financial vehicle that was introduced in 1987 and is defined in the U.S. Internal Revenue Code. They are the most popular means of securitizing mortgages into investment pools due to their preferential tax treatment.

Real Estate Settlement Procedures Act

The Real Estate Settlement Procedures Act (RESPA) is a federal law that was passed in 1974. It is codified at 12 U.S.C. §2601 et. seq. It prohibits kickbacks from lenders to mortgage brokers or other third-parties. It also requires that lenders disclose the costs of a loan via a Good Faith Estimate (GFE) and a final accounting of the loan's costs on the HUD-1 statement provided to borrowers at the loan's closing.

recourse

In a mortgage lending context, a recourse state is a state where the law allows a mortgage lender to pursue a borrower for the balance of a mortgage loan. Illinois is a recourse state. Once a property is sold at a sheriff's sale, the lender has the right to pursue the borrower for any remaining balance due on the loan.

redemption

The process of paying off an accelerated mortgage loan balance. In Illinois, this right is created by statute and has a time limit for its exercise.

red lining

Red lining is a practice where services such as mortgage or other lending are made more costly or are simply denied to an area based on its racial makeup. The practice was once widespread in the United States and is now prohibited by the Fair Housing Act of 1968.

refinance

A refinance loan is a type of loan taken out to restructure an existing mortgage loan. As part of the transaction, the existing loan is paid off and the new loan takes its place. Borrowers often refinance their mortgage loans to extract equity from the property (cashing out) or to obtain a lower interest rate.

reinstatement

The process of curing a default on a mortgage loan. Depending on state laws, this may require the repayment of the missed payments, plus fees and costs. Some rights to redemption may expire over time.

reverse mortgage

A reverse mortgage is a form of mortgage available in the United States. It is available to seniors aged 62 or over and is part of a program regulated by HUD. In a reverse mortgage, the borrower receives the equity in the home up front. The reverse mortgage is not due until the borrower dies, sells the home, or breaches one of the mortgage conditions.

S

sanctions

A type of remedy requested to punish the bad behavior of an opposing party or its attorneys. Typical sanctions are cash sanctions. More extreme sanctions are the dismissal of a case or the entry of judgment in a case.

schedules

Detailed lists filed by the consumer along with the petition showing the consumer's assets, liabilities, and other financial information. *See* Appendix 3.

secured creditor

A creditor holding a claim against the consumer who has the right to take and hold or sell certain property of the consumer in satisfaction of some or all of the claim. The holder of your home mortgage or auto loan are examples of two types of secured creditors.

secured debt

Debt backed by a mortgage, pledge of collateral, or other lien; debt for which the creditor has the right to pursue specific pledged property upon default. Examples include home mortgages, auto loans and tax liens.

securitization

A process by which loans (e.g. mortgage loans, auto loans, credit card debts) are bundled into pools. The pools, which are set up as trusts, issue bonds that represent the right to collect profits generated by the loans. The loans must be "performing" (not in default) in order for a securitization trust to generate wealth for investors.

servicer

A bank or other entity that accepts and processes payments on behalf of the owner of a mortgage loan. Servicers also assess fees and penalties when loans are delinquent.

setoff

A type of claim or defense asserted in response to a lawsuit. A setoff alleges that the amount claimed to be due by the Plaintiff is offset by amounts the Plaintiff would owe to the Defendant.

Sheriff's sale

In Illinois, a sheriff's sale is held after the entry of a judgment of foreclosure and sale. After a sheriff's sale is held, the sale must be confirmed by a judge. Prior to the sale being confirmed, the homeowner retains title to the property.

short sale

A sale of real property where the purchase price is less than the amount the seller owes on his or her mortgage.

special indorsement

A special indorsement is a means of indorsing a negotiable instrument. A special indorsement makes the instrument payable to a specific person or entity. For example, a signature accompanied with the language, "Pay to the order of Bob Smith," would be a special indorsement making the instrument payable only to Bob Smith.

special right to redeem

A statutory remedy in Illinois, the special right to redeem gives some homeowners one last opportunity to avoid foreclosure. After a sheriff's sale is conducted, if the winning bidder is the mortgagee or its agent, and if the sale price is less than the redemption value, then the homeowner has the right to pay the mortgagee the sale price, plus fees, costs and statutory interest.

standing

At law, standing is the legal capacity to bring a lawsuit or to assert a claim against another. This means that a party asserting a claim must be the real party in interest, who has a legally recognized claim that can be resolved by a court. For example, if Bob and Steve enter into a contract, both Bob and Steve have standing to assert a claim against the other if he breaches the contract. However, Alice, who is not a party to the contract, will generally not have the standing to assert a claim against Bob or Steve for breach of the contract.

statement of financial affairs

A series of questions the consumer must answer in writing concerning sources of income, transfers of property, lawsuits by creditors, etc. (There is an official form a consumer must use.)

statement of intention

A declaration made by a chapter 7 consumer concerning plans for dealing with consumer debts that are secured by property of the estate. This generally involves whether the consumer wants to reaffirm specific debts.

statutory damages

A type of damages that are granted to a successful plaintiff by the authority of a statute. These are generally awarded in addition to actual damages.

stripping

In a bankruptcy context, it is possible to remove or "strip" liens from a piece of real property as part of the bankruptcy process.

This is most often done to strip underwater second or third mortgages from a home in a Chapter 13 bankruptcy.

subprime loan

A subprime loan is generally a loan sold to individuals with poor credit scores or limited credit history. During the real estate boom, many borrowers were steered into subprime loans when they qualified for loans with better terms. Subprime loans usually contain features that benefit the bank at the expense of the consumer. For example, a subprime loan may contain a variable interest rate and a prepayment penalty.

summons

A summons is a legal document addressed to the defendant in a lawsuit. It puts the defendant on notice of the lawsuit and states a date on which the defendant must appear in court.

Supreme court

In Illinois and in the federal system, the supreme court is the highest court in the structure. Rulings issued by the Illinois Supreme Court are binding on all courts in Illinois. Rulings issued by the U.S. Supreme Court are binding on all courts in the nation.

T

Tenants by the entirety

A type of tenancy in which a married couple holds land as if both individuals were one person. A tenancy by the entirety includes a right of survivorship – when one spouse dies, the other inherits his or her interest.

Tenants in common

A type of tenancy in which multiple persons or entities each own shares of one piece of property. This type of tenancy contains no right of survivorship, and one tenant in common is permitted to encumber or sell his or her portion of the property without the consent of the other tenants.

title

Having title to something means having the right to possess the thing. In real property, title often refers to the record owner of a piece of land.

title theory state

In a title theory state, the lender retains title to a mortgaged piece of real property. Once the mortgage is paid off, the lender then conveys a deed to the homeowner. Title theory states tend to lack a judicial foreclosure process.

transfer

Any mode or means by which a consumer disposes of or parts with his/her property.

Troubled Asset Relief Program (TARP)

The Troubled Asset Relief Program (TARP) is a U.S. government program that allows the Treasury to purchase distressed assets like mortgage loans.

trust

An entity created by a written instrument. A trust can be used for many purposes. One such purpose would be a mortgage securitization trust, which pools mortgage loans and issues bonds whose value is tied to the performance of the underlying loans.

trustee

The trustee is a private individual or corporation appointed in all chapter 7, chapter 12, and chapter 13 cases and some chapter 11 cases. The trustee's responsibilities include reviewing the consumer's petition and schedules and bringing actions against creditors or the consumer to recover property of the bankruptcy estate. In chapter 7, the trustee liquidates property of the estate, and makes distributions to creditors. Trustees in chapter 13 have similar duties to a chapter 7 trustee and the additional responsibilities of overseeing the consumer's plan, receiving payments from consumers, and disbursing plan payments to creditors.

Truth In Lending Act (TILA)

The Truth In Lending Act is a federal law that was passed in 1968 and requires that lenders give certain standardized disclosures regarding the terms and costs of any credit offered. It is codified at 15 U.S.C. §1601 et. seq.

U

unclean hands

This is an equitable doctrine that states that a party who has done wrong cannot seek an equitable remedy. The defense claims that the party seeking equitable relief has acted in bad faith in relation to the claim being made.

unconscionability

When used in contract law, unconscionability is a defense to the enforceability of a contract. It is generally related to contract terms that are so unfair, they cannot be enforced. There are two types of unconscionability, procedural and substantive.

Procedural unconscionability refers to the conditions of contract formation. It examines the age, intelligence and relative power positions of the parties to a contract. The two main elements of procedural unconscionability are oppression (taking advantage of a disproportionate power relationship) and surprise (hiding terms of a contract from one party).

Substantive unconscionability refers to the unfairness of a contract's terms. It involves contract terms that are so patently unfair that a court may decline to enforce those terms.

undersecured claim

A debt secured by property that is worth less than the full amount of the debt. If your mortgage is for $600,000 and your home is only worth $400,000, the claim is unsecured.

underwater

A term used to describe a house that is worth less than the balance of the mortgage secured against the house.

Unfair acts and deceptive practices (UDAP)

In addition to the federal prohibition against unfair and deceptive business acts and practices encoded in the Fair Trade Commission

Act, most states have their own UDAP statute. In Illinois, our UDAP statute is called the Illinois Consumer Fraud and Deceptive Business Practices Act (ICFA). An unfair business practice may be an action like charging excessive fees to cell phone users. A deceptive business practice may be an action such as advertising a sale item, yet not having the sale item in stock. This kind of deceptive practice is also known as a bait-and-switch.

Uniform Commercial Code (UCC)

The Uniform Commercial Code is a set of laws designed to regulate commerce in the United States. The UCC has been enacted in all 50 States. Louisiana has not adopted Article 2 of the UCC, instead preferring to retain its civil system for regulating the sale of goods.

United States trustee

An officer of the Justice Department responsible for supervising the administration of bankruptcy cases, estates, and trustees; monitoring plans and disclosure statements; monitoring creditors' committees; monitoring fee applications; and performing other statutory duties.

unliquidated claim

A claim for which a specific value has not been determined.

unscheduled debt

A debt that should have been listed by the consumer in the schedules filed with the court but was not. Depending on the circumstances, an unscheduled debt may or may not be discharged.

unsecured claim

A claim or debt for which a creditor holds no special assurance of payment. This is credit which was extended based solely upon the creditor's assessment of the consumer's future ability to pay. One primary example would be credit card debt.

V

Voluntary transfer

A transfer of a consumer's property with the consumer's consent.

Y

Yield Spread Premium (YSP)

A yield spread premium is the practice of paying a mortgage broker or loan officer a kickback for steering a borrower into a mortgage loan that will net a higher yield for the lender. In general, the more exotic the loan, the higher the yield spread premium.

Appendix 3

The Bankruptcy Schedules

Schedule A

On Schedule A, you must list all of your real estate, also known as real property. For each property, you must provide:

- A description and location of the property
- The nature of your interest in the property
- Whether the property is held by a husband, wife, or if it is joint or community property
- The current value of your interest in the property without deductions for secured claims or exemptions
- Whether there is a secured interest in the property (like a mortgage)

Schedule B

On Schedule B, you must list all of your personal property. There are 35 categories of property listed on this schedule. You must provide the following information:

- A description and the location of the property
- The nature of your interest in the property
- Who has an interest in the property
- The current value of your interest in the property without deductions for secured claims or exemptions

Schedule C

On Schedule C, you must list all of the property that you are claiming as exempt. This is property that you are protecting from possible liquidation. You must provide:

- A description of the property
- The law under which you are exempting the property
- The value of the claimed exemption
- The current value of the property without deducting the exemption

Schedule D

On Schedule D, you must list your secured creditors. These are creditors who have secured your debts against your property, like a mortgage or an auto loan.

Schedule E

On Schedule E, you must list priority unsecured creditors. These are creditors who will be paid back first due to the nature of their claim. A good example would be the Internal Revenue Service.

Schedule F

On Schedule F, you must list your unsecured creditors who have non-priority claims. Credit cards are a good example of creditors you would list on Schedule F.

Schedule G

On Schedule G, you must list your unexpired leases and executory contracts.

Schedule H

On Schedule H, you must list your co-debtors. This is generally used by married couples or by people who have co-guarantors on their loans.

Schedule I

On Schedule I, you must list your current income. This is necessary for both the means test and for calculating your disposable monthly income.

Schedule J

On Schedule J, you must list your current monthly expenses. This is important for certain means test analyses and for calculating your disposable monthly income.

Appendix 4

Selected Articles

This appendix contains articles written by the attorneys of Sulaiman Law Group, Ltd. They are intended to discuss specific legal issues in more depth than the main body of this book. Sulaiman Law Group would like to thank attorneys Mohammed Badwan, Nosheen Rathore, and Mara Baltabols for their contributions to this appendix.

Chapter 7 Eligibility

By Mohammed O. Badwan, Attorney At Law

A Chapter 7 bankruptcy also known as a "straight liquidation", liquidates a debtor's non-exempt assets and pays back creditors the proceeds from liquidation, and the rest of the debt is forgiven. Almost all Chapter 7 filings are no asset cases; meaning no assets are liquidated and the debtor keeps all the property they owned at the time of filing. Whether or not assets are liquidated, a successful Chapter 7 filing will result in elimination of almost all of the debtor's pre-petition liabilities (credit cards, contractual liabilities, mortgages, medical bills, etc). The bankruptcy process can be difficult and confusing. One of the first obstacles debtors must overcome is qualifying for a Chapter 7. A debtor's Chapter 7 eligibility is highly dependent on one factor: income. The Bankruptcy Code is very complex to say the least. Congress decided to complicate matters to prevent bankruptcy abuse through the Bankruptcy Abuse Prevention and Consumer Protection Act of 2005 (the "Act"). The Act made qualifying for a Chapter 7 a confusing and daunting task. The Act implemented 11 USC §707(b)(2)(A)(i) which is also known as the "means test" to encourage debtors to reorganize their debts in a Chapter 13 rather than eliminating them in a Chapter 7. Pursuant to 11 USC §707(b)(2)(A)(i) a debtor's Chapter 7 case may be dismissed if the presumption of abuse arises. The presumption of abuse arises if the debtor has disposable income after their necessary expenses are deducted.

The first question that needs to be addressed when determining whether a debtor is eligible for a Chapter 7 is whether they are above or below the median income for their applicable household size. For example, a household of 5 for a family in Cook County has a median income of $87,288. If a debtor within the same county and household size is under the median, then the "means test" is not applicable and there is no presumption of abuse of the bankruptcy code and they are presumably eligible. If a debtor is over the median income for the applicable household size, then there is a presumption of abuse and the debtor must overcome the presumption by passing the "means test".

The "means test" is a Congressional invention that determines whether a debtor is presumably abusing the system. The "means test" only applies to debtors with "primarily consumer debt". It is "supposed" to determine whether a debtor is living beyond their means. In a nutshell, if the debtor's necessary expenses as defined by the means test are close to or outweigh their current monthly income then they pass the test. The nuisance of the "means test" is that debtor's cannot deduct their actual expenses for most deductions. Conversely, the debtor must use IRS standard deductions to determine whether they have disposable monthly income after all their necessary expenses are deducted. However, a debtor can deduct all "contractually obligated" expenses, regardless of how high they are. For example, a $5000 mortgage can be used as a deduction whether or not the debtor wants to keep or surrender the home. Other necessary expenses are determined by IRS standards. For example, a family of 5 can only deduct $1427 for housing expenses (excludes utilities) if they rent. Keep in mind, if you own then you are "contractually obligated" to make that payment and can use the actual expense opposed to the IRS standard for the applicable household size. Once a debtor deducts all the necessary expenses from their income (average of 6 months prior to bankruptcy is used as the current income under the "means test), they will pass the "means test" if the number is around $200 or less. The "means test" was implemented to encourage some repayment to creditors if the debtor has disposable monthly income after all necessary deductions. Therefore, if a debtor has $500 left over each month, then they would have money left over each month to pay creditors in a Chapter 13.

The "means test" has caused confusion and hysteria in the bankruptcy community. Many believe that it does not reflect a debtor's actual circumstance. The Bankruptcy Court is aware of the complex issues produced by the "means test". It is common knowledge that the "means test" has its share of ambiguities. As a result, the Courts are having great difficulty interpreting Congress's intent. Courts are divided on how portions of the "means test" should be interpreted. Consequently, one district may allow an expense where another does not. It has been around 5 years since the "means test" has been implemented and the issues that have spawned from the ambiguities are still far from settled. Therefore, it is of utmost importance that a debtor consults with a competent bankruptcy attorney before even considering filing a Chapter 7.

Passing the "means test" presumably qualifies a debtor for a Chapter 7. However, other major considerations still need to be addressed. As you recall, a Chapter 7 is a liquidation; meaning all non-exempt assets are subject to liquidation. So, just because a debtor qualifies for a Chapter 7 does not mean that debtor should file. For example, if a debtor has $40,000 in credit card debt and has unexempt personal property assets worth $80,000, then the assets will be liquidated. In the example, it would make more sense for a debtor to file a Chapter 13 and protect his assets.

Although income is the most important variable in qualifying for a Chapter 7, the debtor must meet some other qualifications. A debtor who has received a Chapter 7 discharge within the last 8 years does not qualify for a Chapter 7. Furthermore, a debtor who has filed and successfully completed a Chapter 13 in the last 6 years does not qualify for a Chapter 7 unless the debtor paid more than 70% of their unsecured debt in the Chapter 13. There is no debt limit for a Chapter 7. Therefore, whether your debt is $2 or $20 million, you can discharge the debt in a Chapter 7 bankruptcy.

In today's economic climate, most debtors, whether above or below median income, do not have any assets and have considerable debt. A Chapter 7 bankruptcy assures the debtor a fresh start allowing them to proceed with their lives without the stress of creditors. Many high-income debtors assume they are not eligible for a Chapter 7 bankruptcy. Nothing can be further from truth. Although income is the most vital factor, there are numerous other considerations that need to be addressed. The Bankruptcy Code's complexity is not to be taken lightly. The only way to determine your eligibility is to consult with a competent bankruptcy attorney.

Common Scenarios

Scenario 1

Client owns a home and has fallen back on his mortgage payments. The house is worth $350,000 and Client owes $550,000 between his first and second mortgage. Client has decided that the house is a bad investment and wants to walk away. Client is worried that the house will sell for less than it is worth at sale and the bank will go after him for the difference. Client makes about $90,000 between him and his wife and they have 2 kids. Client's mortgage payments are $5000 a month, $6,000 if taxes and insurance are included. Client wants to file a Chapter 7 bankruptcy to ensure the bank will not come after him for the deficiency? Is he eligible?

A: The client will most likely qualify for a Chapter 7 even though his income for a family of 4 is above the median, thus triggering the "means test". His $5,000 "contractually obligated" expense is the main qualifier in this scenario. A salary of $90,000 translates to $7500 a month before taxes are deducted. The necessary expense of $5000 eats up so much of the Client's salary that he would not have any money left over each month to pay creditors after other necessary expenses are deducted (utilities, car payments, food, health care, transportation costs, etc). If the Client's mortgage payment was $1200 a month, he most likely would not qualify for a Chapter 7 assuming he does not have any other mortgages on any other properties.

Scenario 2

Client owns 4 properties, 1 primary residence and 3 investment properties. The investment properties are underwater (worth less than Client owes). Client is having trouble finding renters and has maxed out his credit cards (owes $80,000). Client is married with 1 child. Client's income is $180,000. The mortgages on the investment properties are $12,000 combined and he is not receiving rent on any of the properties. Client wants to surrender the properties to the bank but is worried they will come after him for the deficiencies. Client wants to keep his primary residence and the house is worth equivalent to what he owes. Is he eligible?

A: Once again, the answer is probably yes. For one, the debtors' debts are primarily "non-consumer" and therefore the "means test" does not apply since most of his debt arose from investments. Even if the "means test" applied, he mostly likely would qualify.

Since his "contractually obligated" expenses (all 4 mortgages) are so high, it will eat up his income in the means test leaving no money to pay back creditors in a Chapter 13.

Chapter 13 Lien-Stripping: History and Overview

By Mohammed O. Badwan, Attorney At Law

Although the 2005 amendments to the Bankruptcy Code through the Bankruptcy Abuse Prevention and Consumer Protection Act of 2005 (BAPCPA) made it more difficult for debtors to qualify for Chapter 7 relief; a provision providing substantial relief for debtors with underwater properties (mortgage on property exceeds property value) remained in intact. It is still possible for homeowners to strip off any wholly unsecure liens in a Chapter 13 bankruptcy.[68] A lien is unsecure when the property's value does not cover the value of the lien. This controversial provision resulted in legal warfare between debtors and banks. Banks relied on a bankruptcy provision that prohibits any modification of rights of holders of secured claims.[69] Debtors relied on a provision stating that lien holders are only secured to the extent of the value of the collateral; therefore, if a lien is wholly unsecure, it is void pursuant to the clear and unambiguous language of the statute. Judges had their work cut out for them.

The main issue that had to be decided by the courts was whether a wholly unsecured junior mortgage may be stripped off pursuant to 11 U.S.C. §506(d), notwithstanding the anti-modification protection afforded holders of home mortgages in 11 U.S.C. §1322(b)(2).[70] Section 506(a) of the Bankruptcy Code provides that "an allowed claim of a creditor secured by a lien on property in which the estate has an interest....is a secured claim to the extent of the value of such creditor's interest in the estate's interest in such property....and is an unsecured claim to the extent that the value of such creditor's interest....is less than the amount of such allowed claim."[71] Subsection (d) of Section 506 then provides that "to the extent that a lien secures a claim against the debtor that is not an allowed secured claim, such lien is void."[72]

The banks relied heavily on a Supreme Court case that held when applying the two provisions, "a lien 'strip down' of an undersecured home mortgage lien is impermissible for claims secured by principal residences, because it modifies the total package of rights which such a claim holder bargained. A lien 'strip down' reduces an undersecured lien to the value of the collateral, in contrast to a lien 'strip off', which removes a wholly unsecured junior lien"[73] The *Nobleman* court never addressed the issue of whether a lien 'strip off' is permissible but concluded that a lien 'strip down' is not permissible on a primary residence. It was now up to the courts to decide whether a lien 'strip off' would violate a statutory provision stating that the terms of a secured lien cannot be modified on a primary residence. The majority of courts decided in favor of homeowners and held that wholly unsecured liens may be 'stripped off'.[74]

Allowing the stripping off of wholly unsecure liens was a monumental victory for homeowners across the country. The decision became significant after the housing crisis resulted in the substantial decrease in home values across the country. Many homeowners found their homes to be worth substantially less than what is owed on the mortgages. However, the decision allowed the homeowners to strip off a second mortgage, assuming it was wholly unsecure (balance of first mortgage exceeds value of home), helping them regain value in their homes.

Lien stripping is only permissible in a Chapter 13 bankruptcy. A debtor that files a Chapter 7 may not strip off any non-judgment liens (mortgages) on their homes. A Chapter 13 bankruptcy is a repayment plan that typically lasts for three to five years, depending on the debtor's annual income. The amount repaid in a Chapter 13 depends on how much disposable income a debtor has each month and the value of the debtor's non-exempt assets. The repayment is usually anywhere between 10% to 100% of a debtor's unsecured debt.

When a mortgage lien is stripped, the nature of the debt changes from secured to unsecured. The balance is treated is an unsecured debt just like credit cards. In most cases (depending on disposable monthly income and assets), the debtor only has to repay a portion of the balance of the once secured mortgage. For example, John Debtor owns a home that is worth $200,000. He has two mortgages on the property; a first for $210,000 and a second for $80,000. He can strip the second mortgage since the balance of the first mortgage exceeds the value of the home. So, the $80,000 second mortgage changes from secured debt to unsecured debt. The significance of the transformation is unsecured debt does not have to be repaid in its entirety in a Chapter 13 bankruptcy. Assuming John has $200 of disposable monthly income, he would repay the once secured second mortgage $12,000 (60 months x $200 in disposable monthly income) over the course of a 5-year Chapter 13 plan. Once John completes the plan, the mortgage will be officially stripped from the home.

Lien-stripping can be an extremely useful strategy for homeowners that are underwater; especially since the housing crisis continues to drive home values to the ground. Lien-stripping can benefit many homeowners who have seen the value of their homes plummet in the last couple of years. Not only can a Chapter 13 bankruptcy help the debtor strip a wholly unsecure second mortgage, but also can wipe out credit card debt with minimal repayment. With no end to the recession in sight, many homeowners should consider utilizing the Bankruptcy Code as a source for financial relief.

"Totality of Circumstances" As a Basis for Dismissal in a Chapter 7

By Mohammed Badwan, Attorney At Law

Successfully passing the means test in a Chapter 7 bankruptcy is not the only obstacle on the road to financial freedom. Although passing the means test rebuts the presumption of abuse in a Chapter 7 filing, the U.S. Trustee can still file a motion to dismiss if it believes the totality of circumstances of the debtor's financial situation demonstrates abuse.[75] If the Trustee succeeds, then the debtor must either convert to a Chapter 13 bankruptcy or their bankruptcy will be dismissed without the relief sought. The totality of circumstances provision was added to the Bankruptcy Code through the Bankruptcy Abuse Prevention and Consumer Protection Act of 2005 (BAPCPA).[76] Prior to BAPCPA, the U.S. Trustee could only file a motion to dismiss a Chapter 7 if the case was a substantial abuse of the bankruptcy code. The implementation of the totality of circumstances provision in the Code specifically allows the U.S. Trustee to file a motion to dismiss even if the debtor has passed the means test and rebutted the presumption of abuse. The new provision has resulted in confusion among bankruptcy practitioners and judges.

The new provision fails to expressly define the phrase, "totality of the circumstances," forcing the courts to interpret its meaning with little guidance. Although the phrase is new to the

Code, it has pre-BAPCPA roots.[77] The court in *In Re Zaporski* ruled that the totality of circumstances concept is a judicially created construct for determining substantial abuse under pre-BAPCPA; the case law applying that concept lays out the general scope of the abuse to be determined." [78] Therefore, in analyzing whether dismissal is appropriate under the totality of the circumstances provision, courts focus on the following factors: 1) whether the debtor has the ability to repay a substantial portion of his debts ; 2) whether the petition was filed because of sudden illness, calamity, disability or unemployment; 3) whether the debtor incurred cash advances and made consumer purchases far in excess of his ability to repay; 4) whether the debtor's proposed family budget is excessive or unreasonable; and 5) whether the debtor's schedules and statements of current income and expenses reasonably and accurately reflect the true financial condition of the debtor.[79]

Many bankruptcy practitioners have been highly critical of the totality of the circumstances test. They believe it renders the means test a "mere surplusage".[80] They argue that "to perform the means test and then perform another means test that is more to the U.S. Trustee's liking ignores the plain language of the statute and would be a waste of judicial resources".[81] The *Nockerts* court found the argument persuasive and ruled that a dismissal based on the totality of the circumstances, "requires proof of something more than the ability to fund a Chapter 13 plan in order to avoid rendering the means test a 'mere surplusage'."[82]

Practically speaking, the totality of circumstances test becomes applicable when a debtor passes the means test but has disposable income on Schedule J. Schedule J is a list of the debtor's actual expenses as opposed to the allowable expenses in the means test. If a debtor has disposable income, after all his reasonable and necessary expenses are deducted from his income, then that allows for a meaningful repayment to his creditors in a Chapter 13 plan. The U.S. Trustee, at its discretion, may then file a motion to dismiss the Chapter 7 petition based on totality of the circumstances. The U.S. Trustee would assert that the means test does not reflect the debtor's actual financial circumstances and move the Court to dismiss the Chapter 7 since the totality of circumstances of the debtor's financial circumstances (disposable income) demonstrates abuse of the bankruptcy code.

Case law on the totality of circumstances provision is still in its infancy. When determining whether a case is abusive by applying the totality of circumstances test, the court is ultimately being asked to determine whether the debtor's expenses are reasonably necessary. "There is no bright-line rule for determining what is reasonably necessary."[83] Judges are quick to point out that the "totality of circumstances" test is fact-sensitive and must be decided on a case–by–case basis.[84] Courts have refused to superimpose their values and substitute their judgment for the debtor when determining whether an expense is reasonably necessary.[85] However, courts will substitute their judgment when any one of the following additional factors are present: 1) the debtor proposes to use income for luxury goods or services; 2) the debtor proposes to commit a clearly excessive amount to non-luxury goods or services; 3) the debtor proposes to retain a clearly excessive amount of income for discretionary purposes; 4) the debtor proposes expenditures that would not be made but for a desire to avoid payments to unsecured creditors; and 5) the debtor's proposed expenditures as a whole appear to be deliberately inflated and unreasonable.[86]

It is evident that the application of the totality of the circumstances provision has resulted in a rather large gray area due to its subjective nature. One judge may find an expense to be reasonably necessary while another may find the expense to be unreasonable. The BAPCPA and its ambiguities have resulted in many issues that bankruptcy practitioners and judges alike are having difficulty tackling. When considering bankruptcy, it is imperative that a debtor seek competent bankruptcy counsel, to address the rather ambiguous totality of the circumstances provisions to increase the likelihood of a successful chapter 7 filing.

How to Determine Whether a Lender Has Standing to Foreclose on a Borrower's Home

By Nosheen Rathore, Attorney At Law

In the current foreclosure crisis, it is common to see banks other than the original lender of the loan foreclosing upon borrowers. For this reason, it is important for borrowers to review the complaint and ensure that the plaintiff has standing to bring forth the suit.

To establish standing when bringing forth a foreclosure suit, a lender must have suffered an injury in fact for which a judicial decision may provide a redress or remedy.[87]Further, standing requires that the party requesting relief (or the lender in a foreclosure context) must possess a personal claim, status, or right that is capable of being affected by the grant of such relief.[88] Whether the lender has standing to sue is determined from the allegations contained within the complaint.[89] Further, standing is a jurisdictional requirement which must be continuous throughout the foreclosure suit.[90] In other words, a lender must have proper standing when it files a suit against a defendant and may not retroactively establish its standing to sue.[91]

Section 1504 of The Illinois Mortgage Foreclosure Law ("IMFL") establishes that only "the legal holder of the indebtedness, a pledgee, an agent, or the trustee under a trust deed...." may file foreclosure.[92] If the lender asserts a right to foreclose within its initial complaint, then the records must affirmatively show the capacity in which the lender is suing.[93] The lender must provide adequate proof that it holds legal title from which no other party can recover at the time that it filed its complaint.[94] Therefore, in order to verify whether a lender has proper standing, the first step is to review the allegations of the complaint and the attached mortgage and promissory note.

The most important documents to review is the promissory note which evidences the borrower's obligation to the lender. In order to verify proper standing, a borrower must understand how a promissory note is transferred between banks. The standard promissory note in a foreclosure action is a negotiable instrument under the Illinois Uniform Commercial Code ("IUCC"). A negotiable instrument is an unconditional promise to pay a fixed amount of money. [95] The IUCC states the following in regards to enforceability of a negotiable instrument: A "person entitled to enforce" an instrument means (i) the holder of the instrument, (ii) a nonholder in possession of the instrument who has the rights of a holder, or (iii) a person not in possession of the instrument who is entitled to enforce the instrument pursuant to Section 3-309 or 3-418(d)."[96]

The term "holder," with respect to a negotiable instrument, is defined as the person in *possession* if the instrument is payable to bearer[97] or, in the case of an instrument payable to an identified person, the identified person if that person is in possession.[98] A person can become a holder when a negotiable instrument is either issued to that person, or as the result of a subsequent negotiation that occurs after issuance.[99] Furthermore, when a negotiable instrument is first issued, there must also be a delivery of the instrument, meaning an initial voluntary transfer of possession.[100]

As a negotiable instrument, the subject mortgage is negotiated either by assignment or indorsement.[101] Either way, negotiation always requires a change in possession of the instrument because nobody can become the holder of a negotiable instrument without possessing the instrument either directly or through an agent.[102] Ordinarily, a promissory note is transferred by negotiation, which is effected by delivery alone in the case of a bearer instrument or by indorsement plus delivery in the case of an order instrument.[103] In both instances, possession of the promissory note is a necessity of being a holder of the note.[104]

Therefore, to verify if the suing plaintiff in the foreclosure case is the proper party, a borrower must review the chain of title of the subject foreclosure suit and make sure that the plaintiff has possession of the promissory note. If a promissory note has been properly transferred, the indorsements on a promissory note will establish a chain of ownership leading from the lending bank to the foreclosing bank. However, if the plaintiff cannot show a proper chain of title or produce the original note, the court may dismiss the foreclosure suit for failure to verify that it is the proper party to bring forth the foreclosure suit.

Debt Cancellation: "What is my income tax liability post-foreclosure?"

By Nosheen Rathore, Attorney At Law

When a mortgage lender forgives a borrower's debt through a foreclosure, it elects to discharge the remaining principal of the debt, usually because the lender considers the debt to be uncollectible. After a lender elects to forgive the debt, the borrower as a taxpayer must then determine whether the forgiven debt will become taxable income. To address this issue in the current housing crisis, Congress enacted the Mortgage Forgiveness Debt Relief Act of 2007[105] ("MFDRA") on December 20, 2007 for the purpose of excluding income which may be taxable as a result of debt forgiveness related to foreclosures, short sales, consent foreclosures, and loan modifications.

The concept of debt forgiveness is that the ordinary taxable income of a taxpayer includes the portion of debts which are forgiven by the lender. Section 2 of the MFDRA changes the Internal Revenue Code ("IRC") to allow a taxpayer to exclude income from the discharge of indebtedness under Section 108 of the IRC. [106] Pursuant to the new provision, gross income is no longer included as income if it is "qualified principal residence indebtedness which is discharged before January 1, 2010." [107]

To prevent any abuse of this provision and to ensure that it is used only for its intended purpose, Congress enacted certain qualifying guidelines. First, the provision only applies to qualified

298

principal residence indebtedness.[108] For purposes of debt forgiveness, principal residence shares the same definition that is used in IRC Section 121. Section 121 excludes the first $250,000 ($500,000 in the case of a joint return) in gain from the sale of a taxpayer's principal residence) from taxable income.[109] Therefore, the new Section 108 exclusion would not be applicable to second homes, vacation homes, or investment properties.

Second, the changes to Section 108 cap the amount of qualified principal residence indebtedness at $2,000,000.00 and $1,000,000.00 in the case of a married taxpayer filing a separate return. [110] Basically, what that means is that if a lender forgives the debt on the taxpayer's home mortgage, up to $2,000,000.00 of the amount forgiven will not qualify as taxable income to the taxpayer. However, any amount forgiven that exceeds the $2,000,000.00 cap will count as taxable income on that year's tax return.

The MFDRA also includes home equity debt as part of debt forgiveness. However, only home equity debt that was used to improve the residence where the residence collateralized the loan qualifies for forgiveness under the act. [111]Home equity debt that was used for other expenses, such as personal bills, vacations, or college tuition does not qualify to be forgiven.

Third, this exclusion from income only applies to discharges that arise directly from the declining value of the residence or the distressed financial position of the taxpayer. [112] The following situations are deemed to be qualifying circumstances: 1) modification of the terms of a mortgage, 2) a short payoff, or 3) foreclosure of the taxpayer's principal residence. Although, as mentioned above, only the portion of the discharged loan that is qualified principal residence indebtedness will be excluded from taxable income. [113]

For example, suppose a taxpayer lives in a principal residence with a mortgage of $300,000 and the tax payer takes out a home equity loan for $150,000. The taxpayer uses $100,000 of the home equity loan to add a sunroom to the house and uses $50,000 to start a business. Assuming that the taxpayer's financial condition caused him to go into foreclosure and lose his home, the taxpayer would be able to exclude $400,000 of the discharge of indebtedness from his income. He would still have to pay taxes on the $50,000 that he used to start a business.

Lenders who forgive debt in excess of $600.00 are required to issue a Form 1099-C. This form will reflect the amount of the forgiven debt. Further, the amount of forgiven debt to be excluded from the taxable income of the borrower must be reported on IRS Form 982 and attached to the tax return of the borrower. [114]

Mortgage Escrow Accounts: "Why did my monthly mortgage payment jump so high?"

By Nosheen Rathore, Attorney At Law

In the current housing crisis, many distressed homeowners actively seek alternatives to foreclosure such as loan modifications or other repayment plans. After months of tedious paperwork and phone calls, many homeowners are shocked when their "modified" payment is higher than their regular payment. Often times, the reason behind the increase in a homeowner's monthly payment is an escrow amount that is added to the principal and interest portion of the mortgage payment. This escrow amount can consist of past due and future projected property taxes and insurance, as well as related fees. The primary purpose of such escrow accounts is to ensure that a homeowner's mortgage, tax, and insurance payments are made on a timely basis. [115]

Although mortgage escrow accounts are usually created to protect the interests of both the homeowner and the lender, escrow arrangements can also lead to vulnerability of the interests of both parties. A lender may be compelled to expend its own funds to protect its collateral if the homeowner is not making necessary payments at the appropriate time. On the other hand, a homeowner usually has little control or knowledge of how an escrow amount is calculated. Because of the lack of a homeowner's ability to determine a proper or improper escrow arrangement, a lender has the opportunity to require the homeowner to pay an amount that is more than necessary to cover the tax and insurance obligations on a property. A lender with thousands of customers could stand to gain substantial profits from the use of the funds gained through even small overcharges on escrow accounts.

For this particular reason, and to protect the interests of borrowers, Congress enacted the Real Estate Settlement Procedures Act ("RESPA") [116] to govern the procedures to be followed in connection with mortgage escrow accounts. After a homeowner has defaulted on their loan, RESPA authorizes a loan servicer to estimate the property taxes and insurance that will be due over the following twelve months and to adjust the borrower's monthly escrow payments under the mortgage to cover the estimated expenses, subject to certain limitations. [117] More specifically, Section 10 of RESPA places limits on the amount a lender or servicer may require a homeowner to keep in his or her escrow account to cover the payments of taxes, insurance, or other disbursements.[118] This section also governs a lender's obligations with respect to providing an annual escrow account statement and notice of any shortage in the escrow account. [119]

More specifically, Section 10 of RESPA states that a lender may charge a borrower a monthly sum equal to one-twelfth of the total annual escrow payments that the lender reasonably anticipates paying from the account. [120] A lender may also add an amount to maintain a cushion equal to one-sixth of the estimated total amount of these annual payments from the escrow account.[121] Because of the cushion amount, lenders are allowed to collect monthly escrow payments in excess of the amounts actually necessary to pay the tax and insurance premiums as they become due. Lenders are not permitted to collect greater than a two month cushion on the escrow amount.[122]

Regulation X, RESPA's implementing regulation, further ensures that the correct amount of funds are placed in escrow. Regulation X authorizes a loan servicer to conduct an analysis of the amount of money that will become due into the escrow account at either: 1) the beginning of the loan, 2) at the end of each computation year, or 3) "at other times during the escrow computation year." [123] This limitation is subject to an exception. RESPA and Regulation X authorize a lender to require that the borrower pay additional deposits if a deficiency or shortage exists in the escrow account. [124] If the lender determines that a deficiency amount exists, the lender may require the homeowner to make additional monthly deposits into the escrow account to remedy such deficiency, but must notify the homeowner of any shortage of funds. [125] A deficiency is the amount of a negative balance in an escrow account. [126] A shortage is the amount by which an escrow account balance falls short of the target balance at the time of the escrow analysis. [127] RESPA further authorizes lenders to calculate and collect certain "advance deposits in escrow accounts," or shortage contributions, in order to minimize any negative balance that may occur in a borrower's escrow account over the applicable twelve months. [128]

The two primary calculations for determining whether your account has been properly escrowed are described as follows:

> "Under the first [method], often referred to as the aggregate method, estimated requirements for anticipated disbursements for the next twelve months are added, the balance in the [escrow] account at the time of the analysis is subtracted ... and the result is divided by twelve to arrive at monthly escrow requirements for the coming year.... In other words, all escrow obligations ... are lumped together to determine the required monthly escrow payment from the mortgagor, even if the individual escrow items are of great disparity in the amount and become due on different dates. Under the second method, commonly known as individual item analysis, the lender creates sub-accounts within the escrow account corresponding to each expenditure that must be paid out. The lender then calculates the escrow amount needed to ensure that each escrow sub-account never falls below zero." [129]

Although these particular laws have been put in place to avoid over-escrowing situations, it is important for homeowners to carefully review the escrow provisions within their mortgage, and to monitor escrow accounts if they are put into place. Violations of the above-mentioned law could lead to a homeowner's monthly payment increasing to the point that he or she is forced into default and a subsequent foreclosure. Furthermore, if a lender violates escrow provision laws, it may be held liable for breach of contract, breach of fiduciary duty, unfair and deceptive business acts, claims for equitable and monetary relief, and any related attorney's fees.

Condominium Associations: Do I Pay My Assessments if I'm in Foreclosure?

By Nosheen Rathore, Attorney At Law

As more and more condos are foreclosed upon, unit-owners are often unclear about whether they should continue to pay their association fees. Further, unit-owners are often times surprised to find that the condo association may have filed a separate suit to foreclose on the unpaid association fees and are moving for eviction.

When a unit-owner fails to pay the monthly assessments or fees on time, the association can automatically record a notice of lien against the condo.[130] A lien against a condo for unpaid association fees will take priority over all other recorded or unrecorded liens and encumbrances, except for: (a) taxes, special assessments, and special taxes which are levied by any political subdivision or municipal corporation of Illinois, or any other state or federal taxes which by law are a lien on the interest of the unit owner prior to preexisting recorded encumbrances and (b) encumbrances on the interest of the unit owner recorded prior to the date of such failure to pay association fees or refusal which by law would be a lien thereon prior to subsequently recorded encumbrances.[131] Further, any action brought to extinguish the lien of the association will include the association as a party to the suit.[132]

Once notice of the lien is recorded, the lien may be foreclosed by an action brought by the association in the same manner as mortgage on a property may be foreclosed.[133] Although foreclosing upon the lien is an option, the preferred remedy in Illinois is a forcible entry and detainer action. [134] The Condominium Property Act provides that "in the event of any default by any unit owner in the performance of his obligations under this Act or under the declaration, bylaws, or the rules and regulations of the board of managers, the board of managers or its agents shall have such rights and remedies . . . including the right to maintain an action for possession against such defaulting unit owner . . . for the benefit of all the other unit owners in the manner prescribed by Article IX of the Code of Civil Procedure.[135]

When an association files an action for forcible entry and detainer, it is only seeking possession of the delinquent unit.[136] The unit owner will still retain title and will remain obligated to continue paying his or her monthly mortgage payment. Once the association obtains a judgment for possession, the order can be placed with the sheriff to evict the unit-owner from the premises, as is done with rental property evictions. The unit-owner would have to tender the entire amount due on the lien to halt the association from taking possession of the condo.

In the event that a property is foreclosed upon by the mortgagee, the Condominium Property Act states that "the purchaser of a condominium unit at a judicial foreclosure sale, or a mortgagee who receives title to a unit by deed in lieu of foreclosure or judgment by common law strict foreclosure or otherwise takes possession pursuant to court order under the Illinois Mortgage Foreclosure Law, shall have the duty to pay the unit's proportionate share of the common expenses for the unit assessed from and after the first day of the month after the date of the judicial foreclosure sale, delivery of the deed in lieu of foreclosure, entry of a judgment in common law strict foreclosure, or taking of possession pursuant to such court order." [137] This payment confirms the extinguishment of any lien created for failure to pay association fees where the judicial foreclosure sale has been confirmed by order of the court, a deed in lieu thereof has been accepted by the lender, or a consent judgment has been entered by the court. [138]

The Condominium Property Act also provides that the purchaser of a unit at a foreclosure sale must pay the association up to six months of unpaid assessments owed by the prior unit owner if several conditions are met. [139] First, the condominium association must file a lawsuit to collect unpaid assessments to be entitled to this special relief. Second, the purchaser of the unit must be someone other than a mortgage holder; if a bank or other mortgage holder purchased the unit at a foreclosure sale, the obligation to pay assessments shifts to the third-party purchaser. Third, the new owner is liable to pay past assessments only to the extent that the assessments have not been paid by the previous owner. Finally, a person who buys from a mortgage holder is liable for payment of pre-foreclosure assessments only if the condominium association's paid assessment letter and section 22.1 disclosures specified the amounts that must be paid.[140]

Because legislators have given condo associations a fair amount of power to pursue unit-owners and even subsequent purchasers for unpaid association fees, it is important to consider whether purchasing a condo with an association fee is the best option for you. Even after foreclosure proceedings are over, condo associations will still be able to recover unpaid fees based on a breach of contract. For these reasons, it is usually in a unit-owners best interest to stay current on the association fees or if in default, try to negotiate a payment plan to catch up with past due amounts.

How Do I Answer a Foreclosure Complaint in Illinois?

By Mara A. Baltabols, Attorney At Law

Many homeowners defending foreclosure are left with the inevitable choice of answering the foreclosure complaint without assistance from an attorney. Representing oneself in a legal case is otherwise known as proceeding "pro se." A mortgage foreclosure complaint contains legal language that may be difficult for a non-attorney to understand. A foreclosure defendant that lacks a legal background may, despite his or her best efforts, not answer the complaint properly by either failing to admit or deny allegations contained in the complaint or by not properly pleading a defense or counterclaim. A defendant to foreclosure should sit down with the complaint, read each paragraph, and answer each one by stating that they either (a) admit (agree), (b) deny (disagree), (c) have insufficient information to admit or deny the allegations contained in that paragraph. If a defendant fails to answer the complaint or sufficiently deny certain allegations contained therein, the bank will likely obtain a judgment of foreclosure--either by default (for a failure to answer) or pursuant to summary judgment (for a failure to raise an issue of fact in the answer to the complaint). A borrower should only admit those paragraphs that he or she truly believes to be true, and deny those that he or she has sufficient reason to believe are not true.

To avoid improperly answering a complaint, it is important for a defendant to understand what a bank is required to plead therein. A complaint is presumed sufficient if it contains all of the statements and requests outlined in the Illinois Mortgage Foreclosure Law ("IMFL").[141] The Illinois state legislature provided a short form in the IMFL that almost every foreclosure complaint follows.[142] By using the model form, a bank's complaint will generally be protected from attack for insufficient form.[143] Use of the model form is not required to foreclose, but almost every foreclosure complaint in Illinois follows it.

If a defendant fails to properly answer the complaint the bank will easily obtain judgment for foreclosure against them. Under the IMFL, the foreclosing bank is entitled to what is known as "summary judgment" where the allegations in the complaint are not denied via a verified answer or the borrower states that he or she has insufficient information to admit or deny the allegations contained in the complaint.[144] In other words, the bank will be entitled to a judgment of foreclosure where the borrower only admits or states that he or she has insufficient information to admit or deny the allegations in an unverified answer (an answer that is not signed under oath).[145] A verified answer is sworn to under oath via a signature and affirmation that all of the statements in the answer are true and correct.

A particular paragraph or paragraphs in the complaint that borrower should scrutinize are those stating the amounts alleged as owed. These allegations, including the "default" amounts, are normally set forth in paragraphs 3(J) and 3(K). If the borrower disputes that he or she is in default or the amount of the debt owed, the borrower may choose to deny one or both of these paragraphs. After analyzing the amounts alleged as owed in the complaint, a defendant may wish to dispute whether the bank is the true owner of the subject loan entitled to foreclose.

Whether the bank can foreclose relates to its ownership of the underlying debt or note. Ownership of the note pertains to its "standing" to bring the lawsuit. If the defendant disputes the bank's standing, he or she may be in a position to "deny" paragraph 3(N) of the complaint, or its equivalent. Paragraph 3(N) of the short form complaint reads: "(N) Capacity in which plaintiff brings this foreclosure: plaintiff is the legal holder of the indebtedness."

Also, if the defendant disagrees with the plaintiff's ownership of the loan, the defendant may dispute whether the plaintiff is the "mortgagee." Under the IMFL, "mortgagee" is defined as "the holder of the indebtedness." If the defendant disagrees that that the plaintiff is the owner or holder of the note, it is appropriate to deny that the bank is the mortgagee. In which case, the defendant may choose to deny paragraph 3(D) of the complaint, or its equivalent, which normally reads: "(D) Name of mortgagee: plaintiff inserts its own name, or occasionally the name of the original lender."

Otherwise, the defendant may dispute the bank's ownership of the loan by objecting to whether the bank attaches a "true and correct" copy of the note to the complaint.[146] The requirement that the bank attach a "true and correct copy" or the note, including all current signatures and endorsements (from one lender to another, as a party may endorse a check) is inferred from the language of the IMFL short form complaint. The IMFL model form is deemed to include allegations that the exhibits attached are "true and correct copies of the mortgage and note and are incorporated and made a part of the complaint of foreclosure by express reference."[147] Arguably, the copy of the note and mortgage attached to the complaint should look just like the original documents at the time foreclosure was filed.

The court will generally consider the copies attached to the complaint to be true and correct copies so long as the defendant does not object to their authenticity.[148] The defendant must present a valid dispute that the copies attached are true and correct copies in order to shift the burden back to the plaintiff to prove its case.[149] "Plaintiffs normally bear the burden of proving the elements of their claims."[150]

By attaching true and correct copies of the note, in particular, the bank supports that it is the holder of the indebtedness entitled to foreclose.[151] "Under the *Uniform Commercial Code,* which Illinois has adopted, 810 ILCS 5/1-101 *et seq.,* a key requirement to being a holder is physical possession of the note secured by the mortgage."[152]

Sometimes a plaintiff bank tries to show that it holds the note by bringing the original to court. To prove holder status via possession of the original note it must be either endorsed in blank (containing a blank space, or endorsement to "bearer") or directly to the foreclosing party via single, or multiple specific endorsements, or a combination of both.[153] If the copy of the note attached to the complaint does not appear to be a true and correct copy, the defendant may argue that the bank was not the owner or "holder" of the note at the time that it filed the complaint.

After answering the complaint and signing it under oath and defendant may choose to set forth defenses. It is logical to set forth defenses that relate to denials in the answer. For example, a defendant may allege a defense of "set off" for a failure to properly account for amounts paid under the mortgage or other disputes related amounts alleged as owed. Or, if a defendant objects to the bank's standing to foreclose, or ownership of the loan, a defendant may raise a defense for "lack of standing." These defenses need to be clearly labeled and supported by factual allegations set forth in outline or paragraph form. After pleading the defenses, a defendant should sign and file them along with the answer.

Overall, as intimidating as the legal process may seem, a pro se defendant should not shy away from denying allegations in a foreclosure complaint if he or she has reason to believe that they are not true. If a defendant has a good faith basis to plead a defense or counterclaim they should do so in conjunction with answering the complaint. Especially considering how easily the bank will obtain a judgment of foreclosure where a defendant fails to raise a dispute via his or her answer, defenses, or claims. Properly answering a complaint and raising defenses is an important part of defending against a foreclosure and presenting a dispute to the court. If a defendants fails to properly raise an issue to the court, the court may not be able hear the issue. Where there is no triable issue presented by the defendant, the bank will quickly and easily foreclose.

Does a Defendant in Foreclosure Have a Right to a Jury Trial?

By Mara A. Baltabols, Attorney At Law

Unless a foreclosure defendant pleads certain defenses or counterclaims, he or she has no right to a jury trial in Illinois state court. There are numerous advantages to making a jury demand. A jury of one's peers could relate to the difficulty in keeping up mortgage payments in these tough economic times. A jury may feel the fear of losing a home where countless memories have taken place, compared to a judge focused on the rule of law. Even the added time commitment of a jury trial may influence the other side towards settlement. Unfortunately, a foreclosure defendant generally lacks the right to make a jury demand in Illinois courts.

In Illinois, claims in equity do not allow for a jury trial. The equity court, otherwise known as the chancery court, normally hears equitable claims. Equitable claims are generally claims where monetary damages are insufficient to make a party whole. The concept of "making a party whole" involves placing a party back to the position he or she would have been had they not entered into the transaction or experienced the injury. As such, the court may issue remedies or mandate performance in the interest of a fair and just result. Such remedies include specific performance, injunction, or as relevant to this discussion, foreclosure.

Foreclosure is a claim in equity because instead of seeking monetary damages it requests the sale of a specific property to pay off a debt. Property is considered unique, the value of which cannot be determined by a court of law. The equity court orders sale of the property for its value to the higher bidder. A court may order a monetary judgment after the sale if the property sells for less or more than the amount of the debt. Even so, the foreclosure remains a claim in equity.

By denying a right to a jury trial for equitable claims, the Illinois constitution does not violate the Seventh Amendment federal right to a jury trial. The Illinois Constitution states, "The right of trial by jury as heretofore enjoyed shall remain inviolate."[154] This means that the Illinois constitution does not interfere with the federal right to a jury trial, which existed before the Illinois state constitution was enacted. Illinois recognizes a right to a jury trial in criminal proceedings, under English common law, and where afforded by statute.[155] This provision of the state constitution does not disturb a litigant's right to a jury trial in federal court.

A foreclosure defendant interested in a jury trial must plead certain defenses and counterclaims.[156] Common law claims that the state legislature has not written into statutory law allow for a jury trial.[157] Fraud, waiver, and estoppel all arise under common law and are defenses to foreclosure. Otherwise, if a party pleads only statutory claims, then the statute itself must allow for a jury trial.[158] There are no traditional defenses to foreclosure arising under statute that confer a right to a jury trial. For instance, the Illinois Consumer Fraud Act[159] is a statutory defense to foreclosure, but it does not allow for a jury trial in state court. However, the Seventh

Amendment right to a jury on statutory claims is preserved in federal court. [160] Therefore, the consumer wishing to bring an Illinois Consumer Fraud Act claim before a jury may prefer to sue first and file its complaint in federal court.

A party making a jury demand must do so prior to filing in its complaint or within the time for answering.[161] If a jury trial demand is made, the demanding party need not follow through with the jury demand. The requesting party will have to pay a jury demand fee regardless of whether the matter is ultimately tried before a jury. If a party fails to make a timely jury demand he or she will be considered to have waived the right to do so. [162] For the sake of discussion, claims that allow for a jury trial are generally called "legal claims." Once a party sets forth legal claims in response to equitable claims, the court will decide how to hear each claim and in what order.

Where a case involves legal claims in addition the equitable claims, the action becomes one of multiple issues. The equity court may hear the legal claims along with the equitable claims, divided into claims at law and claims in equity.[163] The court will normally sever the legal claims from the equitable claims and decide them separately. With a proper jury demand, the legal claims are issued to a jury and decided before the equitable claims.[164] The court may take consider jury's factual conclusions in deciding on the equitable claims, but is not required to do so.

It should be noted that conferring jurisdiction over an issue in equity is not necessarily excluding a trial by jury. In the absence of legal claims, an equity court has the option to issue factual questions to a jury at its discretion. The court may weigh the jury's factual conclusions in deciding upon the equitable claims. To reiterate, even where a party brings legal claims or defenses to an equitable claim, it has no right to a jury on the equitable claims. For example, a court will continue to decide a foreclosure, but a party may assert a defense of fraud before a jury. The court has the option to take the jury's factual conclusions on the fraud under advisement in deciding the foreclosure.

There are many factors to consider in bringing claims or defenses to a foreclosure regardless of whether a jury trial is an option. A foreclosure defendant proceeding without an attorney must research and properly plead each claim or defense. Moreover, if a foreclosure defendant has valid defenses and claims to a foreclosure it is important to assert them. A foreclosure defendant should never feel discouraged from pursuing all available claims or defenses under the law. In the event that a defendant wishes to hire an attorney, he or she should do so at the onset of a case. At the very least, so that the attorney may file a timely jury demand if one is available.

How Do I Know if I Can Rescind My Mortgage?

By Mara A. Baltabols, Attorney At Law

A Truth in Lending Act ("TILA"),[165] rescission claim is based upon the original lender's failure to provide the borrower with the required disclosures at closing of a mortgage loan refinance that secures a principal dwelling.[166] TILA provides a consumer with an unconditional right of rescission within three (3) business days following consummation of a residential loan refinance. TILA rescission rights apply to loans that are **not** used to fund the construction or purchase of property therefore it is generally required that they be a refinance.

For the applicable transactions, there is an unconditional right to rescind through midnight on the third business day following consummation of the loan. Where certain material disclosures were not provided, this three-day right to rescission never begins to tick and can extend up to three years.[167]

Due to the violations apparent on the face of the TILA disclosures documents, or lack thereof, a borrower may have a cause of action to rescind their mortgage pursuant to the Truth in Lending Act, 15 U.S.C. § 1601 et seq. ("TILA"), and Federal Reserve Board Regulation Z, 12 C.F.R. § 226 et seq. ("Regulation Z"). Even a technical violation in a material disclosure will give rise to a three-year extended right of rescission.

The material disclosure required for a refinance loan that secures a principal dwelling, are:

> [T]he annual percentage rate, the method of determining the finance charge and the balance upon which a finance charge will be imposed, the amount of the finance charge, the amount to be financed, the total of payments, the number and amount of payments, [and] the due dates or periods of payments scheduled to repay the indebtedness....
>
> 15 U.S.C. § 1602(u).

A borrower may rescind for a failure to provide TILA disclosures that contain the required material information. For example, the disclosures did not provide clear payment schedule information, an understated finance charge, or an inaccurate APR.[168] Other actionable disclosure violations include a lender's failure to provide each person with a security interest in the home with two copies of the Notice of Right to Cancel.

The purpose of rescission is to place the parties back to the positions they held prior to the extension of the loan. A successful rescission operates to void the bank's security interest in the borrower's home, and allow for the recovery of statutory damages for any failure to honor rescission. To effectuate rescission, a borrower must send a notice of rescission outlining the material violations under TILA and explicitly requesting rescission of the loan. The borrower should send the notice of rescission to the current mortgage holder, servicer *and* the original lender, just to be safe. If the borrower is unsure of the address where to send the notices, the borrower may call the bank to request the appropriate mailing address. The borrower *must* send the notice of rescission within three-years of consummation of the loan or he or she will lose the right to rescind pursuant to the statute of limitations.[169]

Despite that it is the original lender's failure to supply accurate material disclosures, TILA allows the borrower to rescind against the assignee of the loan. A notice of rescission under TILA is effective against assignees of the loan. [170]

Upon receipt, the mortgage holder has twenty (20) days to comply with the request, void its security interest in the home and return any interest and finance charges paid by the borrower. To effectuate rescission the mortgage holder must release its security interest in the home and return all funds that that the borrower paid over the course of the loan, including interest and costs. At which point, the borrower must tender either loan proceeds or the property to mortgage holder. In other words borrower must be prepared to either (1) give the property to the mortgage holder, (2) obtain a loan to repay the mortgage holder the remaining principal balance of the loan (of course with better terms than the rescinded loan). If the borrower is unwilling to tender the property, and cannot obtain another loan to pay back the mortgage holder, the borrower must seek a repayment plan by settling with the mortgage holder or pursuing assistance from the courts. In the event that the mortgage holder disputes the borrower's right to rescind or if it is unwilling to tender first, the mortgage holder is obligation to seek assistance from the courts.

Where mortgage holder will reject rescission and does not itself seek a declaratory judgment or other assistance from the courts, the borrower must take legal action to enforce rescission. If after 20 days the mortgage holder rejects, fails to honor rescission or fails to seek a rescission modification from the courts, then the borrower must file a complaint to enforce rescission. The complaint should join the mortgage broker, the original lender, and the current servicer as defendants. The complaint should allege rescission and damages against the mortgage holder for a failure to honor rescission.

TILA rescission is a powerful tool, but notable limitations are that a borrower must rescind within three-years, for material violations of TILA, and only for a refinance of a mortgage securing the borrower's principal dwelling. Otherwise, TILA rescission is beneficial to a borrower not interested in keeping the property, because the borrower may tender the property and receive a return of all interest and other costs he or she paid over the course of the loan. The mortgage holder and other servicer is then required to cure all bad credit marks associated with the loan. Therefore, a borrower with a mortgage eligible for rescission may want to consider looking over their documents from the closing for TILA violations or have a qualified attorney consider their case for rescission.

Can A Foreclosure Court Deny A Deficiency Judgment?

By Matthew Hector, Attorney At Law

The July 2011 Illinois State Bar Association Commercial Banking, Collections, and Bankruptcy Section newsletter included an article entitled, "Taking deficiency judgments in foreclosure."[171] Its main premise is that the Illinois Mortgage Foreclosure Law (IMFL) does not give courts discretion to refuse to enter deficiency judgments. I disagree. While the author is correct that section 15-1508 of the IMFL states that a court "shall" enter a personal judgment for deficiency, the equitable powers of the court can still trump the command language of section 15-1508.

It is well-established that courts hearing mortgage foreclosure actions have broad discretion in approving or denying the confirmation of a mortgage foreclosure sale.[172] The IMFL provides that a court may deny confirmation of sale if "justice was otherwise not done."[173] This catch-all phrase allows the court to consider the totality of the circumstances surrounding the foreclosure action and the sheriff's sale. More often than not, the foreclosing lender is repurchasing the property at the sheriff's sale. The sheer volume of foreclosures and the instability of the housing market has kept many investors away from foreclosure auctions. What was once a lucrative way to acquire property is now a coin toss – it is entirely possible that the purchased property will lose equity as the market continues to deteriorate.

The declining housing market is also indicative of the artificial inflation of property values in Illinois. The housing bubble drove prices up higher than they should have been. As more loans are scrutinized, it also seems that a significant amount of mortgage fraud took place. In many instances, this mortgage fraud was used to inflate a property's value, allowing buyers to cash out money at closing. These inflated values served as comparison values for further fraudulent appraisals, creating a perpetual motion machine designed to artificially inflate housing prices. When 49% of Chicago mortgages (not including the suburbs) are underwater, it becomes readily apparent that the market couldn't truly support those inflated values.

These inflated values become particularly important when reviewing the case law that discusses section 15-1508. A good starting point is *JP Morgan Chase Bank v. Fankhauser.*[174] In *Fankhauser*, the court examines several other cases where courts refuse to confirm a sale based on the discrepancy between the amount bid at auction and the value of the debt. That number is the potential deficiency. It is also interesting that the *Fankhauser* court holds that a mortgagor is entitled to an evidentiary hearing as to the fairness of a judicial sale, even when that mortgagor has failed to appear in the case until after the foreclosure sale's conclusion.[175] The case clearly establishes the broad, equitable powers of trial courts.

But do those powers allow trial courts to avoid the "shall" language of section 15-1508(e)? The article[176] cites two cases that predate the IMFL to support its position that whether a deficiency issues is not a matter of equity, but one of contractual interpretation.[177] The fact that both cases predate the IMFL, is merely an interesting footnote, at least as far as the article is concerned.[178] It would appear that when a promissory note allows for a deficiency against its maker, or that when a statute allows for the pursuit of a deficiency judgment, then so-called fairness does not come into play. Or does it? Section 15-1508(b) gives the court broad powers to deny confirmation of sale.[179] Section 15-1508(b)(iv)(2) provides that the confirmation order *may* include a deficiency judgment.[180] This language seems to suggest that including such a judgment is not required. The article, however, soldiers on.

The article argues that even more potentially fatal to the pro-equity argument is the holding in *Bank of Benton v. Cogdill*, which also predates the passage of the IMFL.[181] The *Bank of Benton* court held that, "the right to secure a deficiency judgment in any foreclosure proceeding is clear, provided that the mortgagee receives only one full satisfaction."[182] Certainly, we don't want to abrogate anyone's rights. Instead, let's examine the context of these opinions. In each and every one of these cases, the IMFL did not apply. None of the cases recite the standard for confirming a judicial sale. None of the cases even mentions the confirmation of the sale. Each case discusses something akin to a report of sale. Many of the issues in these deficiency judgment cases arose at what would be a modern confirmation of sale hearing. Moreover, the cases cited in the article[183] were decided at times when the nation was not experiencing the utter collapse of a housing bubble that artificially inflated home values. The deficiencies mentioned in the cases do not "shock the conscience."[184]

As *Fankhauser* establishes, trial courts have broad, equitable powers when it comes to deciding whether to confirm a sheriff's sale.[185] This may leave many judges stuck with a Hobson's choice. If they confirm the sale, they may be bound by the mandatory language of section 15-1508(e), utterly unable to deny a deficiency, no matter how large. If they refuse to confirm sales where the property is significantly underwater, the property may become stuck in a loop where it can never be sold. Each day that a property is in foreclosure adds to the total amount due under the note. Per diem interest accrues faster than one would imagine. Continually denying confirmation would result in an ever-increasing amount due, creating larger and larger disparities between the sale price and the loan balance. Add to that the fact that our trial courts are flooded with foreclosure matters. There is almost an incentive to confirm and get cases off the docket.

Granted, lenders could stop repurchasing the properties for less than a full credit bid. Certainly, the lender believed that the property was worth that inflated price when the loan was issued.

327

Property values have yet to stabilize, and the added volume of foreclosures means that we may see further decline before the market rebounds. The debate really shifts to the question of, "who bears the burden of the depressed market?" This is where the court's equitable powers can truly come into play. There is nothing in the law that prohibits courts from conditioning confirmation in such a way that maximizes fairness. If a judge conditioned confirmation of a sale upon the bank not seeking a deficiency in the foreclosure matter, then that would theoretically be within the court's powers. That conditioned confirmation would not preclude the lender from later pursuing the borrower for his obligations under the note. If the note provides for recourse, then certainly the lender may attempt to pursue that debt in a separate lawsuit.

The current urban legend is that lenders aren't pursuing deficiency judgments. The article[186] indicates something a bit different – a frustration with a system that is not granting such judgments. The truth is likely somewhere in between. Based on my reading of the law, there is no clear precedent under the IMFL that prohibits courts from refusing to grant a deficiency judgment. The standard mortgage foreclosure complaint seems to hedge as to whether the plaintiff will seek a deficiency. Either it states, "no deficiency will be sought against those who have received a Chapter 7 discharge," or perhaps "a deficiency judgment may be requested against those who have not received a Chapter 7 discharge." Very rarely does the complaint specifically request the remedy. Section 15-1598(e)(ii) seems to require that a deficiency be "requested in the complaint." Language that hedges, hems and haws about whether a deficiency will ultimately be requested, and language that seeks to avoid violating the protections of the automatic bankruptcy stay does not amount to a request.

Given that there is limited IMFL case law on this point, and given that many mortgage foreclosure complaints do not specifically request a deficiency judgment, this issue is far from settled. If the court's equitable powers allow it to deny confirmation where an unconscionable result would issue, what is preventing it from conditioning confirmation upon not issuing a deficiency judgment? As mentioned above, it would not preclude a separate lawsuit sounding in breach of contract. Foreclosure defense attorneys and consumer protection attorneys alike would do well to fight excessive deficiency judgments.

Can I Stop the Confirmation of My Home's Sale? 735 ILCS 5/15-1508 Explained

By Matthew Hector, Attorney At Law

An Illinois foreclosure lawsuit does not end with a sheriff's sale of the home. Although a judgment of foreclosure and sale is a judgment, it is not a final judgment. Before a foreclosure case is finalized, the sheriff's sale must be judicially confirmed.[187] Sheriff's sales are almost always confirmed. However, there are several reasons why a sale may not be confirmed.[188] Most of the objections to confirmation involve the nature of the sale.[189] A recent addition to the Illinois Mortgage Foreclosure Law (IMFL) creates an objection that is unrelated to the sale itself. These objections are powerful because they represent one of the last opportunities a home owner has to defend his home from foreclosure.

Denying confirmation of sale can be powerful because it can improve a home owner's bargaining position in settlement negotiations. It may not seem like it, but attempting a loan modification is essentially a settlement negotiation. The extra time gained can be crucial. Preventing the confirmation of a sale does not vacate the judgment of foreclosure, but it does prevent the lender from enforcing that judgment. Recent changes to the IMFL have added extra protection for home owners seeking a loan modification under the Making Home Affordable (MHA) program established by the Obama administration.

Pursuant to §15-1508(d-5), if a home owner has applied for assistance under the MHA program, and the property was sold in violation of the program's guidelines, then the sale will not be confirmed.[190] For example, a loan servicer is not allowed to file a foreclosure action until it has evaluated a home owner's Home Affordable Mortgage Program ("HAMP") eligibility.[191] If the home owner is eligible, then the servicer must offer a trial modification before proceeding to sale.[192] It is worth noting that while HAMP is the most visible MHA program, it is not the only one that triggers §15-1508(d-5). The Home Affordable Foreclosure Alternatives program ("HAFA") also limits when a servicer may proceed to foreclosure.[193] In order to be protected by MHA programs, the home owner must apply for them. Complacency does not trigger the protections of §15-1508(d-5). Although HAMP's overall success has been underwhelming, it certainly cannot hurt to apply. Being denied a HAMP modification also triggers HAFA, which requires that servicers evaluate several options before proceeding to foreclosure. Even though an order denying the confirmation of sale won't re-open the main case, a denied sale still buys valuable time.

Using §15-1508(d-5) as a basis for denying the confirmation of sale will not necessarily provide a basis for vacating the judgment of foreclosure. As an end-of-case strategy,

331

delaying the confirmation of sale is a last-chance measure. It is very difficult to present a credible motion to vacate a judgment if it has been more than thirty days from the entry of that judgment. If the home owner has largely ignored the case up to this point, only a few fact patterns will justify the attempt. In those situations where it is possible to vacate the judgment, facts will generally exist that establish significant problems with the lender's case.

When significant problems exist with the lender's case, §15-1508(b) becomes the more important section. The "if justice was not done" provision of §15-1508(b) is a catch-all that includes many defenses and fairness-based arguments. Even if a party makes its first appearance at the confirmation of sale hearing, it may challenge the sale's confirmation.[194] Although much of the case law on this subject relates to the sale price of the property, other arguments may be made to defeat the confirmation of sale.[195] Courts are to view the terms of the sale in their entirety when determining whether a sale should be confirmed.[196] Illinois courts have indicated that sales price is one part of the overall terms of the sale.[197] Therefore, the identity of the seller would also be part of the terms of the sale. This means that a home owner can assert the plaintiff-lender's lack of standing to sue at the time of the confirmation of sale.

If a lender cannot demonstrate that it owns the loan associated with the property, it cannot prove that it has standing to sue. If the lender lacks standing to sue, the lender also lacks the ability to sell the house. This is because the lender must have owned the loan, and have been able to demonstrate ownership, at the time it filed the lawsuit. If a lender cannot demonstrate ownership at the time of filing, the case must be dismissed and re-filed as a new case. If a home owner can successfully challenge the lender's standing at the confirmation of sale hearing, then the case against him must be dismissed. Since the judgment of foreclosure has already been entered at this stage in litigation, a motion challenging the confirmation of sale on these grounds should also be accompanied by a motion to vacate the judgment of foreclosure. If the lender lacked standing at the time of the sale, the lender also lacked standing at the time the case was filed.

In general, a motion to deny confirmation of sale is useful for giving the home owner more time to work out a loan modification or find a new place to live. Using §15-1508(d-5) to deny confirmation also forces lenders to complete their obligations pursuant to MHA's guidelines. Similarly, barring a serious issue with the lender's case, or some underhanded dealing on its part, using §15-1508(b) will only buy time. In some specific instances, it may represent a final chance to put facts in front of the judge that merit vacating the judgment of foreclosure and sale. In those instances it can be a powerful tool.

Standing, Securitization, and "Show Me the Note"

By Matthew Hector, Attorney At Law

If you spend some time researching foreclosure defense, sooner or later, the "show me the note" defense will make its appearance. It's a perfectly valid means of defending against a foreclosure lawsuit, and is useful where even a traditional attack on a plaintiff's standing to sue is inappropriate. Simply demanding to see the original note is good practice, even if the plaintiff bank is the home owner's original lender. Without the original note, the plaintiff bank cannot demonstrate that it has the power to enforce the note. Does this mean that it lacks standing? If there is no evidence that the note was ever conveyed to a third party, maybe not. A lost note affidavit may provide enough evidence that a note existed to defeat the standing issue. Even in original-lender-as-plaintiff situations, demanding to view the original note makes good sense. You never know if it was negotiated to a third party.

During the real estate bubble, mortgages and their associated notes were sold and re-sold, then pooled into trusts. These trusts then sold bonds that entitled purchasers to a portion of the yield of the pooled mortgages. It turns out that many of the mortgages that were pooled were horribly underwritten – many did not even come close to conforming with the issuing bank's lending standards. It also turns out that many lenders did not follow basic rules for buying and selling all of these mortgages and notes.

Although many attorneys think of secured transactions as something that bored them to death in law school, the law of secured transactions is very much alive in modern foreclosure defense.

For purposes of this discussion, how a note is negotiated from one party to another is the key to understanding "show me the note" arguments as well as standing. As stated above, only the holder of the original note may enforce that note against its maker. The maker is the home owner who signed the note. The note is a promise to repay a specific amount of money to a specific entity at specified times. If the note is indorsed, it becomes negotiable, which means that it can be freely transferred to other parties.

For instance, Bob decides to purchase a starter home for $170,000. He has $20,000 in savings as a down payment. His local bank issues him a loan for the remaining $150,000 that Bob needs to purchase the house. To commemorate this loan, Bob signs a note and a mortgage. The note designates Bob as the maker/borrower. Bob promises to repay the $150,000 over a term of 30 years at 5% interest. His monthly payment will be $500.[198] The bank keeps the original note in a secure location. Over time, Bob makes payments. Eventually the note is paid off and the bank releases the mortgage it holds on his house. This was how things worked before securitization really took off.

Securitization made it possible for banks to sell their loans to the secondary market. This freed up capital at the bank, allowing it to make another loan to someone else. At first, there were strict guidelines regarding securitization. Over time, those guidelines were loosened. Securitization boomed. Lenders couldn't originate loans fast enough to keep up with the demand. In order to meet that demand, many lenders loosened their lending standards. Thus began the rise of the sub-prime mortgage market. Many sub-prime loans were bundled together into the trusts that are the backbone of the mortgage-backed security market.

In a perfect scenario, National Bank, N.A. would issue the loan. It would then sell the loan to National Bank Holding, Inc. That sale would ideally be for the value of the loan and commemorated with physical documentation. Specifically, National Bank would indorse the note "Payable to National Bank Holding, Inc." National Bank Holding, Inc. would then sell the loan to National Bank Holding II, LLC. That sale would also be documented and the note indorsed over to National Bank Holding II, LLC. At that point, National Bank Holding II, LLC would deposit the loan into a trust. Once fully funded, the trust would then sell bonds to investors seeking a stable, long-term investment.

It turns out that there were very few perfect scenarios. Mortgage-backed trusts are established via documents called Pooling and Servicing Agreements. These PSAs govern the ins and outs of the transactions that are needed to establish the trust. More

336

often than not, the original lender would retain the servicing rights to the loan. This means that although the lender no longer owned the loan, it had the right to collect payments, assess late penalties, foreclose, etc. It turns out that the original lenders frequently retained the physical loan documents themselves. No indorsements were made, and the documents never changed hands.

Why is this a problem? If the physical note was never negotiated down the chain and into the trust, then the trust never actually held the note. It also means that the original lender, who allegedly no longer owns the loan, still has documents that make it appear as if it still owns the loan. These defective transfers are at the heart of the current mortgage foreclosure fiasco. This is also why it is vital that home owners demand to see the original note when their lender seeks to foreclose.

Even if a loan was never sold into the secondary market, the lender needs to demonstrate that it is in possession of the original note in order to enforce the note against a home owner. If a loan was sold on the secondary market, and especially if the loan was securitized, proving that possession becomes orders of magnitude more difficult. If a loan was sold from A to B and B to C and C to D, it must bear indorsements that demonstrate those transfers. If there is a gap in that chain of ownership, the current holder of the note will have a difficult time proving that it has the authority to foreclose upon the mortgage.

No matter what the facts of your foreclosure case may be, it is imperative that you always demand to see the original note. It could be the difference between losing a home and securing a loan modification or other settlement.

How Long Do I Have In My Home? Scenarios for Home Owners Facing Foreclosure

By Matthew Hector, Attorney At Law

Potential clients have lots of questions. "How long do I have in my home?" tends to be the most frequently asked. As is true with many legal questions, the answer is, "It depends." Litigation can be a lengthy process. While some cases are similar, no two cases are the same. Many factors can affect how long resolving a foreclosure can take. This article will give some sample scenarios and timelines.

Some clients come to us before they are served with a summons. They are likely behind on their mortgage payments and may have received a demand letter from the lender's attorneys. People at this stage are in the best possible position. Once a home owner is served with a foreclosure summons, Illinois state law gives him twenty-eight days to respond to the complaint. The first hearing date is usually thirty to forty days after the case is filed. In this situation, a borrower can remain in his home up to eighteen months before the lender acquires possession of the property. It all depends on the litigation strategy and the goals of the home owner.

If walking away from the property with dignity is the primary goal, this timeline can grow considerably shorter. Depending on the lender and its willingness to negotiate, a consent foreclosure can be processed in a matter of months. This means that an eighteen month timeline may contract down to three to six months. The ability to dictate your departure date is one of the big advantages to acting early.

If keeping the property is the primary goal, eighteen months can grow to three to five years, depending on the strategy. For example, if a loan modification is not possible due to a home owner's income being too high, filing a Chapter 13 bankruptcy plan may take three to five years to complete. At the end of the plan, the back payments are paid off and the mortgage is current. If a loan modification is possible, a successful litigation strategy may help speed the process along. It may also buy the necessary time to compile the required documentation for the application process.

When a home owner acts at the beginning of a foreclosure case, the litigation timeline can be very long. For example, suppose that a home owner named Dave is served with a summons with a hearing date of January 2. Dave begins shopping around for an attorney but fails to find one before the first hearing date. Dave attends the hearing and asks for more time to find an attorney. Normally, the judge will grant between 21 and 28 days to do this. The case will be set for a status date shortly after that period of time expires. On the 27th day, Dave hires an attorney. The attorney appears at the next hearing, which is set for February 7. At the February 7 hearing, Dave's attorney asks the judge for time to file an appearance and to answer or otherwise plead in response to the bank's complaint. The judge grants the attorney's request. The case is set for a status hearing on March 14.

Dave's attorney finds a defect in the lender's complaint and files a motion to dismiss before his 28 day deadline to file lapses. At the March 14 hearing, the attorneys agree to file responsive briefs setting forth their arguments regarding Dave's motion to dismiss. Both sides take 28 days to draft and file their responsive briefs. The motion is set for a hearing on May 16. At the May 16 hearing date, Dave's motion is granted. Because Dave's motion points out a defect that can be repaired, the lender is granted 28 days to amend its complaint. The case is set for a status hearing on June 20. At the June 20 status hearing, Dave's attorney is granted 28 days to respond to the lender's amended complaint.

At this point, the case is almost six months past the first hearing date and Dave has yet to file an answer to the lender's complaint. Although every case is different, this is a rather typical scenario. This is a great example of why acting early is the best plan. Home owners who act early have the power of courtroom procedure on their side. Most people do not defend their foreclosures. Actively fighting against a foreclosure slows down the process and extends the amount of time a home owner has in his home. In the previous example, Dave could have up to another year in his home before having to move out.

When a foreclosure case is past judgment, it can be very difficult to defend. If a default judgment has been entered within the last 30 days, judgments are normally vacated simply by filing a motion to vacate. If the judgment is more than 30 days old, it will be more difficult to vacate. This is because a home owner must demonstrate a valid defense to the foreclosure and a valid reason why he never presented that defense. Most reasons that an average person would consider to be "valid" do not meet the requirement. For instance, hiring a bad attorney is not a valid reason. Applying for a loan modification and assuming the lawsuit could be ignored is not a valid reason. Aside from improper service of process, there are very few situations that satisfy this requirement.

As a general guideline, if a home owner waits until after a judgment is entered, he has considerably less time in his home than if he had acted when the case was filed. Once a lender has obtained a judgment of foreclosure and sale, the sale can take place as early as 30 days post-judgment. In order to proceed to sale, a notice of the sale must be published in a local newspaper for three consecutive weeks. The notice cannot begin to run more than 45 days before the sale date. If a judgment is entered on July 1, the sale will generally take place no earlier than the second week of August. After the sale, a confirmation hearing is held. Once the sale is confirmed, an order of possession can take effect in as few as 30 days from the date of confirmation. In some situations, a home owner can request more time and receive a 60 to 90 day stay on the order of possession. If a home owner waits until after a judgment is entered, he may only have 90 days left in the home.

When considering how to handle a potential or current foreclosure lawsuit, it is important to think about your primary goal. Some people don't want to keep their homes. Some people want to keep their homes, even if that means remaining in an underwater property. Every case is different, and every client's goals are personal choices. Regardless of the goals, understanding how a litigation strategy can change the timeframe for achieving those goals is important. Even more important is the understanding that acting early is better than acting late. Those who act early can almost dictate their move out date. Those who act late generally act too late.

Reopening A Bankruptcy Case –A Debtor's Liability Considerations

By Matthew Hector, Attorney At Law

Why Reopen A Closed Bankruptcy Case?

Debtors may want to reopen a closed bankruptcy case to seek relief from the misconduct of their creditors. For example, if a creditor violates the bankruptcy discharge by attempting to collect a discharged debt, it would be necessary to reopen the case to pursue damages for that violation. Pursuant to 11 U.S.C. §350(b), it is possible to reopen a closed bankruptcy case to (1) administer assets, (2) accord relief to the debtor, or (3) for other cause. Although the Code does not define "other cause," "a decision to reopen a case for "other cause" lies within the discretion of the bankruptcy court."[199] This discretion is based on the bankruptcy court's equitable powers, allowing "the bankruptcy judge broad discretion to weigh the equitable factors in each case."[200] This relief is available to debtors, the trustee, or any party in interest.[201] Before reopening a bankruptcy case, there are some considerations that must be addressed. These considerations are going to be highly dependent on the facts of the individual case.

It is possible for creditors to reopen a bankruptcy case to seek "recovery from a previously undisclosed asset of the debtor."[202] In *Shondel*, a judgment creditor/injured party sought to reopen the debtor's Chapter 7 case to see recovery from debtor's insurance policy, which was not listed as an asset in her Chapter 7 petition. Although the debtor's personal liability was not affected by reopening the case, it was proper to reopen the case to allow the creditor to pursue relief from debtor's insurer.

The case law on the issue indicates that it is possible for creditors to pursue newly discovered assets, but the cases all speak to assets that existed prior to the debtor's petition, not after-acquired assets. Potential assets, e.g. pre-petition causes of action, are included in this category if debtor was aware but did not properly schedule the cause of action.[203] The *Lopez* court held that even once the ability to revoke the discharge had passed, reopening and allowing the administration of a previously undisclosed claim was warranted as it would provide the estate additional assets that could be distributed to the benefit of the creditors.[204]

For undisclosed assets, the *Lopez* court also provides insight into how those assets would be administered. A trustee would be appointed upon reopening, and it would be allowed to evaluate whether the Action had value, then prosecute the action and settle, abandon or arrange for the debtor to prosecute the action in exchange for the estate receiving a share of the proceeds. *Id.* For the purposes of a debtor seeking to reopen a case for other reasons, e.g. violation of the automatic stay or discharge, motion to quit-claim real property, it is important for the bankruptcy practitioner to determine whether any undisclosed assets exist that may give rise to a claim by discharged creditors. This is doubly important when the case was previously filed by a different attorney – never assume that previous counsel's work was 100% accurate.

Revocation of Discharge

Another consideration for a debtor seeking to reopen his case is whether it would give rise to a reason to revoke the debtor's discharge. 11 U.S.C. §727(e) provides that the trustee, a creditor, or the U.S. Trustee may request a revocation of a Chapter 7 discharge up to 1 year after the date of discharge if the discharge was obtained through an unknown fraud of the debtor[205], or up to one year from the date the case was closed if the debtor acquired property that is property of the estate or was entitled to acquire property and knowingly and fraudulently failed to report the property or surrender it to the trustee.[206] A Chapter 7 discharge may also be revoked up to 1 year after the case is closed if the debtor has refused to obey any lawful order of the court, or refused to testify after being granted immunity from self-incrimination.[207] Once the case is over a year past the date is was closed, the discharge cannot be revoked. As such, there is no opportunity for scheduled creditors to attack the discharged based on a fraudulently concealed asset.

Chapter 13 debtors seeking to reopen their case post-discharge run into a similar, but less comprehensive revocation of discharge issue. Pursuant to 11 U.S.C. §1328(e), a party in interest can, within one year of discharge, request the revocation of a discharge if the discharge was obtained via fraud and the party in interest was unaware of the fraud until after the discharge was granted.[208] Ultimately, for both Chapter 7 and Chapter 13 debtors, it is important to determine whether there was fraud in the underlying petition. For Chapter 7 debtors, it is also important to determine whether there were any undisclosed assets that could be described as knowingly and fraudulently withheld. If the one-year statute of limitations has run, creditors cannot bring an action to revoke the discharge or revoke confirmation of a plan.[209]

Given that the grounds for revocation of discharge are so limited, it is highly unlikely that a debtor seeking to reopen his case for any of the purposes listed in §350(b) of the Code will face renewed liability to his creditors. The discharge injunction is permanent and can only be disturbed for the ground enumerated in §§727 and 1328 of the Code.[210] This is further supported by the intention underlying the Code, that the honest but unfortunate debtor be afforded a fresh start.[211] It would fly in the face of the equitable powers conferred by §350(b) to think that a debtor reopening his case to pursue a discharge violation would suddenly be subject to renewed claims by his creditors if the petition was accurate and complete when filed.

Post-Petition or Post-Discharge Assets

Some debtors may wonder whether reopening the case will bring assets acquired after the bankruptcy was filed, or after the discharge is granted, back into the bankruptcy estate. 11 U.S.C. §541 describes the property of the bankruptcy estate. The Code provides that an interest in property that would have been the property of the estate becomes property of the estate if it is acquired within 180 days after the case is filed. These interests include inheritances, divorce property settlement agreements, and life insurance benefits.[212] It also covers any interest in property that the estate acquires after the commencement of the case.[213] This does not appear to cause a problem for a debtor seeking to reopen his case because scheduled assets not administered at the closing of the case are abandoned to the debtor.[214] The only true risk would be an asset acquired pursuant to §541(a)(5) where the debtor seeks to reopen the case post-discharge but within the 180-day look back period.

Post-discharge assets would not be reabsorbed into the case upon being reopened – this would both frustrate the fresh start provided by the discharge and significantly chill any debtor's attempts to pursue post-discharge claims. Moreover, once the case is closed, the estate ceases to exist but for the limited of property that is not abandoned, nor administered in the case, which remains property of the estate.[215]

Barring a situation where a debtor has willfully or fraudulently failed to schedule pre-petition assets, and attempts to reopen the case within one year of discharge, it is extremely unlikely that the debtor risks any negative affect to his discharge. As to assets acquired post-discharge the Code indicates that those assets cannot become a part of the bankruptcy estate. Likewise, assets that were abandoned by the trustee or abandoned by operation of law, those assets revert to property of the debtor post-discharge. If the trustee failed to administer those assets, it stands to reason that they are also safe from interference when a debtor seeks to reopen his bankruptcy case. It is important, however, to fully analyze the debtor's petition, in particular during the 180-day look back period described in 11 U.S.C. §541(a)(5) and during the 1-year statute of limitations period established for revoking a discharge. Cases where reopening the bankruptcy may be necessary should be evaluated on a case-by-case factual basis before filing the motion. In situations where reopening the case could expose the debtor to further liability, it may be wise to wait until the appropriate time bar has passed.

About The Authors

MATTHEW HECTOR is an attorney licensed to practice in the State of Illinois. He received his Bachelor of Arts with honors from the University of Alabama in 1998. He received his Juris Doctor *cum laude* from The John Marshall Law School in 2004 and his Master of Law with honors from The John Marshall Law School in 2007. Matthew has published extensively and maintains the Sulaiman Law Group blogs. He would like to dedicate this book to his daughter, Molly, who scribbled on an early manuscript version with crayon. Her work vastly improved the contents of this guide.

AHMAD SULAIMAN is an attorney licensed to practice in the State of Illinois and is the managing partner of Sulaiman Law Group, Ltd. He received both his Bachelor of Arts *magna cum laude* and his Juris Doctor from Loyola University in Chicago, Illinois. Mr. Sulaiman founded Sulaiman Law Group based upon the core principles of Dedication, Innovation, Compassion and Excellence. These four core principles inform every action taken by the firm.

Main Text Endnotes

[1] Leicht, Kevin T., "Borrowing to the Brink," *Broke, How Debt Bankrupts The Middle Class*, edited by Katherine Porter, Stanford University Press, 2012.

[2] Cauchon, Dennis, "Student loans outstanding will exceed $1 Trillion this year," October 25, 2011, available at: http://www.usatoday.com/money/perfi/college/story/2011-10-19/student-loan-debt/50818676/1 (last visited January 3, 2012).

[3] Humphries, Stan, "No Respite From Housing Recession In First Quarter," May 8, 2011, available at: http://www.zillow.com/blog/research/2011/05/08/no-respite-from-houslng-recession-in-first-quarter/ (last visited January 3, 2012).

[4] Guzzardi, Will, "Chicago Mortgage Crisis: Nearly Half Of Borrowing Homeowners Are Underwater, Says New Report," May 10, 2011 (updated July 10, 2011), available at: http://www.huffingtonpost.com/2011/05/10/chicago-mortgage-crisis-n_n_860068.html (last visited January 3, 2012).

[5] U.S. Department of Labor, "Economic News Release," December 2, 2011, available at: http://www.bls.gov/news.release/empsit.nr0.htm (last visited January 3, 2012).

[6] Simon, Ruth, "Thinking Deeply On Risky Lending," The Wall Street Journal, December 12, 2011, available at: http://online.wsj.com/article/SB100014240529702037648045770563308695 12216.html (last visited January 30, 2012).

[7] "Facts for Consumers," available at: http://www.ftc.gov/bcp/edu/pubs/consumer/credit/cre19.shtm (last visited January 3, 2011).

[8] DebtSettlers, Inc. is a fictitious debt settlement company. Any similarity to an actual debt settlement company is purely coincidental.

[9] *Id.*

[10] *See* 735 ILCS 5/2-1303.

[11] Christie, Les, "Foreclosure free ride: 3 years, no payments," January 1, 2012, available at: http://money.cnn.com/2011/12/28/real_estate/foreclosure/index.htm?iid=HP_LN (last visited January 5, 2012).

[12] U.S. Departments of Treasury and Housing and Urban Development, "Home Affordable Modification Program," available at: http://www.makinghomeaffordable.gov/programs/lower-payments/Pages/hamp.aspx (last visited January 5, 2012).

[13] It can be found here: http://www.makinghomeaffordable.gov/get-started/contact-mortgage/Pages/default.aspx

[14] Being underwater is not necessarily a "financial hardship" under the HAMP

guidelines.

[15] U.S. Departments of Treasury and Housing and Urban Development, "Second Lien Modification Program," available at: http://www.makinghomeaffordable.gov/programs/lower-payments/Pages/lien_modification.aspx (last visited January 5, 2012).

[16] U.S. Departments of Treasury and Housing and Urban Development, "Home Affordable Foreclosure Alternatives Program," available at: http://www.makinghomeaffordable.gov/programs/exit-gracefully/Pages/hafa.aspx (last visited January 5, 2012).

[17] U.S. Departments of Treasury and Housing and Urban Development, "Home Affordable Refinance Program," available at: http://www.makinghomeaffordable.gov/programs/lower-rates/Pages/harp.aspx (last visited January 5, 2012)

[18] U.S. Departments of Treasury and Housing and Urban Development, "FHA Short Refinance," available at: http://www.makinghomeaffordable.gov/programs/lower-rates/Pages/short-refinance.aspx (last visited January 5, 2012).

[19] U.S. Department of Treasury and Housing and Urban Development, "Home Affordable Unemployment Program," available at: http://www.makinghomeaffordable.gov/programs/unemployed-help/Pages/up.aspx (last visited January 5, 2012).

[20] See 735 ILCS 5/15-1401.

[21] Internal Revenue Service, "Home Foreclosure and Debt Cancellation," available at: http://www.irs.gov/newsroom/article/0,,id=174034,00.html (last visited January 5, 2012).

[22] P.L. 110-142.

[23] See 735 ILCS 5/15-1402.

[24] See Federal Housing Administration Frequently Asked Questions, available at http://portal.hud.gov/FHAFAQ/controllerServlet?method=showPopup&faqId=1-6KT-188 (last visited January 30, 2012).

[25] See In re Kemp, 440 B.R. 624 (Bkrtcy. D. N.J. 2010).

[26] A document custodian is an entity assigned with the responsibility of maintaining and storing documents.

[27] See Metrobank v. Frank R. Cannatello, 2012 IL App (1st) 110529, Case No. 1-11-0529, decided January 9, 2012.

[28] See 735 ILCS 5/15-1602.

[29] See 735 ILCS 5/15-1603.

[30] See 735 ILCS 5/15-1603(c).

[31] See 735 ILCS 5/15-1604.

[32] This value is established by statute. See 735 ILCS 5/15-1603(d).

[33] PL 111-22.

[34] Local Loan Co. v. Hunt, 292 U.S. 234, 244 (1934).

[35] Local Loan Co. v. Hunt, 292 U.S. 234, 244 (1934).

[36] *See* 11 U.S.C. §109(e).

[37] U.S. Courts, "The Chapter 13 Discharge," available at: http://www.uscourts.gov/FederalCourts/Bankruptcy/BankruptcyBasics/Chapter13.aspx (last visited January 5, 2011).

[38] *See* Federal Housing Administration Frequently Asked Questions, available at http://portal.hud.gov/FHAFAQ/controllerServlet?method=showPopup&faqId=1-6KT-188 (last visited January 30, 2012).

[39] *See* 28 C.F.R. §58.3.

[40] *See* Fed. R. Bankr. P. 3015

[41] Fed. R. Bankr. P. 2002(b).

[42] U.S. Courts, "The Chapter 13 Discharge," available at: http://www.uscourts.gov/FederalCourts/Bankruptcy/BankruptcyBasics/Chapter13.aspx (last visited January 5, 2011).

[43] *See* 11 U.S.C. § 1328(a)

[44] *See* 11 U.S.C. § 523.

[45] *See* 11 U.S.C. §362.

[46] Kumar, Kavita, "Complaints about aggressive debt collectors on the rise," January 12, 2012, available at: http://www.stltoday.com/business/local/complaints-about-aggressive-debt-collectors-on-rise/article_f4a3dd7a-3e2f-11e1-b2e5-0019bb30f31a.html (last visited January 27, 2012).

[47] *Id.*

[48] U.S. Courts, "Discharge in Bankruptcy," available at: http://www.uscourts.gov/FederalCourts/Bankruptcy/BankruptcyBasics/DischargeInBankruptcy.aspx (last visited January 31, 2011).

[49] *See* 15 U.S.C. §1681 et. seq.

[50] *See* 15 U.S.C. §§1692 – 1692p.

[51] 15 U.S.C. §§1692-1692p.

[52] 15 U.S.C. §1692a(6).

[53] 15 U.S.C. §1692d(5).

[54] 15 U.S.C. §1692e.

[55] 15 U.S.C. §1692f.

[56] 815 ILCS 505/1 et. seq.

[57] 815 ILCS 505/2.

[58] 15 U.S.C. §45.

[59] *See* 815 ILCS 505/2A – 505/2MMM.

[60] 815 ILCS 505/10a.

Chapter 13 Lien Stripping: History and Overview Endnotes

[61] 12 U.S.C. §2601 *et. seq.*

[62] 12 U.S.C. §2605.
[63] 12 U.S.C. §2605(e)(1)(A).
[64] Pub. L. No. 111-203, 124 Stat. 1376 (July 21, 2010).
[65] 12 U.S.C. §2605(f).
[66] Pub. L. No. 111-203, 124 Stat. 1376 (July 21, 2010).
[67] Federal Trade Commission, "FTC Policy Statement on Deception," October 14, 1983, available at http://www.ftc.gov/bcp/policystmt/ad-decept.htm (last visited May 10, 2012).
[68] 11 U.S.C. §506(d)
[69] 11 U.S.C. §1322(b)(2)

[70] *In Re Waters*, 276 B.R. 879, 880 (Bankr.N.D.Ill.2002)
[71] *Id.*
[72] *Id.*
[73] *Nobleman v. American Savings Bank,* 508 U.S. 324 (1993)
[74] *In Re Waters*, 276 B.R. 879, 881 (Bankr.N.D.Ill.2002)

"Totality of Circumstances" As a Basis for Dismissal in a Chapter 7 Endnotes

[75] 11 USC 707(b)(3)
[76] *Id.*
[77] *In Re Zaporski,* 366 B.R. 758, 769 (Bankr.E.D.Mich.2007); *In re Nockerts,* 357 B.R. 497, 505 (Bankr.E.D.Wisc.2006)
[78] *In Re Zaporski,* 366 B.R. 758, 769 (Bankr.E.D.Mich.2007)
[79] *In re Lorenca,* 422 B.R. 665, 669 (Bankr.N.D.Ill.2010)
[80] *In re Nockerts,* 357 B.R. 497, 506 (Bankr.E.D.Wisc.2006)

[81] *Id.*
[82] *Id.*
[83] *In re Nicola,* 244 B.R. 795, 797 (Bankr.N.D.Ill.2000)
[84] *In re Lorenca,* 422 B.R. 665 (Bankr.N.D.Ill.2010)
[85] *In re Navarro,* 83 B.R. 348, 355 (Bank.E.D.Pa.1988)

How to Determine Whether a Lender Has Standing to Foreclose on a Borrower's Home Endnotes

[87] *P & S Grain, LLC v. County of Williamson*, 399 Ill. App. 3d 836, 842 (5th Dist. 2010).
[88] *Id.* at 844.
[89] *Id.*
[90] *Italia Foods, Inc. v. Sun Tours, Inc.*, 399 Ill. App. 3d 1038, 1069 (2nd Dist.

2010).

91 *Id.*

92 *See* 735 ILCS 5/15-1504(a)(3)(N).

93 *Bayview Loan Servicing, LLC v. Nelson,* 382 Ill. App. 3d 1184, 1188 (5th Dist. 2008).

94 *Ray v. Moll,* 336 Ill. App. 360, 364 (4th Dist. 1949).

95 *See* 810 ILCS 5/3-104(a).

96 *See* 810 ILCS 5/3-301.

97 A negotiable instrument is payable to bearer if it is not indorsed (i.e. signed) to a specific entity.

98 *See* 810 ILCS 5/1-201.

99 *See* 810 ILCS 5/3-201, Official Comment 1.

100 *See* 810 ILCS 5/3-105(a).

101 *See* 810 ILCS 5/3-201, *See also Lewis v. Palmer,* 20 Ill. App 3d 237, 240 (4th Dist. 1974).

102 *See* 810 ILCS 5/3-201, Official Comment 1.

103 *See generally* 810 ILCS 5/3-205.

104 *Id.*

Debt Cancellation: "What is my income tax liability post-foreclosure?" Endnotes

105 Pub.L. No. 110-142, 121 Stat. 1803.

106 Mortgage Forgiveness Debt Relief Act of 2007 §2(a).

107 *Id.*

108 *Id.*

109 Section 2(b) amended subsection (h)(1) of I.R.C. §108. I.R.C. §121(a) to define property as "principal residence" if "during the 5-year period ending on the date of the sale or exchange, such property has been owned and used by the taxpayer as the taxpayer's principal residence for periods aggregating [two] years or more." Mortgage Forgiveness Debt Relief Act of 2007 §2(b).

110 Section 2(b) amended subsection (h)(2) of I.R.C. §108 to define "qualified principal residence indebtedness" as "acquisition indebtedness" under I.R.C. §163(h)(3)(B), which "(I) is incurred in acquiring, constructing, or substantially improving any qualified residence of the taxpayer, and (II) is secured by such residence" and also includes "indebtedness secured by such residence resulting from the refinancing of indebtedness meeting the requirements of [I.R.C. §163(h)(3)(B)(i)]...but only to the extent the amount of the indebtedness resulting from such refinancing does not exceed the amount of the refinanced indebtedness." Mortgage Forgiveness Debt Relief Act of 2007 §2(b).

111 I.R.C. §163(h)(3)(B)(i)(I) (2008).

112 Section 2(b) amended subsection (h)(3) of I.R.C. §108: exception for certain

discharges not related to taxpayer's financial condition.--Subsection (a)(1)(E) [of I.R.C. §108] shall not apply to the discharge of a loan if the discharge is on account of services performed for the lender or any other factor not directly related to a decline in the value of the residence or to the financial condition of the taxpayer. Mortgage Forgiveness Debt Relief Act of 2007 §2(b).

[113] Mortgage Forgiveness Debt Relief Act of 2007 §2(b) amended subsection (h)(4) of I.R.C. §108.
[114] http://www.irs.gov/newsroom/article/0,,id=174034,00.html

Mortgage Escrow Accounts: "Why did my monthly mortgage jump so high?" Endnotes

[115] *GMAC Mortg. Corp. of Pa v. Stapleton*, 236 Ill. App. 3d 486, 489 (1st Dist. 1992).

[116] *See* 12 U.S.C. §§ 2601-2617.
[117] *See id.* § 2609(a)(1)-(2).
[118] *See* 12 U.S.C. § 2609(a).
[119] *See* 12 U.S.C. § 2609(b).
[120] *See* 12 U.S.C. § 2609(2).
[121] *Id.*
[122] *Id.*
[123] *See* 24 C.F.R. Sect. 3500.17 (f)(1)(H).
[124] *Id., see also* 12 U.S.C. § 2609(a)(2).
[125] *See* 12 U.S.C. § 2609(a)(2), (b).
[126] *See* 24 C.F.R. Sect. 3500.17.
[127] *Id.*
[128] *In re Rodriguez,* 391 B.R. 723, 727-28 (Bankr.D.N.J.2008).
[129] *Aitken v. Fleet Mortgage Corp.,* 1992 U.S. Dist. LEXIS 1687, at 5, n. 1.

Condominium Associations: Do I Pay My Assessments if I'm in Foreclosure? Endnotes

[130] *See* 765 ILCS 605/9(g)(1).
[131] *Id.*
[132] *Id.*
[133] *See* 765 ILCS 605/9(h).
[134] *See* 765 ILCS 605/9.2.
[135] *See* 765 ILCS 605/9.2(a).
[136] *Id.*

[137] *See* 765 ILCS 605/9(g)(3).

[138] *Id.*
[139] *See* 765 ILCS 605/9(g)(4).
[140] *See* 765 ILCS 605/22.1

How Do I Answer a Foreclosure Complaint in Illinois? Endnotes

[141] *See* 735 ILCS 5/15-1501, et seq. *See also Mortgage Electronic Registration Systems, Inc. v. Barnes,* 406 Ill.App.3d 1, 6-7 (1st Dist. 2010).
[142] 735 ILCS 5/15-1504(a).
[143] 735 ILCS 5/15-1504(a), 5/15-1105(a). *See Land of Lincoln Savings & Loan v. Michigan Avenue National Bank of Chicago,* 103 Ill.App.3d 1095, 1099 (3d Dist. 1982).
[144] 735 ILCS 5/15-1506(a)(1).
[145] *See First Federal Savings & Loan Association of Ottawa v. Chapman,* 116 Ill. App. 3d 950, 953-54 (3d Dist. 1983) (finding that an answer to a verified foreclosure complaint should itself be signed under oath or supported by affidavit).
[146] 735 ILCS 5/15-1504(a)(2).
[147] 735 ILCS 5/15-1504(c)(2).
[148] *See U.S. Bank National Ass'n v. Sauer,* 392 Ill. App. 3d 942, 946 (2d Dist. 2009) (stating that it is defendant's burden to prove lack of standing).
[149] *See id.*
[150] *Cogswell v. Citifinancial Mortgage Company, Inc.,* 624 F.3d 395, 401 (7th Cir. 2010), citing *TAS Distrib. Co. v. Cummins Engine Co.,* 491 F.3d 625, 633 (7th Cir.2007); *Midland Hotel Corp. v. Reuben H. Donnelley Corp.,* 118 Ill. 2d 306, 315-16 (1987); *Dyduch v. Crystal Green Corp.,* 221 Ill. App. 3d 474, 477-78 (2d Dist. 1991).
[151] *Cogswell,* 624 F.3d at 402 ("Generally speaking, only a mortgagee can foreclose on property, and a mortgagee must [] be 'the holder of an indebtedness ... secured by a mortgage.'").
[152] *Id.* citing 810 ILCS 5/1-201(b)(21)(A).
[153] 810 ILCS 5/1-201(b)(21)(A) (defining a holder as "the person in possession of a negotiable instrument that is payable either to bearer or to an identified person that is the person in possession.").

Does a Defendant in Foreclosure Have a Right to a Jury Trial? Endnotes

[154] Ill. Const.1970, art. I, § 13.

[155] Ill. Const. 1970, art. VI, § 9. *Martin v. Heinold Commodities, Inc.,* 163 Ill. 2d 33, 71 (1994).

[156] "A plaintiff desirous of a trial by jury must file a demand therefor with the clerk at the time the action is commenced. A defendant desirous of a trial by jury must file a demand therefor not later than the filing of his or her answer. Otherwise, the party waives a jury. If an action is filed seeking equitable relief and the court thereafter determines that one or more of the parties is or are entitled to a trial by jury, the plaintiff, within 3 days from the entry of such order by the court, or the defendant, within 6 days from the entry of such order by the court, may file his or her demand for trial by jury with the clerk of the court. If the plaintiff files a jury demand and thereafter waives a jury, any defendant and, in the case of multiple defendants, if the defendant who filed a jury demand thereafter waives a jury, any other defendant shall be granted a jury trial upon demand therefor made promptly after being advised of the waiver and upon payment of the proper fees, if any, to the clerk." 735 ILCS 5/2-1105(a).

[157] *Fisher v. Burgiel,* 382 Ill. 42, 54-55 (1943); *Martin, supra* at n. 2.

[158] *Id.*

[159] 815 ILCS 505/1 *et seq.*

[160] *See Martin, supra* at n. 2.

[161] *Id.*

[162] *See id.*

[163] Once it is determined which claims are at law or chancery, Illinois Supreme Court Rule 135(b) provides that when a party pleads actions at law and actions at equity in a single complaint, the pleading party may separate the claims into distinct counts of "separate action at law" and "separate action at chancery." Il. Sup. Ct. R. 135(b).

[164] If a single pleading contains both actions in equity and actions at law, Supreme Court Rule 232(a) requires the court to decide if the actions at law and equity are severable and, if so, whether they should be tried separately and in what order. Il. Sup. Ct. R. 232.

How Do I Know if I Can Rescind My Mortgage? Endnotes

[165] 15 U.S.C. §1601 *et seq.*

[166] *See* 15 U.S.C. § 1635 and 12 C.F.R. § 226.23.

[167] 15 U.S.C. § 1635(f); 12 C.F.R. §§226.15(a)(3), 226.23(a)(3).

[168] *See* 15 U.S.C. §1602(u) and 12 C.F.R. § 226.18(g).

[169] 15 U.S.C. §1635(f).

[170] *Schmit v. Bank Uninted FSC,* 2009 WL 320490 at *3 (N.D.Ill. Feb. 6, 2009) ("Assignees...may not 'hide behind the assignment'; timely notice to the original creditor rescinds the transaction in its entirety.") *quoting Hubbard v. Ameriquest Mortgage Co.,* 2008 WL 4449888 (N.D.Ill. Sept. 30, 2008).

Can A Foreclosure Court Deny A Deficiency Judgment? Endnotes

[171] Available at http://www.isba.org/sections/commercial/newsletter/2011/07/takingdeficiencyjudgmentsinforeclos (last visited August 12, 2011).
[172] *See JP Morgan Chase Bank v. Fankhauser,* 383 Ill. App. 3d 254 (2nd Dist 2008).
[173] 735 ILCS 5/15-1508(b)(iv).
[174] *See* fn2.
[175] *Fankhauser,* 383 Ill. App. 3d at 265.
[176] *See* fn1.
[177] *See Eiger v. Hunt,* 282 Ill. App. 399 (1st Dist. 1935)(holding that the right to a deficiency judgment does not rest on equity principles, but on the legal obligations of the note's maker); *see also Farmer City State Bank v. Champaign National Bank,* 138 Ill. App. 3d 847 (4th Dist. 1985)(following *Eiger v. Hunt).*
[178] *See* fn1.
[179] *See* 735 ILCS 5/15-1508(b).
[180] 735 ILCS 5/15-1508(b)(iv)(2).
[181] *Bank of Benton v. Cogdill,* 118 Ill. App. 3d 280 (5th Dist. 1983).
[182] *Id.* at 289.
[183] *See* fn1.
[184] *Fankhauser,* 383 Ill. App. 3d at 264.
[185] *See* fn5. *See also Citicorp Savings of Illinois v. First Chicago Trust Company of Illinois,* 269 Ill. App. 3d. 293, 300 (1st Dist. 1995)(holding that "a court is justified in refusing to approve a judicial sale if unfairness is shown which is prejudicial to an interested party").
[186] *See* fn1.

Can I Stop the Confirmation of My Home's Sale? 735 ILCS 5/15-1508 Explained Endnotes

[187] 735 ICLS 5/15-1508.
[188] 735 ILCS 5/15-1508(b).
[189] A sale will not be confirmed if it was not properly noticed, if the terms of the

sale were unconscionable, if the sale was conducted fraudulently, or if justice was not done. 735 ILCS 5/15-1508(b)((i)-(iv).

[190] 735 ILCS 5/15-1508(d-5).

[191] *See* Homeowner Frequently Asked Questions, Home Affordable Modification Program (HAMP), "What if I am facing foreclosure?," available at http://www.makinghomeaffordable.gov/faqs/homeowner-faqs/Pages/default.aspx (last visited February 20, 2011).

[192] *Id.*

[193] *See* Homeowner Frequently Asked Questions, Home Affordable Foreclosure Alternatives (HAFA), "How can I be considered for HAFA?," available at http://www.makinghomeaffordable.gov/faqs/homeowner-faqs/Pages/default.aspx (last visited February 20, 2011).

[194] *See JP Morgan Chase Bank v. Fankhauser*, 383 Ill. App. 3d 254, 265-66 (2nd Dist. 2008)(holding that an interested party's failure to defend a case did not preclude it from challenging confirmation of sale).

[195] *See generally Commercial Credit Loans, Inc. v. Espinoza*, 293 Ill. App. 3d 915, 927-30 (1st Dist. 1997).

[196] *Id.*

[197] *Id.*

Standing, Securitization, and "Show Me The Note" Endnotes

[198] This may not be an accurate number based on loan value and APR, but this is an example, not an amortization exercise.

Reopening A Bankruptcy Case –A Debtor's Liability Considerations Endnotes

[199] *In Re: Shondel*, 950 F. 2d 1301, 1304 (7th Cir. 1991).

[200] *Id.*

[201] Fed. R. Bankr. P. 5010.

[202] *Id.*

[203] *See In re Lopez,* 283 B.R. 22 (9th Cir. BAP 2002)(debtor was allowed to reopen her case to schedule a non-scheduled pre-petition sexual harassment claim as it provided a benefit to the creditors); *In re Upshur*, 317 B.R. 446 (Bankr. Ct. N.D. GA 2004)(pre-petition EEOC claim was grounds to reopen case and add to Schedule B as it provided a benefit to the creditors).

[204] *In re Lopez*, 283 B.R. at 28.

[205] 11 U.S.C. §727(d)(1).

[206] 11 U.S.C. §727(d)(2).
[207] 11 U.S.C. §727(d)(3).
[208] 11 U.S.C. §1328(e)(1)-(2).
[209] *In re Berry*, 190 B.R. 486, 490-91 (Bankr. Ct. S.D. GA 1995).
[210] 11 U.S.C. §524.
[211] *Marrama v. Citizens Bank of Massachusetts*, 549 U.S. 365, 367 (2007).
[212] 11 U.S.C. §541(a)(5)(A)-(C).
[213] 11 U.S.C. §541(a)(7).
[214] 11 U.S.C. §554(c).
[215] 11 U.S.C. §544(d).

Made in the USA
Charleston, SC
24 January 2013